Bessie A Dalzell

from

Stanley

Christmas

1961

# America's Wonderlands

CONTRIBUTORS: *Daniel B. Beard, William Belknap, Jr., Jack Breed,
Andrew H. Brown, Lewis F. Clark, Robert T. Cochran, Jr.,
Frank and John Craighead, Willard R. Culver, Ralph Gray, Robert F. Griggs,
Elsie May Bell Grosvenor, Gilbert Grosvenor, Melville Bell Grosvenor, Val Hart,
E. "Tex" Helm, Paul Jensen, John M. Kauffmann, Eugene Kingman,
Bates Littlehales, Justin Locke, George W. Long, Bart McDowell, Carl F. Miller,
Adolph Murie, Edwards Park, Kathleen Revis, J. Baylor Roberts,
Louis Schellbach, Merle Severy, Robert F. Sisson, Bob and Ira Spring,
B. Anthony Stewart, Mason Sutherland, Frederick G. Vosburgh,
Bradford Washburn, Don Watson, Paul A. Zahl,* and others.
Wildlife paintings by *Walter A. Weber;* decorative maps by *Irvin E. Alleman.*

# America's

## THE SCENIC NATIONAL PARKS

PREPARED BY THE

FOREWORD BY

INTRODUCTION BY

THE NATIONAL

MOUNTAIN GOAT IN GLACIER NATIONAL PARK BY WILFORD L. MILLER

RHODODENDRON BY PAUL JENSEN, NATIONAL GEOGRAPHIC STAFF

# Wonderlands

## AND MONUMENTS OF THE UNITED STATES

*National Geographic Book Service,* MERLE SEVERY, CHIEF

*Melville Bell Grosvenor,* PRESIDENT AND EDITOR, NATIONAL GEOGRAPHIC SOCIETY

*Conrad L. Wirth,* DIRECTOR, NATIONAL PARK SERVICE

GEOGRAPHIC SOCIETY, WASHINGTON, D. C.

**Spires of the Tetons** pierce the Wyoming sky. Jackson Lake mirrors rivers of snow on the mountain flanks in Grand Teton National Park.

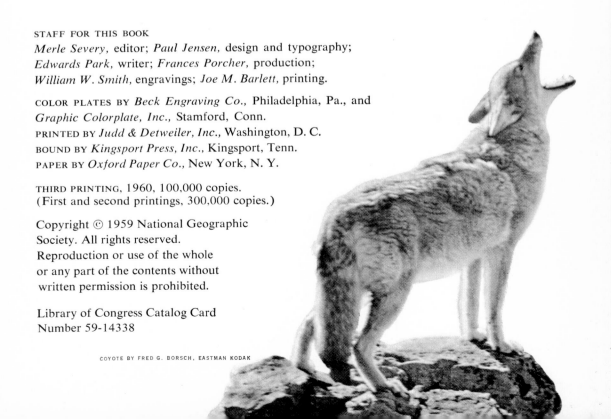

STAFF FOR THIS BOOK
*Merle Severy*, editor; *Paul Jensen*, design and typography;
*Edwards Park*, writer; *Frances Porcher*, production;
*William W. Smith*, engravings; *Joe M. Barlett*, printing.

COLOR PLATES BY *Beck Engraving Co.*, Philadelphia, Pa., and
*Graphic Colorplate, Inc.*, Stamford, Conn.
PRINTED BY *Judd & Detweiler, Inc.*, Washington, D. C.
BOUND BY *Kingsport Press, Inc.*, Kingsport, Tenn.
PAPER BY *Oxford Paper Co.*, New York, N. Y.

THIRD PRINTING, 1960, 100,000 copies.
(First and second printings, 300,000 copies.)

# Foreword

"BRING ME MEN TO MATCH MY MOUNTAINS!" These words of poet Sam Walter Foss ring in my ears as I leaf the pages of this book. Only through the efforts of courageous men of vision have America's wonderlands been preserved for all to enjoy. Without men like John Muir, Stephen T. Mather, Horace M. Albright, and John D. Rockefeller, Jr., without conservation-minded patriots in Congress and the White House, our national parks could never have been created. Men like Conrad L. Wirth carry on the crusade for an unspoiled America.

Fortunate we are, too, in our national park rangers. They spare these precious parklands from becoming shopworn and trampled by millions. And with what patience they keep us visitors from feeding ourselves to the bears!

This unique book, the most complete and lavishly illustrated volume in its field, is made possible by vast resources of text and color plates produced over the years by the non-profit National Geographic Society and its famed Magazine. Hence its moderate cost. To cover all facets of the National Park System would mean to give none its full due. Therefore we concentrated on areas of outstanding scenic and archeological interest. America's historic shrines and landmarks we have reserved for a companion volume.

*America's Wonderlands* is the loving creation of skilled editor Merle Severy and his associates in the National Geographic's Book Service. Park superintendents, naturalists, historians, archeologists—National Park Service Director Conrad Wirth himself—checked every page to ensure authenticity.

Going over this material reminded me of how my father, Gilbert Grosvenor, fired my enthusiasm for these scenic sanctuaries when I was a boy. I recall Stephen Mather, the Park Service's first Director, with whom my father, as President of the National Geographic Society, worked so closely to save our Nation's wilderness domain. In nearly half a century of cooperation with the Park Service, The Society has contributed in extraordinary ways: the first expedition to explore Carlsbad Caverns; the discovery of the Valley of Ten Thousand Smokes; the donation to the American people of a large tract in Sequoia's Giant Forest; the recent gift of the scientific trove, Russell Cave; the unearthing of Pueblo Bonito, and now the excavations at Wetherill Mesa.

During these same years the *National Geographic* has published more than 100 articles portraying the glories of our national park lands.

For me the book has stirred warm memories: the Utah and Mount Holyoke girls who waited on our table at Grand Teton and Yellowstone; the University of Arkansas football star who carried our luggage at Yosemite. As I met fellow tourists enjoying their heritage, it struck me again and again—there's something about these parks that brings out the finest in people.

The Society proudly presents *America's Wonderlands* to its members and to the public, so that all may know our national parks and how well the men dedicated to them serve our Nation. These parks "strengthen bodies, refresh minds, uplift the spirits . . . enrich leisure." I echo the invitation Conrad Wirth extends in his Introduction: "Come, use and enjoy them."

*Melville Bell Grosvenor*

MULE DEER BY J. BAYLOR ROBERTS, NATIONAL GEOGRAPHIC PHOTOGRAPHER

# CONTENTS

BALD EAGLE BY IKE VERN

TOKLAT GRIZZLY BEAR
IN MOUNT MCKINLEY NATIONAL PARK
BY WARREN F. STEENBERGH

INTRODUCTION

# THE
# NATIONAL
# PARKS

## Our heritage of beauty and history

*By CONRAD L. WIRTH*
*Director, U. S. National Park Service*

IN SPRING, snow melt makes torrents of Rocky
Mountain streams, the elk move from Jackson
Hole to the high meadows of Yellowstone, and
the Director of the National Park Service goes
missing from his usual haunts in Washington, D. C.

"No, sir, he's out of town," my secretary tells the
telephone. "Inspection trip, you know. Oh, no, sir, I'm
sure he didn't take any fishing tackle with him...."

11

ELK IN YELLOWSTONE PARK BY ANDREW H. BROWN, NATIONAL GEOGRAPHIC STAFF

But then again maybe he did. How can I know whether to stock a Glacier National Park trout stream unless I see how many fish are in it?

Seriously, trying to manage your 24-million-acre estate, the National Park System, entirely from a desk in Washington would be unthinkable, and none of my predecessors ever attempted it. I make no apologies for my trips to the field, even those that include an hour or two on a trout stream.

As a matter of fact, I'd be happy to have you along on one of my swings. Let's begin at Grand Canyon National Park in Arizona (see National Parks map in pocket at back of book). That's where I started when I first went to work for the Park Service in 1931.

"Before you get settled behind your desk," said Horace Albright, then Director of National Parks, "you'd better find out what a park looks like. Here's a ticket to Grand Canyon."

The chief ranger met me at the train. With a scornful look at my eastern clothes, he ordered me aboard a mule parked nearby, mounted another one himself, and led the way to a thrilling experience. We went right over the rim

**Parks Director Wirth hits the trail** whenever office duties permit. Here he inspects a remote area with Yellowstone Superintendent Lemuel Garrison (right) and Associate Director E. T. Scoyen (left).

J. BAYLOR ROBERTS, NATIONAL GEOGRAPHIC PHOTOGRAPHER, AND (RIGHT) GRANT SHARPE

**Mountain goats** nimbly play follow-the-leader across a six-foot chasm in Glacier National Park. Under park protection, wild animals flourish in their natural settings and frolic fearlessly before visitors' eyes.

of the canyon, down the Bright Angel Trail. No matter how hard I tried to make my mule walk close to the inside of the zigzagging, sloping path, he always stayed on the edge of a sheer precipice.

Somehow we made it to the bottom. We crossed the Colorado River, brown with silt, and rode halfway up to the North Rim, then came back down to the bottom for an overnight stop at Phantom Ranch. As I recall it—and believe me, I recall it—the chief impression of the park that day was on the seat of my inadequate trousers.

"If anybody is going to carry anybody back up to the South Rim tomorrow," I announced as I ate my dinner standing up, "I'm going to carry the mule!"

Tomorrow, of course, was a brighter day. We rode uneventfully back up the trail, as thousands of tourists have done, and from the comfort of park headquarters I looked back upon a memorable experience.

The greatest benefit I received from the trip was a heightened awareness of what was mine as an American. There on the Bright Angel Trail I felt a    13

**Grand Canyon's strata,** like pages in a book, reveal the history of the earth. This mightiest of gorges, still being cut by the Colorado River, bares rocks formed a billion and a half years ago.

JUSTIN LOCKE

little bit like a pioneer, aware of dangers the first settlers faced as they subdued a wild land. My existence, I could see, was only a continuation of theirs in the pageant of the Nation's history. What they struggled to build I must help preserve, as a Park Service man and as a citizen of the United States.

More than likely your own first visit to a national park was quite different, but it does not really matter where you start. The important thing is for you to receive a full dividend from your experience, as I did, not only through lungs filled with clean air and eyes soothed by natural beauty, but in spirits enriched perhaps beyond immediate understanding.

I MYSELF don't know how to describe this ability of the parks to lift up the soul. One of the best writers on the parks, Freeman Tilden, refers to an ancient undefined Greek concept of a "fifth essence," beyond fire, air, earth, and water, and quotes the English historian Trevelyan as to what this essence is:

"The effect of natural beauty is immense. Many regard it as the best thing in life. One motive for preserving places of historic interest and natural beauty is to cultivate in our people the historic sense, the vivid realization of the life of our ancestors and all former inhabitants as a reality lovingly pictured in the mind, not merely an abstraction read of in history books."

Grand Canyon not only helps cultivate a historic sense, but takes us far back into ages past as well. Better than any other place in the world, we believe, it tells the story of the earth during the last billion and a half years or so. The Colorado River has uncovered, at the bottom of its gorge, rocks in which scientists have never found any evidence of primal life.

Higher in the walls geologists have discovered some of the oldest known traces of life, in the form of fossilized plants and marine animals. Even the canyon's rims are not really contemporary, for the topmost layers in this part of Arizona long ago eroded away. To see the sort of layers that once overlaid the canyon rims, we'll have to journey to three parks in Utah.

These parks interlock in telling the story of the earth itself. Lower rock levels of Zion Canyon in Zion National Park are about the same age as those that once formed the top of Grand Canyon. Bryce Canyon and Cedar Breaks combine with Zion to bring the story closer to the relatively recent era when humanity came on the scene. I think these parks together make up one of the most important museums in the world.

These natural wonders are easily grasped and appreciated, but they are just half the picture. The Park System also includes 90 historic areas, which offer greater intellectual challenge and reward to the visitor. It has been stimulating to watch the growing interest in our historic areas because, to me, it reflects a deepening understanding on the part of Americans of the heritage of freedom, valor, and patriotism handed down to us.

16    **Fireman's holiday:** a summer lookout rappels down a cliff in Mount Rainier Park. Crowned by 40 square miles of glaciers, Washington's 14,410-foot peak rises beyond flowered, forested Paradise Valley.

RUTH KIRK

One time somebody asked me: "What kind of people visit the national parks?" "What kind don't?" I parried, thinking of the more than 60 million park visits each year. Mill hands and office clerks. Tycoons and poor folk. Lawyers, doctors, and thieves. Some are fond of flowers, some like snow and ice. Some prefer snakes, though most are amazed that we protect even rattlers. Bears are liked by everybody—except the hundred or so people each year who get mauled or bitten for ignoring our warnings about them.

THE PARKS mean different things to different people. For instance, in Glacier one day I ran across a middle-aged couple who were packing their car, getting ready to leave.

"Good morning to you," I said. "How do you like the park?"

"Best of the 10 we've seen this vacation," the man replied. "But mister, please don't keep me from my packing. We have only three more days of vacation and three parks still to see." While he bustled around, I found out from his wife that they had arrived in Gla-

**Ice-sculptured peaks
mount a blue jewel:
St. Mary Lake**

Indians believed that the Wind Maker, their underwater god, lived in St. Mary and spoke to them when his waters were ruffled. Glacier National Park's Montana skyline includes Little Chief (far left), Citadel, Gunsight, Fusillade, Reynolds, Going-to-the-Sun, and Goat.

RAY ATKESON

19

cier the night before. "We drove by one of those glaciers," she said, "and we saw Indians on the hotel lawn. This is a wonderful place."

Too rushed to get much out of a national park? Maybe. But this couple, who probably couldn't tell a coyote from a collie dog, were having the time of their lives. I defend their right to see Glacier any way they want. The Park Service does not tell people how to take their pleasure.

At the same time, we feel that the parks repay close acquaintance. For the visitor who takes his time we offer the knowledge of Park Service naturalists, historians, and archeologists, as well as our ranger force. We maintain more than 100 park museums. We provide campfire programs, conducted walks and caravans, trailside exhibits, recorded talks, and a great deal of literature.

At the other extreme from the Glacier couple were two boys I met at the ranger patrol cabin on the Southeast Arm of Yellowstone Lake one summer. They had the barest amount of worn-out camping gear. Untrimmed hair and bushy beards gave them the look of old-time mountain men.

"How long have you fellows been out?" I asked.

"Two months," said one. "And what a time we've had! A cow moose kept us treed all one night. We can tell you, I bet, where the biggest cutthroat trout in the world live. We've gained 15 pounds apiece on beans, bacon, sourdough biscuits, and fish." They had a canoe, and they were planning to paddle back to their car. I took a look at the thing. It was more patches than canoe.

"Maybe you could take these fellows over in the patrol boat," I told the ranger. "If you do, find out for me where they caught those trout."

I don't know who will talk the longest and loudest about their trip, the couple at Glacier or the two boys. I'm sure they all had experiences best suited to their natures. I have faith in the ability of the parks to spray some of Freeman Tilden's "fifth essence" on every visitor.

SOONER or later each visitor meets a ranger. His full title is United States Park Ranger and he is one of the key men in the Park Service. He is the visitor's friend. He shows the guest how to reach the interesting places, warns him against feeding the bears, finds him when he is lost, and deals firmly with him when he violates the regulations, which are few and reasonable.

A ranger is a man's man. He likes animals and flowers. He can spend all day on a horse and half the night on a square-dance floor. He comes in two styles, the year-round career man and the "90-day wonder," the seasonal ranger who works only during rush tourist seasons. Either kind talks facts and listens well. Don't try to bluff a ranger. I made that mistake once.

We were in the high country of Kings Canyon National Park, seeing if dude horses were damaging delicate California mountain meadows. In nature, not enough deer would congregate here to destroy the grass. But let man, the changer of nature's face, destroy the ecological balance—say by running in

**Soft as snow, fine as sugar,** gypsum dunes at New Mexico's White Sands National Monument make perfect teen-age romping grounds.

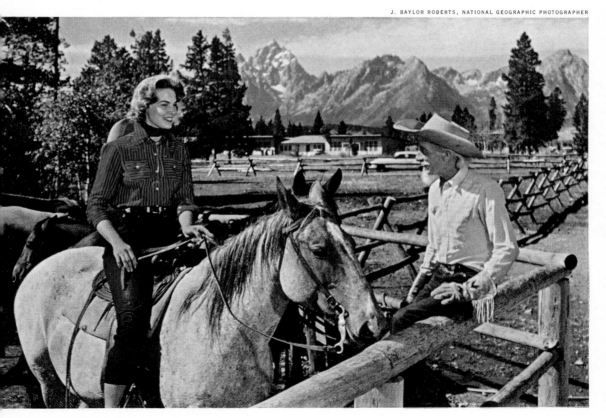

**A character out of the Old West,** Col. Idaho Ellison greets a visitor to Grand Teton National Park, Wyoming. He entertains dudes with tales of daring stagecoach runs, gunslingers, and border fights.

21

**Yosemite's granite fantasy:** Half Dome turns a stony shoulder as the Merced

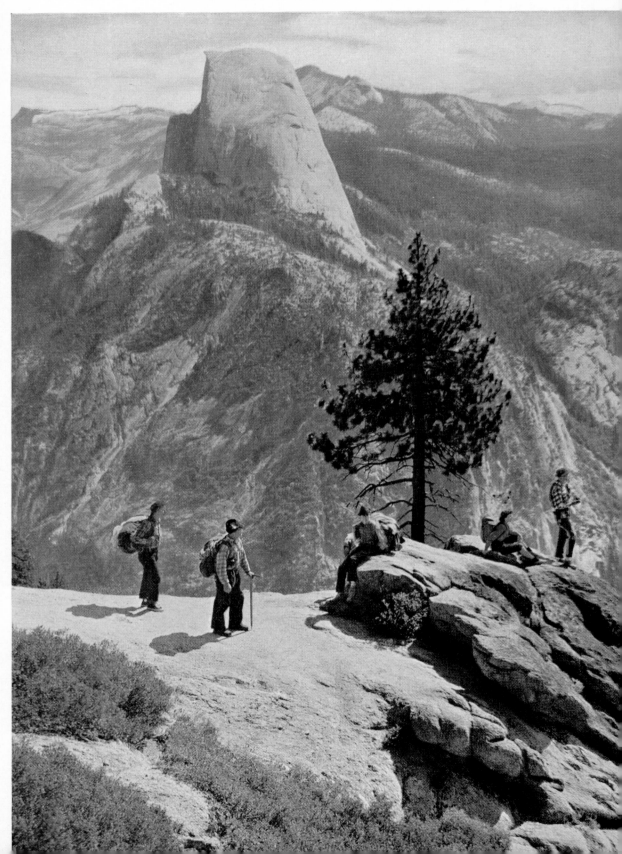

River surges over Nevada and Vernal Falls, then tumbles into the valley. Hikers pause at Glacier Point.

**Custodians** of the Nation's scenic treasures, park officials and Director Wirth (center) confer at Yosemite's park ranger school.

**Official greeter** to all comers, a ranger at Sequoia National Park's entrance station checks in a late-arriving raccoon guest.

too many horses—and you have trouble. We camped by a stream brimming with snow melt. Cold winds whistled through the stunted pines at timber line. I looked around at my companions stretched wearily on the ground after a hard day in the saddle, and I thought I had them sized up.

"Personally," I said, "I could go for a nice bath in that pool down there. But of course you fellows are too tired, and I don't want to go alone, so I guess I'll have to do without."

To my horror, the ranger in our party rose and started peeling off his shirt. The icy water nearly killed me. As I said, don't try to bluff a ranger.

When the time arrives, a ranger becomes a hero—quietly, as befits a man who feels he is only doing a job he is getting paid for. Take Ranger Jack Cahoon, a seasonal who taught school nine months of the year. From the beach at Cape Hatteras he saw a swimmer drifting helplessly out to sea. A storm was raging and the

J. BAYLOR ROBERTS, NATIONAL GEOGRAPHIC PHOTOGRAPHER, AND (BELOW) KENNETH FINK

**Designers,** preparing for the future, shape new buildings for Olympic National Park. Anticipating 80 to 100 million visitors a year by 1966, the Service instituted multi-million-dollar Mission 66 to increase facilities, extend trails and roads, and enlarge staffs.

**Official banisher** of all offenders, a ranger releases a black bear in a remote section of Yellowstone. After the bear had proved a chronic nuisance around campsites, rangers trapped him in a honey-baited pipe. Red paint daubed on his head marks his disgrace.

surf ran high. Ranger Cahoon threw off shirt and shoes, swam out, and brought the man to safety. The Department of the Interior gave him the Valor Award, its gold medal for exceptional bravery.

Three airmen parachuted from a disabled plane and landed in a part of the Grand Canyon nobody had ever reached from the rims above. Ranger Ed Laws and Dr. A. A. MacRae, an experienced Canyon hiker, set out to descend a 550-foot sheer cliff, most formidable in the canyon. Then Ranger Laws noticed deer tracks converging into a single trail. Following it, the men found a dizzy path leading to the stranded fliers. At great danger, the pair clambered down and arranged to bring the aviators up.

Rangers regularly risk their lives to save climbers in trouble on the heights of the Tetons and other ranges. Being trapped in the wilderness by blizzards is routine for Yellowstone ski patrols. The patrol ranger's wife, meanwhile, may be snowbound herself in their isolated cabin home. She, too, is a hero.

Many of our first rangers were simple outdoorsmen without much formal education. Some, like Billy Nelson of Yosemite, would be called "characters" today. He had King Albert of the Belgians out on a pack trip. Billy was cooking under the giant sequoias of the Mariposa Grove. "Hey, King," he suddenly shouted over the crackle of the campfire, "shoot me that side of bacon, will you?" Members of the royal party and the Yosemite superintendent blanched. But the King cheerily threw Billy the bacon. From then on it was "King" and "Billy" in conversation between the two men.

Present-day rangers are college men and have more polish, but are just as good in the wilds as their predecessors. In the fall of 1957, furthermore, we started a special school for new rangers in Yosemite.

When they graduate after three months of training, they know Park Service regulations and objectives, how to look after a horse, how to fight forest fires and find lost people, and how diplomatically to keep visitors from picking flowers. They also learn the history of the National Park System.

THE IDEA came to fruition at a campfire in Yellowstone on the night of September 19, 1870. While the flames danced under the starry sky, the men discussed what should be done with this astounding country they had been exploring for nearly five weeks. In the group sat Gen. Henry D. Washburn, Surveyor-General of Montana Territory; Nathaniel P. Langford, vigilante law enforcement officer who later became Yellowstone's first superintendent; and 2d Lt. Gustavus C. Doane, U.S. Army. At first they argued about staking personal claims, but Cornelius Hedges, a judge in Montana Territory, advanced the idea that Yellowstone's unique natural beauty not be owned by a few individuals. "I feel it should be a national park," he said.

The other leaders were persuaded and promised to urge the proposal as

**Rivers, gorges, and falls** show at a glance on a relief map of California's 760,951-acre Yosemite Park. Granite-walled Yosemite Valley cuts horizontally at center. Red lines are roads; yellow, trails.

J. BAYLOR ROBERTS, NATIONAL GEOGRAPHIC PHOTOGRAPHER

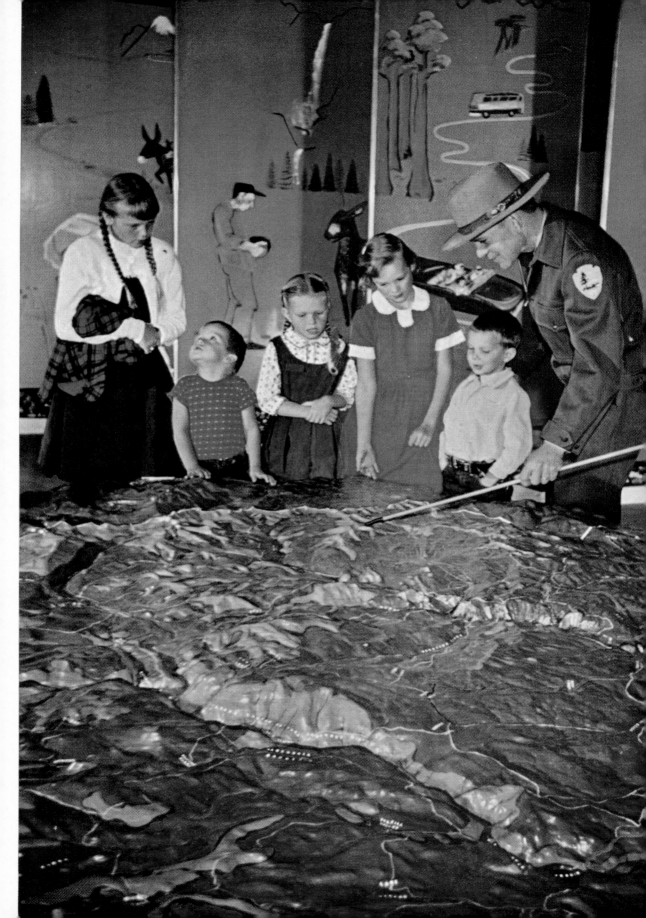

## Yellowstone campers re-enact the drama that gave birth to the park

On September 19, 1870, 15 men pitched tents on this meadow after a month-long journey through the spectacular Yellowstone country.

Braving hostile Indians and riding through early snows, Gen. Henry D. Washburn's party had circled Yellowstone Lake, seen the roaring geysers, and explored the canyon and falls. This was a wonderland, they agreed, and spoke of staking private claims.

But Judge Cornelius Hedges urged that the area be preserved as a park. His companions, persuaded, later worked vigorously for the idea, despite jeers that greeted their reports. "Champion liar of the Northwest" one leader was called.

Their work bore fruit: in 1872 Congress created Yellowstone National Park, the Nation's first.

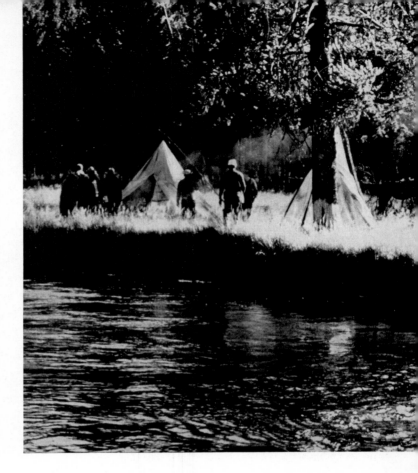

vigorously as they could. These men kept their word, and such was their prominence that Congress two years later established Yellowstone as the first national park in the world. I know of nobody today who seriously questions the wisdom of that Congressional decision. Further, each succeeding Congress and every administration since 1872 has strengthened the concept proclaimed around the Yellowstone campfire.

Curious visitors started coming to the first national park right away. Yellowstone became a huge success, and Congress created more parks. Sequoia, Yosemite, and Mount Rainier came into the new system of "pleasuring grounds," as they were first known, before the turn of the century. The year 1906 saw passage of the Antiquities Act. It permits Presidents to make national monuments of historically and scientifically interesting places by simple proclamation. This important law has given the Nation about half its National Park System. It was conceived originally to protect the Indian ruins of the Southwest from souvenir hunters.

The Park Service was created as a bureau of the Department of the Interior in 1916. Until that time Interior had been running the parks as a sort of extra chore. Most of the work fell to W. B. Acker, an assistant attorney for the department. Working devotedly, but only part time, he could not please everybody. One of his critics was Stephen T. Mather of Chicago, possessor of a borax fortune. Mather wrote his old college friend Franklin K. Lane, Secretary of the Interior, that he thought the department was doing a pretty poor job with the parks.

Retorted Lane: "If you don't like it, come and run the parks yourself." Mather accepted.

One of the first men he met in Washington was Gilbert Grosvenor, then Editor, later President and Chairman of the Board of Trustees of the National Geographic Society. Dr. Grosvenor enthusiastically supported Mather's plan for a specialized Park Service, helped write the legislation that created it, and guided the National Geographic Society to a friendship with the parks that is as firm today as it was in the beginning.

In 1915 Dr. Grosvenor went on a camping trip Mather arranged in California's Sierra Nevadas for some influential people he hoped would help sell his park ideas. Mather and Grosvenor, scorning tents, spread their blankets on the forest floor beneath a giant tree and talked probably half the night about the Park Service. One result of this trip was a contribution by the

29

National Geographic Society to help the Park Service acquire this magnificent grove of ancient sequoias.

In 1958 The Society gave the American people Russell Cave in Alabama. Here the Smithsonian Institution excavated Indian homesites 9,000 years old. It is one of the few properties in the Park System that memorialize North American man from the time of his arrival here from Asia, more than 25,000 years ago, and the time he built villages in the Southwest, about the beginning of the Christian Era.

In 1933 President Franklin D. Roosevelt consolidated under our care a whole host of national monuments, military parks, memorials, and cemeteries previously administered by the War Department and the Department of Agriculture. Two years later Congress passed legislation authorizing the establishment of national historic sites, and 23 areas have been so designated by Secretaries of the Interior.

Among the responsibilities we assumed in the thirties was the park system of Washington, D. C. It contains 792 pieces of property, including the Washington Monument, the Lincoln Memorial, Rock Creek Park, parts of the Chesapeake and Ohio Canal, and so many statues I've lost count. We have the White House on our books, too. We don't tell the First Lady how to run her household, of course, but we keep the gardens neat and the lawns mowed.

The Park Service looks after 24 million acres of land in 181 units scattered throughout the continental United States, Puerto Rico, Hawaii, and the Virgin Islands. Yellowstone was the first park; Russell Cave is the newest. Katmai

30

GILBERT GROSVENOR

## General Sherman: Sequoia's giant among giants

When California's Giant Forest was threatened by lumbering in 1915, Stephen Mather, then Assistant to the Secretary of the Interior, invited a group of eminent Americans to visit the grove. One of these was Gilbert Grosvenor, Editor of the *National Geographic,* who made this dramatic picture as 20 men, fingertip to fingertip, encircled General Sherman's 102-foot waist.

**A picnic among the big trees** saw Mr. Mather at head of table with Dr. Grosvenor on his left. The Society and some of its members later contributed $100,000 to preserve 2,239 acres of *Sequoia gigantea.*

**"Within these plantations of God,** a decorum and sanctity reign":

Emerson's words sound a blessing for dinner amid Giant Forest in Sequoia National Park.

National Monument, with 2,697,590 acres, is the largest; the House Where Lincoln Died in Washington, D. C., the smallest.

Only 29 areas bear the official designation "national park," but I often use the word "park" in its generic sense, to cover any of the units. Scenic values primarily distinguish about a third of the 181.

Beginning in 1956, every area of the National Park Service was scheduled for overdue improvements under a long range program called Mission 66— the most comprehensive improvement program the parks ever had. To understand the need for Mission 66, let's go to Yosemite in California, where Billy Nelson flouted protocol, and recall a time I stood by the road.

"More than 7,000 cars, carrying maybe 25,000 people, are in the valley today," the superintendent told me. "The tent people are overflowing the camp grounds. Every hotel room and cabin is taken. Fishermen stand shoulder to shoulder in the streams. Traffic crawls bumper to bumper on the road up to Glacier Point. Connie, they are mashing the valley flat—God bless 'em!"

There's our problem. Creating our Park Service in 1916, Congress bade us "conserve the scenery and the natural and historic objects and the wildlife therein and . . . provide for the enjoyment of the same . . . by such means as will leave them unimpaired for the enjoyment of future generations."

How do you "conserve" the natural things with 25,000 people milling about on 4,500 acres? You could do it by fencing the people out, but what happens to the "enjoyment"? From the very beginning the Park Service has been protecting the fragile and irreplaceable, but at the same time it has been building roads, trails, hotels, campgrounds, and information centers so the people can come and enjoy the wonders we protect for them.

For some years it had been obvious that the use-versus-preservation conflict in the Park System was not being resolved. In 1925 the parks drew 2,054,000 visits. By 1966 we'll be having somewhere between 80 million and 100 million visits a year! Truly the parks are being loved to death.

Mission 66 will end in 1966, the service's 50th anniversary year. That's why we call it Mission 66. Already we have completed Stevens Canyon Road in Mount Rainier National Park, a job begun in 1931. Yellowstone early acquired its Canyon Village, and Grand Teton a new campground with ingenious parking facilities for trailers at Colter Bay.

But Mission 66 is much more than the physical-improvements program it appears at first glance to be. It includes adequate park staffs, better use of the system for the benefit of more visitors, better interpretation, and, most important, safeguarding of park wilderness, most prized element of all.

In a few areas we frankly try to entice people away from the most crowded places. At Mesa Verde, for instance, cliff dwellings and mesa top sites presently closed to visitors are now being excavated and eventually will be opened to the

Piper bellflower blooms only in the cloud-high gardens of Washington's Olympic National Park. Here enlarged 3½ times, *Campanula piperi* nestles amid lichen-splotched rocks on a windy ledge.

**Campers ring a fire** on Tuolumne Meadows, at 8,500 feet in Yosemite. "Camp out among the

public. The National Geographic Society has contributed $50,000 to aid the scientific aspects of this work. And at Yosemite the Tioga Road has been improved to give visitors an opportunity to see and enjoy the lovely high Sierra country, and at the same time help to relieve the concentration in the relatively small area of Yosemite Valley.

36

CHARLES E. MOHR

grass and gentians of glacier meadows," wrote John Muir. "Cares will drop like autumn leaves."

A fine new Mission 66 visitor center stands in Dinosaur National Monument, which sprawls across the Utah-Colorado line along the Green and Yampa Rivers. The building includes part of the dinosaur-bone "quarries" that are a main feature; visitors see the big fossil bones still in the rock face.

From Dinosaur to Mesa Verde National Park in the southwest corner of

37

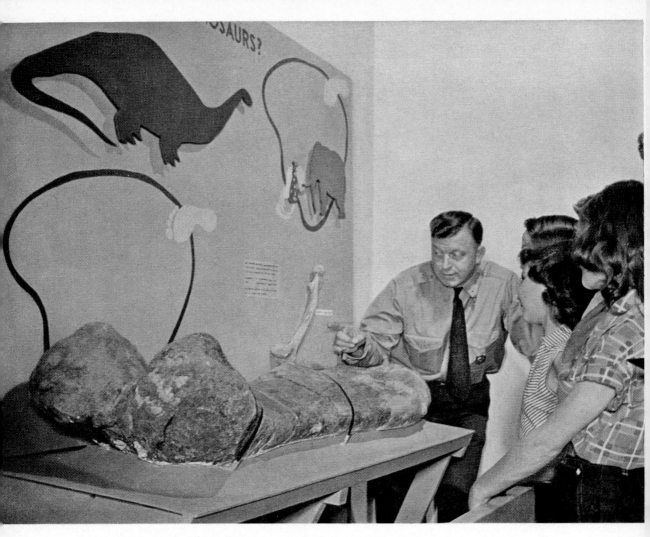

**Dinosaur thighbone,** preserved for some 120 million years, dwarfs that of a human (on wall) at Dinosaur National Monument in Utah.

Colorado is a few hundred miles in distance but millions of years in time—from the age of reptiles to the age of man. Archeologists tell us Mesa Verde dates from about A.D. 1, when primitive Indians wandered in, saw a land then verdant and suitable for farming, and settled down for 1,300 years.

The first settlers lived in simple pit houses with crude roofs, but their descendants built great masonry and adobe pueblos. They made beautiful pottery and feather-cloth garments and wove colored designs into cotton cloth. And they fashioned jewelry from local turquoise. Their decline began in the 13th century. A long drought spurred the Indians to move; nobody much saw the mesa again until the 1880's, when cowboys found it and spread the news.

I love these ruins. I stand on Park Point at the top of the mesa, and I know I stand where bronze warriors once kept lookout for raiding nomadic enemies.

**Indian petroglyphs** on Newspaper Rock record events 800 years past. The undecoded carvings challenge young visitors in Petrified Forest, Arizona. Father prefers a paper he can read.

I see the cliff dwellings stuck like swallows' nests to the yellow sandstone. I can imagine Indian women grinding corn, and I can see fat children playing on the patios hundreds of feet above the canyon floor. And in the visitor center, I see the story of their lives in the finest display of its kind I know.

To the south and east lies Carlsbad Caverns in New Mexico, our biggest underground wonder; in fact, it is one of the world's largest caves. The things visitors see defy description: the Big Room, a mile and a quarter around and 285 feet high in places; the King's Palace and Queen's Chamber with gleaming stone draperies and curtains; tremendous stalagmites such as the Giant Dome, thousands of years old.

Water made Carlsbad by dissolving limestone—actually an ancient, buried coral reef. Unless water flows in still unplumbed depths, Carlsbad has stopped growing. Mammoth Cave in Kentucky, on the other hand, has underground rivers we know about; we can be sure it is still undergoing some change.

Wind Cave, South Dakota, is our only cave with boxwork. To make these lovely formations, water deposited calcite in intersecting limestone cracks, then dissolved the limestone leaving the translucent calcite veins crisscrossing

EDWARDS PARK, NATIONAL GEOGRAPHIC STAFF, AND (LEFT) JUSTIN LOCKE

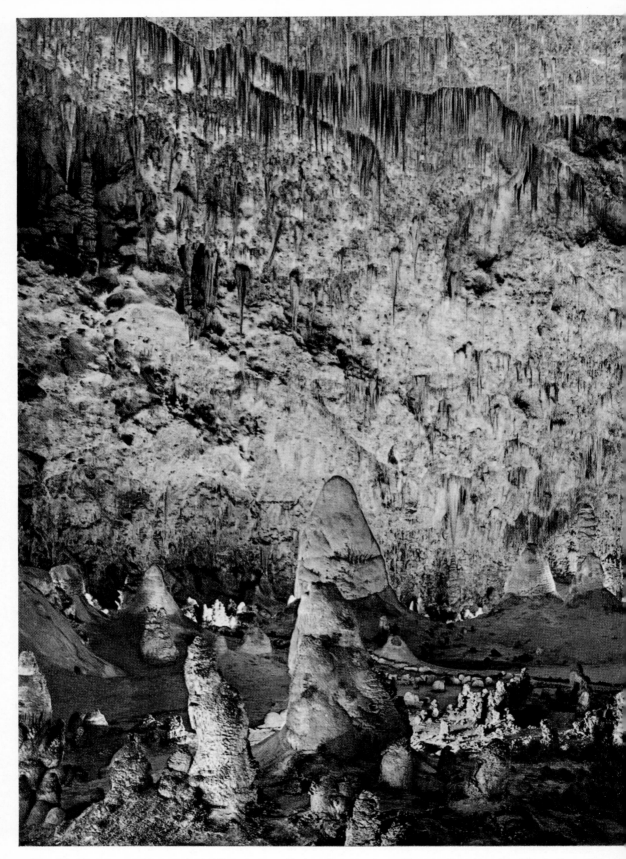

**The Big Room at New Mexico's Carlsbad:** stalactites festoon the ceiling; stalagmites ride like icebergs in a colored sea. Visitors a fifth of a mile back appear ant-size in world's largest known underground chamber.

the walls like cells of a huge honeycomb.

Wind Cave National Park also has 28,059 acres of rolling range and forest land on which the buffalo roam and the antelope play, to say nothing of the prairie dogs. Farmers and stockmen have waged war on prairie dogs so long and so effectively that the pert little rodents have become almost extinct on the ranges where they had thrived. At Wind Cave they are protected as part of the natural scene.

For the sassiest prairie dogs in the National Park System I nominate the ones at Devils Tower National Monument in Wyoming. There they stand begging beside the road in a well-drilled line. I have seen people ignore the striking Tower entirely and spend the day feeding the prairie dogs.

I F WE WANT to see truly wild animals, we'll go to Alaska, where the influence of man has been felt the least. Mount McKinley National Park, which contains the highest mountain on the North American continent, offers a varied assortment of wild creatures.

The Barren Ground caribou lives here, and in no other park. So does the Toklat grizzly

**A hoary marmot** surveys his domain in Mount McKinley Park.

bear; the Alaska moose, largest of its kind; the timber wolf; and the Dall sheep, kin to the Rocky Mountain bighorn. These animals need wilderness for survival. Mount McKinley furnishes a fine example of the way in which animals live together successfully under the stern laws of nature.

To put it in its simplest terms for brevity's sake, wolves eat Dall sheep. But men also like to hunt these same Dall sheep, and in the late 1930's the rivalry between men and wolves over the sheep became rather intense. We don't allow hunters in national parks, of course, but the animals cross boundaries as they please. The men came to us. "You're protecting the wolves so well," they told us, "they're overrunning the country and killing your sheep and ours too."

We undertook a study that revealed a fairly simple explanation. The Dall sheep were declining not from wolf depredations, but from poor grazing due to a prolonged spell of adverse weather. So the wolves had to prowl far and wide to eat, and people mistook a few fast-ranging animals for whole packs. As a matter of fact, the wolf population had actually dropped.

**Mount McKinley's snowfields** glow with sunset gold at noon. In central Alaska the December sun barely skims the horizon at midday. A cloud halo caps the 20,320-foot peak, loftiest in North America.

43

ERNEST GRUENING AND (ABOVE) WARREN F. STEENBERGH

**Snowshoe hare** sits statue-still to escape detection. Outsized feet enable it to run on the crest of the snow.

**A bull moose** wades Wonder Lake in a two-million-acre

Since then the grass has come back, and the sheep have increased—all in the course of natural events. We expect the wolves to increase too. We hope so. To have true wilderness we must have all the parts of an ecological pattern.

Now I want to fly you over Katmai National Monument, country so wild that until just a few years ago when we put our own explorers in, the most reliable information we had on the area came from quarter-century-old records of seven National Geographic Society expeditions, five of them led by Dr. Robert F. Griggs.

Here even such cataclysmic events as volcanic explosions can take place un-sanctuary guarded by the snowy ramparts of Mount McKinley. Antler spread may exceed six feet.

heard and unseen. A mountain erupts. Smoke and ash drift over some settled parts of Alaska. A military plane then goes in to see what happened, but by the time it arrives the volcano may already have started to simmer down.

A concessioner has built comfortable camps on the area's blue lakes in recent years. Guests come in uneventfully by seaplane, the only way they can get there without walking. One inspection flight I made was unusual in that it almost ended in disaster.

Five of us made a full load for the aircraft. We flew first into the Valley of Ten Thousand Smokes. Earth's inner fires were banked; only a relatively few steamy plumes rose from the desolate wilderness below us. Climbing in tight circles, we topped Mount Katmai and looked down into the green lake that never freezes, even in the toughest winters, because of the volcanic heat rising from deep within the slumbering mountain.

We started away. Suddenly the seats dropped from under us. Our cameras and loose gear banged about in the cabin as though weightless. Later the pilot told us we had struck a violent downdraft and dropped like a stone for 2,000 feet.

45

"I leveled off just above some of the wickedest terrain I ever saw," he said.

On the way back to King Salmon Airport, I thought of the endless variety of the National Park System. Here in Katmai, had we crashed, only a prowling fox or bear might ever have found us. Inside the Statue of Liberty—yes, that's a national monument too—I could not even have tripped and fallen; somebody would have caught me before I hit!

Where Katmai's volcanoes are wild things, Hawaii's Kilauea, Mauna Loa, and Haleakala are fairly well domesticated. The first two, the most active ones, are on the island of Hawaii. Haleakala, believed nearly dead, is on Maui. Volcanologists have been studying them all for many years and know when they are about to get dangerous, enabling people to escape their fiery lava flows.

Islanders call Halemaumau, the crater of Kilauea, the "drive-in volcano." A highway runs almost to the edge of the bubbling, steaming pit. The visitor runs his car onto a handy parking lot, then walks a few feet to the brink of eternity. Between him and eternity, however, stands a stout wire fence.

Established in 1916, Hawaii National Park is the most distant and one of the first established on donated private land. All the early ones on the mainland, unlike Hawaii, came out of tracts of land already owned by the Federal Government. All were in the West, for the simple reason that the East never had any substantial amount of public domain.

WHEN the time came to create eastern parks, private owners held the land from which parks could be made. When Congress declined to buy any with taxpayers' money, private philanthropy stepped in. Substantial folk from Boston and New York gave their summer-home property on Maine's Mount Desert Island, and Acadia National Park joined the people's estate.

The Rockefeller family's magnificent contributions to the Park System began at Acadia. John D. Rockefeller, Jr., donated the properties necessary to round out the Federal holdings. A family gift of $5,000,000 to match state and other contributions helped establish Great Smoky Mountains National Park in Tennessee and North Carolina, the most visited of all national parks.

We owe Linville Falls on the Blue Ridge Parkway to Mr. Rockefeller, and he contributed thousands of acres in Jackson Hole for Grand Teton National Park. His son Laurance, a National Geographic Trustee, gave us our newest national park, Virgin Islands, a tropical playground dedicated in 1956. In both a quantitative and a qualitative sense, the Rockefeller family has been the greatest single private benefactor of the Park System.

Foundations established by Mrs. Ailsa Mellon Bruce and Paul Mellon—the Avalon and the Old Dominion—donated half the purchase price of the 28,500-acre Cape Hatteras National Seashore Recreational Area on the Outer Banks of North Carolina, the first seashore in the Park System. The State of North

46    **A fiery geyser** of lava spurts 500 feet above a recent crater on Mount Kilauea in Hawaii National Park. Incandescent river of rock bursts from the cone at left. Surf whitens the distant shore.

THOMAS J. HARGRAVE

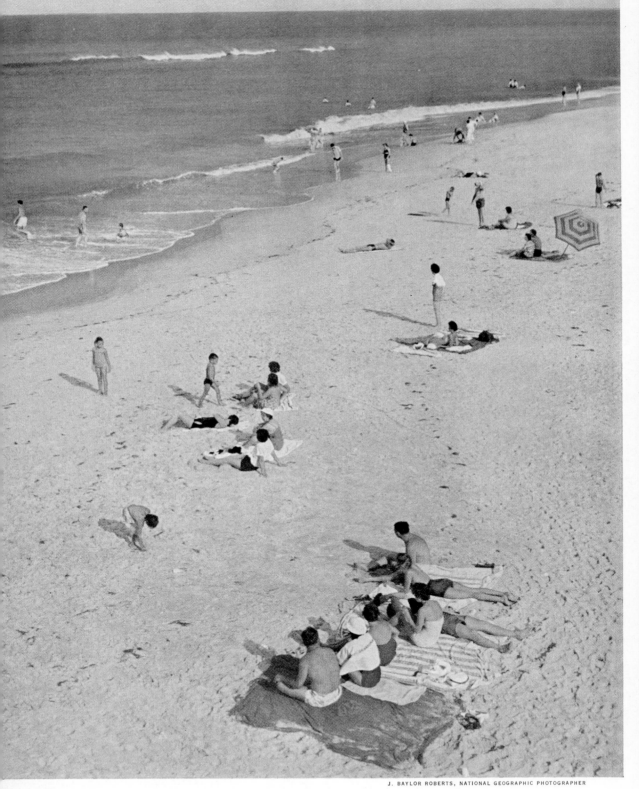

**Sun-drenched sands and restless seas** invite bathers to the Outer Banks. Cape Hatteras National Seashore Recreational Area preserves an 80-mile stretch of North Carolina's pencil-thin isles.

Carolina gave the other half, which means that every one of its citizens played a part in this generous act. The foundations also gave us the money for studies designed to show us where we can acquire other seacoast areas before all the shorelines of the United States pass into the hands of private developers.

Several parks given by states are on our itinerary. One is Big Bend National Park on the Mexican border. We have the State of Texas to thank for these 708,221 acres of glorious desert-mountain scenery. Mexico has plans for establishing its own park just across the Rio Grande. We would like that, for then we could work out arrangements with Mexico for another international park like the one straddling the Montana-Canada line. We call that one Waterton-Glacier International Peace Park, made up of the Canadian Water-

**Conch shell** echoes the crash of surf in the Atlantic playground.

ton Lakes National Park and our Glacier National Park. People cross the border at will, symbolizing the good relations between the United States and her neighbor to the north.

Big Bend is one of our four living-desert museums; others are Death Valley National Monument; Saguaro National Monument near Tucson, home of a magnificent stand of saguaro cactus; and Organ Pipe Cactus National Monument, a section of the great Mexican desert which protrudes into Arizona.

Shenandoah, second national park in the East, came as the welcome gift of Virginia. It was quite a chore rounding up the land, for on it lived hundreds of proud mountaineers who built their own log cabins and could shoot a squirrel in the eye from as far away as they could see him. One owner wouldn't sell. No native mountaineer was he, but former President Herbert Hoover. "Take it as a gift," he said, and deeded over his Camp Rapidan, where he fished and rested during vacations from the White House.

In the fall the hardwood forest along the famous Skyline Drive blazes with red and yellow of changing leaves. The park staff that must handle traffic has no trouble believing that a third of the country's population lives within a day's journey by automobile.

Senator Harry Flood Byrd of Virginia, when governor, played an important part in the drive to acquire land for Shenandoah. A real parks enthusiast, he has been my companion on more than one wilderness trip. One time I had him on a hike in Glacier. We came to a sign reading "4 Miles to Pinnacle Wall." We walked for two hours, then came to another: "3½ Miles to Pinnacle Wall."

50       **A mantle of snow** quiets the vibrant colors of Utah's Bryce Canyon.

Whipped cream clouds, hovering low, creep into each rocky crevice and alcove.

The senator flopped down beside the trail. "How in the world do you measure distances here?" he panted.

"We have a bicycle wheel on a stick, with a meter hooked to it," replied Park Superintendent Jack Emmert. "Ours is right old, and I guess there's some slack in the gears."

"Go get a new one," said the senator. "I'll personally see to it there's an extra $1.50 in the next Park Service appropriation for it." I guess the senator delivered. The sign was fixed by the next time I visited Glacier.

Everglades National Park, gift from Florida, is a subtropical wonderland, a place of mystery. Strange hammocks, islands of rank vegetation, stud its flat expanses of waving marsh grass. I can imagine thin smokes rising from these hammocks—campfire smokes of the Seminole Indians who once roamed this region. Never defeated by the United States although thousands of soldiers hunted them, the brightly clad Seminoles no longer live inside park boundaries, but visitors sometimes see them going about their business.

Not all gifts are on the scale of Everglades or Acadia. The Park System is indebted to hundreds of other contributors. Large or small, every donation is welcome. To receive and care for contributions from citizens, Congress has established the National Park Trust Fund. Anyone wishing to become a donor should write to me, and I will be happy to acquaint him with all details.

52

**An enchanted wood** bewitches children exploring Olympic's luxuriant rain forest.

PAUL A. ZAHL, NATIONAL GEOGRAPHIC STAFF, AND (LOWER RIGHT) M. E. BEATTY

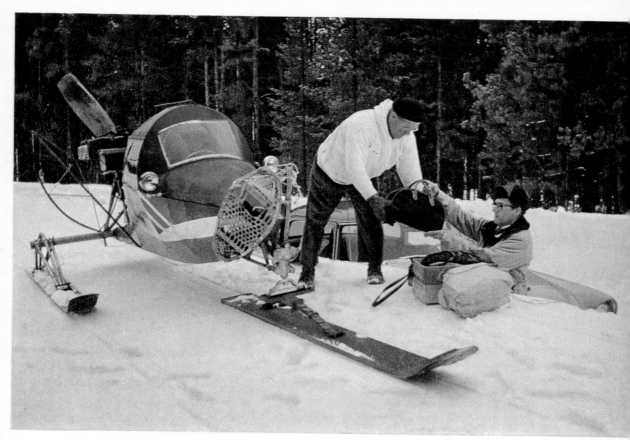

**Homemade snowscooter** with an airplane propeller meets National Geographic biologist Paul A. Zahl for a research trip deep into Yellowstone Park's snow-smothered wilderness.

**Prominent visitors tread Glacier's floral carpet**

U.S. Senator Harry F. Byrd of Virginia hikes third in line. His son Richard and Blackburn Moore break trail beneath the jagged profile of the Garden Wall. Director Wirth and Glacier Park's superintendent and chief ranger close file.

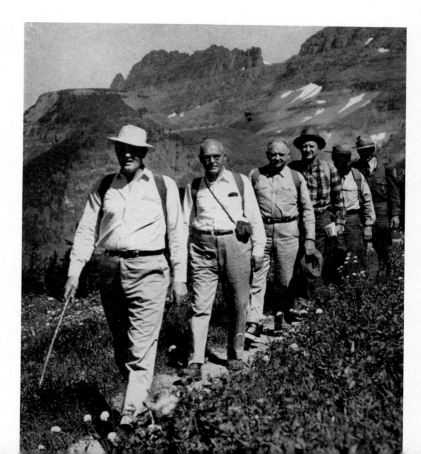

Everglades is a nature park and so are the others we've visited thus far—even the Indian ruins, for the Indian lived close to nature and rarely upset its delicate balance. This book is primarily concerned with these works of nature, rather than historic deeds. The landmarks of American history—battlefields, historic buildings, sites, monuments, memorial parks, and cemeteries comprise a vast subject in themselves and will be dealt with in another book.

OTHER THINGS about the Park Service might surprise you. We are the country's largest manufacturer of museum exhibits; we use the product in visitor centers, formerly called museums. In the Nation's Capital we operate the United States Park Police; some of the men patrol their beats in Rock Creek Park on horseback. We stock zoos with surplus elk and bears which have formed the habit of associating too closely with people. We do this free. We conduct no businesses ourselves; we have under contract some 175 private concessionaires who annually furnish upward of $45,000,000 worth of goods and essential services to park visitors. We cooperate with scientific organizations, such as the Smithsonian Institution and state universities, in excavating archeological sites threatened by new dams, pipelines, or highways. We help other Federal agencies plan recreational use for lands under their primary jurisdiction; Lake Mead, in Arizona and Nevada, is an example.

I hope we'll round out the Park System with more seashore areas and possibly a few more full-sized parks. We don't have a grasslands national park, for example, and I'd like to see one established out in the prairie country.

Once in a while we hear somebody say that the National Park System "locks up" valuable resources. Almost always the charge comes from someone who wants the park forests logged, or their mountain meadows opened for grazing, or dams built in their valleys. Well, to all such we say, "Yes, the parks are locked up—to you." But to everybody else we say, "No, the charge is untrue, the parks are not locked up. Come, use and enjoy them."

Parks exist to strengthen bodies, refresh minds, uplift the spirits. They enrich leisure, and I believe that the way Americans use their ever-increasing leisure will determine, more even than how we work, what kind of Nation this will be fifty or a hundred years from now.

Stephen Mather thought visiting parks was well worth while, and I'll just let him sum it up for me. "Who will gainsay," Mather said, "that the parks contain the highest potentialities of national pride, national contentment, and national health? A visit inspires love of country; begets contentment; engenders pride of possession; contains the antidote for national restlessness.

"A visit to a park teaches love of nature, of trees and flowers, the rippling brooks, the crystal lakes, the snow-clad mountain peaks, the wildlife encountered everywhere amid native surroundings. He is a better citizen with a keener appreciation of . . . living here who has toured the national parks."

**The snakebird spears a dinner of fish.**

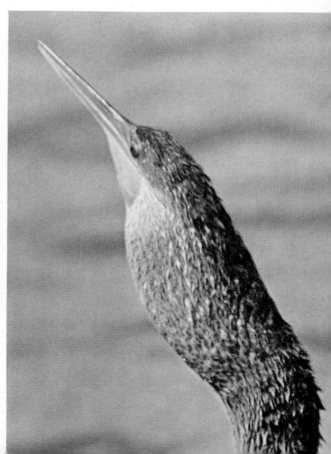

**Going—going—gone!** After stabbing the bream, a female anhinga in Everglades National Park, Florida, takes her catch ashore, shakes it violently, and gulps it. Anhingas swim with body submerged and neck up like a periscope.

## PART ONE

# THE ROCKY MOUNTAINS

Scouts and mountain men, treading these craggy high-lands, called them the Stony Mountains. Today they are the Rockies, and no longer need the feet be bruised by travel through them. What was once a grim barrier to all but the most adventurous is now a rampart of another sort, preserving precious areas of wilderness.

And what a wilderness! Torn by ancient volcanoes, sculptured by glaciers and rushing rivers, sheared by stupendous earth-fault, the Rockies are indeed a marvel to the eye. But this savage marvel has a gentle aspect, too. Beneath the crystalline peaks lie sparkling lakes, meadows strewn with wildflowers, and forests threaded by tumbling streams—a natural balance of land and water and sturdy vegetation, of prey and predator in undisturbed exchange.

A museum, a haven, a place to test the muscle, to study the way of natural things; all these the parks of the Rockies are. But they are more: a place where a man can regenerate his spirit, and see with quiet clarity the size and meaning of his world.

57

NORTH DAKOTA
SOUTH DAKOTA

*Missouri River*

∴ Bismarck

∴ Pierre

**Badlands**
NATIONAL MONUMENT

SOUTH DAKOTA
NEBRASKA

*Platte River*

NEBRASKA
KANSAS

0    STATUTE MILES    150

© N.G.S.
Irvin E. Alleman

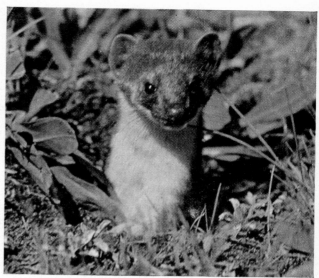

**Perky weasel** wears coat of summer brown; for winter's snows he dons pure white.

# YELLOWSTONE

*By FREDERICK G. VOSBURGH, Associate Editor, National Geographic*

**M**EN CAME OUT OF THE WEST with wild, incredible tales. High in the Rockies, they said, was a land where the earth boiled under your feet, where spouts of hot water as tall as a flagpole came roaring out of the trembling ground, and whole valleys steamed with sulphurous fumes as if the lid over Hell itself had been shot full of holes.

"Out thar in the Yellowstone," Jim Bridger related, "thar's a river that flows so fast it gets hot on the bottom."

Boiling springs bubbled by an icy lake, and a man could catch and cook a trout without moving a step or taking the fish off the line. There were mountains of glass and mountains of sulphur and mountains that spoke with growling voices.

A galloping river leaped over a cliff and landed in a gorge a thousand feet deep all lined with yellow stone. Down a terraced mountainside ran the waters of immense hot springs, scalding at first and cooling as they flowed, so a man could take a bath of any temperature he chose.

Thus ran the tales of the mountain men, long-haired, leather-garbed scouts and trappers such as John Colter, Joe Meek, and Bridger, who ranged westward from St. Louis early in the 19th century.

Today a million and a half visitors to Yellowstone National Park every year see for themselves that many of the old-timers' yarns were the truth and that there are more wonders in Yellowstone than even Jim Bridger knew.

**Queen of geysers,** Old Faithful performs on the average every 64.5 minutes. Named by General Washburn in 1870, she has never been known to miss a cue.

of 308-foot-high Lower Falls. The rim road winds past Lookout Point (right) to Canyon Hotel.

You can wade in the river that "gets hot on the bottom"—the Firehole River near Old Faithful. But the heat comes from hot springs in the bed, not from friction of water on rock.

At Fishing Cone beside Yellowstone Lake almost anybody can catch and cook a fish without moving out of his tracks; or, rather, he could if the rangers would let him, for park rules forbid putting anything into the hot pools.

Glass mountains? There's Obsidian Cliff, of black volcanic glass. There's Sulphur Mountain; and Roaring Mountain, named for the steam vents near its top. And in the awed accounts of the early trappers the present-day visitor recognizes such familiar yet marvelous features as Old Faithful and the great geyser basins, Mammoth Hot Springs, and that colorful, unbelievable canyon "where falls the Yellowstone."

L IKE MOST VISITORS to the park, my family and I were eager to watch Old Faithful in eruption and see a bear.

"Bears?" said the ranger at South Entrance. "They'll be holding you up before you have driven very far in the park."

As we neared Old Faithful, we found he was right. A black bear and her cinnamon cub were holding up all cars.

"Do not feed the bears," the rangers warn. Yet some heedless visitors feed and even fondle these dangerous wild animals, and every summer scores of persons are bitten or clawed. Sometimes bears get so bold and destructive that they have to be trapped and hauled by truck to exile in a distant corner of the park, or even, in extreme cases, sentenced to become a rug.

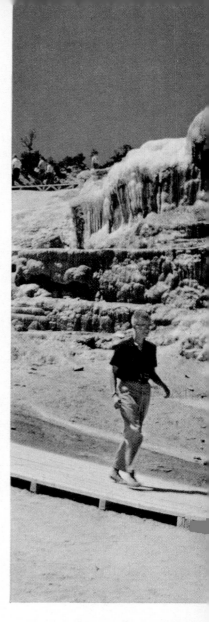

**Minerva Hot Spring startled the eyes of mountain men**

Past more of the furry official greeters we rolled at last to Old Faithful where the queen of Yellowstone rises each hour in draperies of steam.

In only three places in all the world can you see the never-forgotten sight of tons of hot water shooting out of the earth, propelled by the awesome explosive force of nature's hidden fires. One is Iceland, whence came the word "geyser," from an Icelandic verb meaning to gush. Another is New Zealand. But the biggest geysers and the largest number are here in Yellowstone.

Little did they suspect that here at Mammoth Hot Springs "a mountain was turning itself inside out." Welling up from the cavernous depths of Terrace Mountain, lime in solution forms draped balconies like this.

Deep under this ground—perhaps a mile down, the geologists tell us—seethe superhot magmas left from the days when belching volcanoes were building up these mountains. Cold ground waters, trickling downward, strike rising vapors of indescribable heat. They boil, flash into steam. If the explosion takes place in a tube of rock hard enough to stand the strain, the cooler water above is driven out in a geyser eruption.

Such manifestations of nature's power are found throughout much of Yellowstone's area of 3,472 square miles—ten thousand or more hot pools, gey-

## By land or water
## Yellowstone visitors
## enjoy a varied wonderland

A panorama of mountains and pine-clad slopes flashes past the eyes of vacationers speedboating on Yellowstone Lake, a mile and a half high. Other boats from the docks at Lake Hotel (in background) introduce sportsmen to the scrappy trout of America's oldest and largest national park.

**Begging bear** stops Loop Road traffic. Creatures of the wilderness roam this sanctuary free and unafraid. When a bear or deer strolls the highway, motorists stamp on the brakes and spill from cars, cameras in hand. These roadblocks, nicknamed "animal jams" by tolerant rangers, are an everyday sight.

Park Service signs in big bold letters warn not to feed or approach the bears. They are wild animals, even though they appear tame. But each year a number of heedless visitors are clawed or mauled.

ANDREW H. BROWN, NATIONAL GEOGRAPHIC STAFF

sers, and patches of boiling mud. Most of the big "hot water volcanoes" are here in Upper Geyser Basin. Giant, Giantess, Beehive, and Grand Geyser all erupt higher than Old Faithful, but you may have to wait days to see them. More gracious is the queen.

"Next eruption of Old Faithful about 6:40," read a sign at the visitor center. Near a low gray cone of geyserite a ranger naturalist was speaking:

"Old Faithful plays as regularly and as high as it did when discovered. . . . Height varies from 115 to 150 feet and once a 180-foot eruption was measured with a transit. Intervals between eruptions average 64.5 minutes. . . . The source of heat——"

But what was that? From beneath the earth came a rumbling sound, as if a giant were preparing to speak. From the top of the cone welled a little water. Higher it rose, fell back, then triumphantly tons upon tons of steaming water surged toward the darkening sky. From hundreds of throats came an exclamation, a gasp. Great billows of steam rolled off on the breeze.

Higher, yet higher, leaped the column, a hundred feet, a hundred and fifty, still higher, while the billowing steam rose far above, a pillar between the earth and sky.

65

**Old Faithful's steaming column** casts a cool shadow over Old Faithful Inn, "world's largest log cabin." Early risers watch as 10,000 gallons of water roar 150 feet into the air in the four-minute spectacle.

UNION PACIFIC RAILROAD COLORPHOTO

**Patriarch of the plains,** the buffalo once roamed North America more than

Four minutes, and the spouting flood had spent its power. Old Faithful's high plumed head sank lower, and slowly she withdrew to her home in the earth, like a genie into its box. Again people spoke; the spell was broken.

Two other favorites are Daisy and Riverside. Daisy first became famous in 1892, when it began to play regularly. Riverside's slanting stream, like a huge fire hose, pours into the Firehole River.

"Doesn't that hot smelly water kill the fish?" asked a visitor, sniffing the sulphurous fumes.

"Not at all," said the ranger. "You'll find plenty of trout here. The river temperature rises about six degrees as it flows through this area, but that isn't enough to hurt the fish. And bad as it smells, geyser water is pure; it tastes about like water boiled in your teakettle. In fact, geyser drainage is good for fishing. It helps produce a supply of food, and the fish grow all year round."

At Gibbon Geyser Basin, believe it or not, are steam-heated bear dens! Wise bruins have found that vapor-warmed rocks make a snug hideaway.

68

**A ten-point** elk rests on a steam-heated range. In winter, animals replace tourists at geysers and hot springs, gathering like country folks around a pot-bellied stove. Grassland is limited, so Yellowstone's elk herds must be thinned annually to prevent overgrazing.

50 million strong. Here members of Yellowstone's remnant herd find snow-free forage near a geyser's heat.

PAUL A. ZAHL, NATIONAL GEOGRAPHIC STAFF, AND (ABOVE) GEORGE D. MARLER

70      **Ghostly images peer** from the limpid waters of Emerald Pool. Algae tint the scalding depths green. Other species of this microscopic plant life lend brighter color to the shallows and edges, where the

ANDREW H. BROWN, NATIONAL GEOGRAPHIC STAFF

slow-flowing spring cools enough to touch. In ages past, volcanoes
spewed lava over the Yellowstone plateau. Today its volcanic heritage shows in more than 10,000 hot springs, geysers, and steam jets.

71

Steam-heated birds' nests are another Yellowstone oddity, several species making their homes within reach of the warm drifting vapor from geyser basins.

Geysers of the fountain type—as opposed to the nozzle type such as Old Faithful—are often glassy pools until almost the instant of eruption. A good example is Grand Geyser. One minute it is a placid mirror; the next the water is blasting into the air as if propelled by dynamite. The flying rocketlike jets suggest a fireworks display.

One of the best known pools is Morning Glory, around which a superstition centers. Somehow the idea has spread over the country that tossing a penny into Morning Glory brings good luck. Bad luck is much more likely, for the tosser may be fined for defacing the pool.

Periodically, a ranger cleans out Morning Glory with a kitchen spoon on the end of a pole. "The superintendent sends the money to Washington," he said, "and the U. S. Treasury logs it in as an increase in national wealth."

One of the strangest things about these hot pools and geysers is the effect that ordinary soap has upon them. Like small boys they can't seem to stand it. Many of the pools are in delicate hair-trigger balance, so that a slight change in pressure will turn them into geysers.

A dramatic example is Chinaman Spring, a few steps from Old Faithful Geyser. A Chinese laundryman at the hotel many years ago thought it a shame to let all this hot water go to waste. He put up a tent over the pool, tossed in the clothes, added soap, and was rubbing his hands in satisfaction when suddenly up roared the pool—tent, laundry, laundryman and all.

"Soaping" today, of course, is strictly forbidden.

The vicinity of these hot pools is no place for the absent-minded. Anybody who walked into one would parboil in a trice. In Skeleton Spring are skeletons of two boiled bison which have been there since the early days of the park.

AT OLD FAITHFUL, as everywhere in Yellowstone, wild animals are constantly appearing. A big elk bound for the river strolled past a crowd at Grand Geyser. Under the porch at the lodge lived golden-mantled marmots, grandfatherly little dignitaries who ate from visitors' hands. During an eruption of Old Faithful a black cub ambled by—and promptly stole the show.

At night at a campfire session I looked at the strangely assorted people singing "Home on the Range"—tenderfeet on their first trip west, schoolteachers, businessmen, doctors, clerks, lawyers, engineers.

> *Oh, give me a home where the buffalo roam,*
> *Where the deer and the antelope play. . . .*
> *Where the graceful white swan goes gliding along*
> *Like a maid in a heavenly dream.*

"That's a good song to be singing here," said the ranger, "for Yellowstone

**Wary pronghorns** stand hillside sentinel. North America's fastest mammal, *Antilocapra americana* can sprint 50 miles an hour. His bobbing white rump flashes danger to the herd. Both male and female have hollow, branched horns, which they shed every fall.

PAUL A. ZAHL, NATIONAL GEOGRAPHIC STAFF

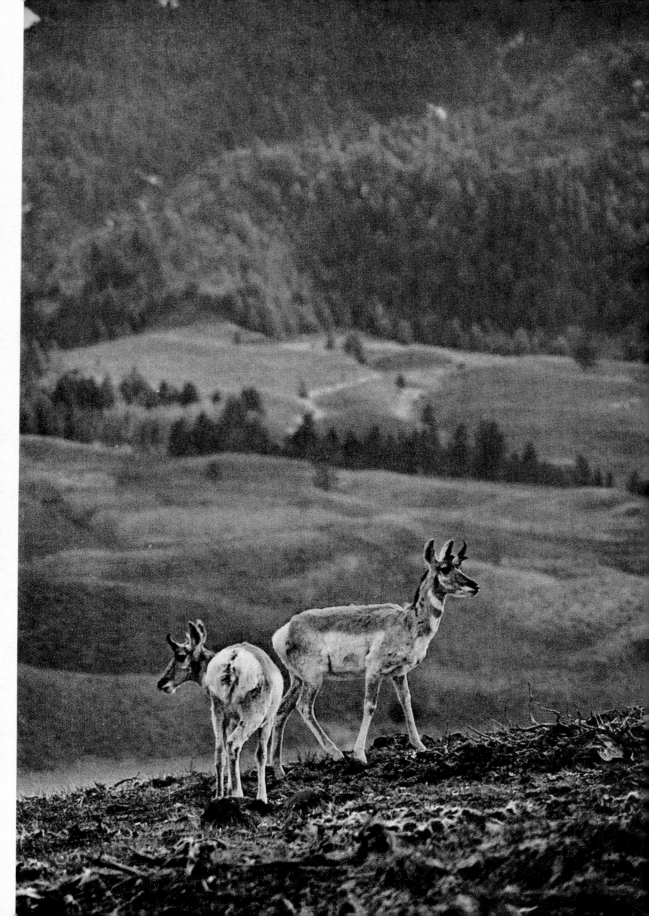

is one place in the world where all of those creatures are still to be found, even the rare trumpeter swan. Up near the Gardiner entrance plenty of 'antelope play,' and on Mirror Plateau hundreds of 'buffalo roam.' "

Old Faithful Inn, dear to countless honeymooners, was hacked from forests in 1903 to become one of the world's largest wooden buildings. No guest will forget its sprawling, gingerbread charm, its 92-foot-high entrance hall, ringed by five tiers of rustic balconies.

Many rooms face the geyser, offering a midnight view of Old Faithful unfolding her stately dance by the light of the moon. Her performance gains glory when nothing moves on the chalky geyser mounds but the prima donna herself.

Fifty-four miles away, another huge hostelry, Canyon Hotel, has long stood as a landmark beside the Grand Canyon of the Yellowstone. During the winter of 1910-11, six-horse sleds groaned over ice-locked hills hauling 5,000 tons of materials for this half-million-dollar building.

Remembered for its vast, raftered lounge and birch-paneled dining room, Canyon Hotel could not keep pace with the rising tides of visitors. So, in the 1950's, the Park Service designed a modern village with hundreds of cottages, a visitor center, shops, campgrounds, and a streamlined lodge decorated with striking murals. Canyon Village was carefully planned to avoid marring its setting. It lies well back from the canyon rim, screened by pines.

**A Shiras Moose scans his domain for rivals**

I F COLTER had ever told in St. Louis that out in the Yellowstone there was a mountain that was turning itself inside out, he would have been laughed out of town. Yet that is exactly what is happening at Mammoth Hot Springs.

It is autumn in Yellowstone, the mating season, and this lordly bull jealously guards his harem. Light-hued *Alces alces shirasi* was named after George Shiras 3d, for 31 years a National Geographic Trustee.

Out of the depths of Terrace Mountain, hot springs are bringing lime in solution from limestone beds hundreds of feet down and depositing it on the outside in the form of travertine (calcium carbonate). This light porous rock builds up fast—six inches to a foot a year—compared to a mere thirty-second of an inch for the hard geyserite of the geyser basins.

Huge terraces have been formed on the mountainside—and one can imagine caverns, correspondingly huge, deep in the earth below.

On one of these travertine terraces stands the little town of Mammoth Hot Springs, the park headquarters. Soil was hauled in by horse and spread

**Nature's dining room:** lodgepole pines whisper luncheon music beside the gentle Yellowstone,

**Floral treasures** spangle upland meadows—pink monkey flower above its thundering falls (page 80).

over the rock when this was Fort Yellowstone.

Down the face of the mountain we wound to Mammoth, past Jupiter Terrace and the other formations standing like pulpits above the town. Over them ran steaming hot water, and many wore mantles of vivid algae. Far down at the base of the lowest terrace emerges Hot River, the subterranean stream draining this eccentric mountain.

Climbing the terraces, we found in one pool an egg someone had left to boil. Farther on, a new spring had broken out in the middle of the path.

"They change course overnight," said the ranger naturalist.

"Why aren't there any geysers here? Because the rock is soft. The water just boils up and flows away. There's no hard, siliceous sinter here to form breeches and barrels for water cannon like Old Faithful."

Jim Bridger, in his best romancing mood, used to tell that out in the Yellowstone there were not only "peetrified" trees but on their branches perched "peetrified birds a-singing' peetrified songs."

No "peetrified" birds or stone songs have been found, but the truth is almost as strange. Science knows, for example, that there are not one but a dozen petrified forests piled

77

wild aster

wild geranium

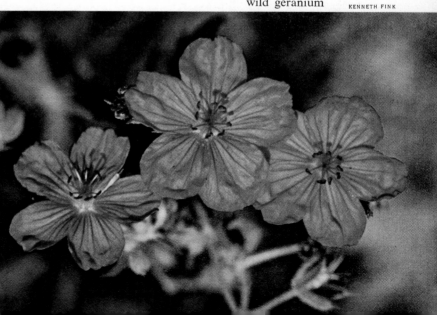

**Anglers gang up on cutthroat trout at outlet of Yellowstone Lake. Snow lingers on Mount Sheridan**

Fish braving the headwaters of the Yellowstone River face triple jeopardy: boatmen dangle tempting bait; shore-based sportsmen wade deep to cast their lures; others throng Fishing Bridge (where picture was taken). Boats may be rented, but many vacationers bring their own atop cars or trailers.

Below: A happy angler displays her catch of brown trout from Shoshone Lake. Isolated Shoshone is accessible by trail or by small boat dragged up the swift outlet stream. No fishing license is required in the park.

Lower right: A sight-seeing cavalcade led by a bus from Yellowstone's famous yellow fleet threads the Hoodoos, stark blocks of ancient travertine that tumbled from Terrace Mountain, three miles south of Mammoth Hot Springs.

ANDREW H. BROWN, NATIONAL GEOGRAPHIC STAFF

one on top of another. Giant trees were smothered by ashes and lava spewed out by thundering volcanoes, and on the debris new forests grew, until there were a dozen of them, like layers in a cake. Now the Lamar River has cut the cake for the wondering eye to see.

But of all the wonders of wonderland, none hit this beholder with a stronger impact than the Grand Canyon of the Yellowstone.

Awed Indians untold years ago peered into a golden gorge where a river leaped like a plume of smoke from the top of a high cliff. They called it the river of the yellow stone. Restrained and simple, the name is perfect, but it fails to prepare you for the tremendous sight that inspired it.

Yellow it is, this breathtaking gorge, and myriad blending shades as well, from ocher to orange and deep, rich red. "Land of sand and ruin and gold. . . ." Somehow the line from Swinburne kept running through my mind. But this was rock and ruin and gold—ruin wrought by a river on solid rock with the aid of hot water and steam.

Ospreys usually look down on man. Here the tables are turned as the big fish hawks soar below in the gorge and nest in plain sight on pinnacles of rock. Many visitors mistake them for eagles.

If you descend into the canyon, and if you are lucky, you may see the little water ouzel, or dipper, dive into the Yellowstone's foam-flecked torrents to "fly under water" in quest of aquatic food.

Most of the Nation's surviving grizzly bears find sanctuary in Yellowstone. Near the canyon, at Trout Creek dump, they feast on table scraps. A mother grizzly sniffed suspiciously before leading off her three butterball cubs.

"Know how to tell a grizzly from a black bear?" asked the ranger. "Let the bear chase you up a tree. If it comes up after you, it's not a grizzly."

Past Mud Volcano and Dragons Mouth Spring, with its flickering tongue of hot water and steam, we drove upriver from Canyon to Yellowstone Lake. On Fishing Bridge anglers almost elbow to elbow were casting for cutthroats, the gorgeous native Yellowstone, or Montana black-spotted, trout.

One of the highest big lakes in the world, Yellowstone today drains to the Atlantic via the Yellowstone River, the Missouri, Mississippi, and Gulf of Mexico. But centuries ago glacier ice blocked the outlet and the lake drained to the Pacific through the Snake and the Columbia. That explains the presence of Yellowstone's cutthroat trout, a distinct species, but related to Pacific coast cutthroats.

Which of all the marvels of Yellowstone, I wondered, makes the greatest impression? I asked this question at each of the five gates where cars pour in and out of the park.

"What hit me hardest?" said an easterner. "Old Faithful, of course."

**A giant unchained,** Lower Falls on the Yellowstone dwarfs visitors who walk its brink. During June run-off, 60,000 gallons a second thunder through this huge spout, carved in a rib of volcanic rock.

ANDREW H. BROWN, NATIONAL GEOGRAPHIC STAFF

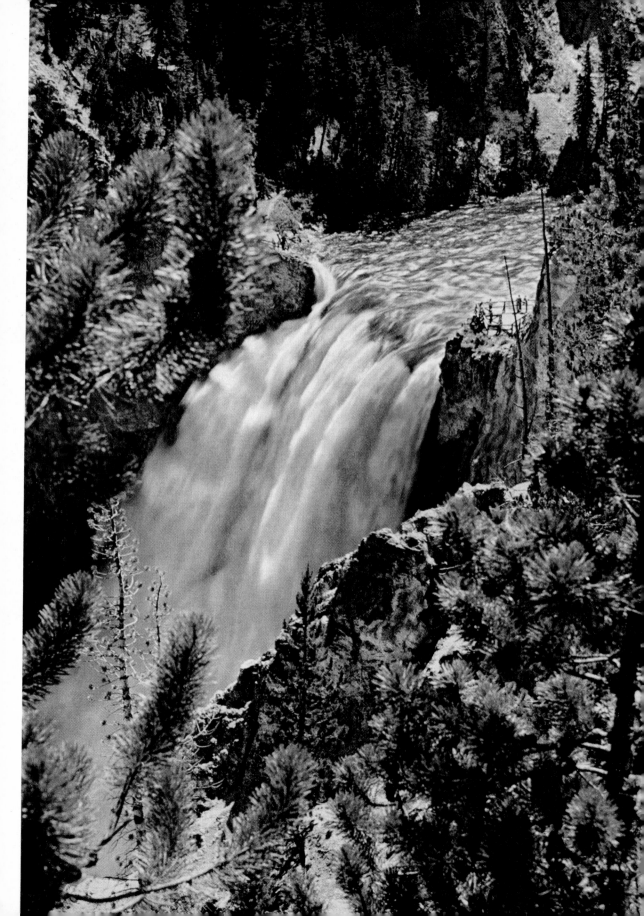

"Bears!" yelled another.

"That wonderful canyon!" a woman exclaimed.

"The unparalleled thermal activity," said a serious-minded student.

But I think the best reaction to Yellowstone is that of old White Hawk, a Bannock Indian. At Old Faithful someone once asked White Hawk whether it was true that Indians used to shun the geyser areas, believing them the abode of evil spirits.

The old chief shook his head and gazed with practical eye at the plumes of hot water, the gemlike seething pools.

"Ugh," said he. "Good place cookum meat."

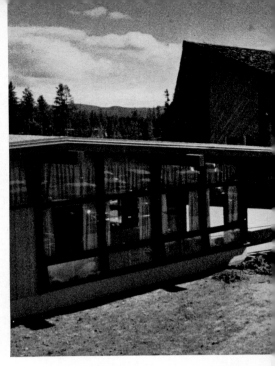

**The new look** in park architecture,

ANDREW H. BROWN AND (ABOVE) J. BAYLOR ROBERTS, NATIONAL GEOGRAPHIC STAFF

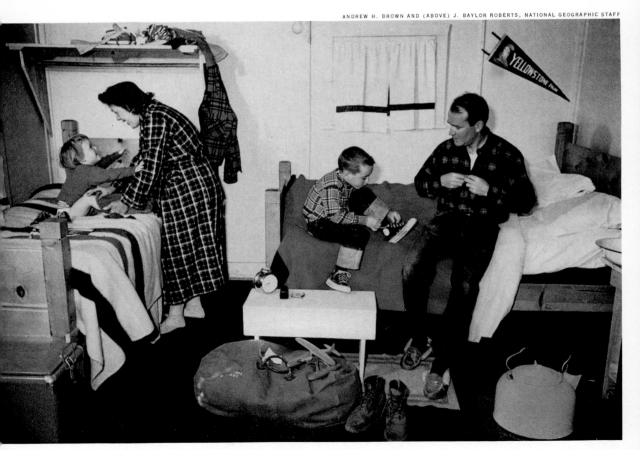

**Snug in a cabin** at Canyon, the Browns, from sweltering Washington, D. C., dress for an active day. Heavy blankets ward off mile-and-a-half-high chill.

Canyon Village Lodge houses dining room, cafeteria, lounge, and shops for 500 motel units.

## YELLOWSTONE NATIONAL PARK *Northwestern Wyoming. Area 3,472 sq. mi.*

**Features:** World's most spectacular thermal area, with more than 10,000 geysers, hot springs, pools, steam jets, mud volcanoes. Largest mountain lake in North America (elev. 7,731 ft.). Grand Canyon of the Yellowstone. Upper, Lower, and Tower Falls. Obsidian Cliff; standing petrified trees. Black and grizzly bears, moose, deer, elk, pronghorn, bighorn, coyote, bison; some 240 species of birds.

**Activities:** Visitor centers. Grand Loop Road (142 mi.) connects major features. Sightseeing bus trips; 1,000 mi. of hiking and riding trails. Campfire programs, guided walks, exhibits. Trout fishing, boating, wilderness camping, wildlife photography.

**Season:** Park open May 1—Oct. 31; most facilities June 1—Sept. 15.

**Weather:** Warm, sparkling days, cool evenings (average elev. 7,500 ft.).

**What to bring:** Hiking shoes and rough-it clothing; woolens for evening. Raincoat, camera and light meter, binoculars.

**How to get there:** Major highways converge on Yellowstone's five entrances (see map at back of book). Consult touring services on routes and snow conditions in high passes during May, June, and September. Park buses connect with trains and buses. Write Yellowstone Park Co., Yellowstone Park, for schedules. Northwest, Western, Frontier, and United Airlines serve nearby cities; surface connections to park.

**Accommodations:** Make reservations early; opening and closing dates for each place vary; write Yellowstone Park Co. for list. Hotels: Old Faithful (Inn), Lake, Mammoth Hot Springs. Lodges: Old Faithful, Lake, Canyon, Roosevelt. Campers cabins: Old Faithful, West Thumb, Fishing Bridge, Canyon. 16 camp and trailer grounds: first come, first served.

**Services:** Main centers provide restaurants, stores, garages; car rentals at Old Faithful, Canyon, Mammoth. Hospital with surgeon at Mammoth; physician at Old Faithful Inn. Religious services in park; interdenominational chapel at Mammoth.

**Park regulations:** Campfires outside campgrounds by permit only. No feeding or molesting animals or defacing natural features. Daily maximum five fish, no fishing license required. Ask for fishing regulations. Boat permits required; no boat over 32 ft., no sailboats because of squalls. Pets allowed on leash, but not in boats or on trails.

*For further information write Superintendent, Yellowstone National Park, Wyoming*

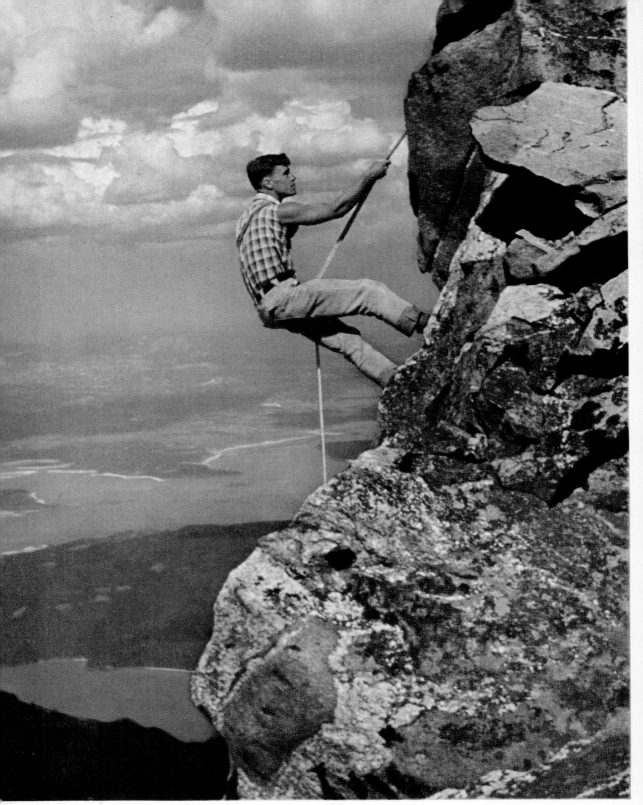

84    **Life hanging by a slender rope,** Frank Craighead rappels down the rock face of Mount St. John. Below lie Leigh Lake (foreground) and Jackson Lake. Guided parties of park visitors swarm up the Teton's major peaks every summer. The Craigheads have scaled them all.

**A mule deer** searches her snowbound home for a cold dinner of serviceberry and bitter brush.

# GRAND TETON

## NATIONAL PARK

*By FRANK and JOHN CRAIGHEAD*
*Photographs by the authors*

FRENCH-CANADIAN TRAPPERS more than a hundred years ago gave the Tetons their name. Gazing in awe at that spectacular granite skyline, they dubbed three towering summits the "Trois Tetons," for their fancied resemblance to a woman's breasts.

Later explorers thought "Tetons" a misnomer. "He indeed must have been long a dweller amid these solitudes who could trace in these cold and barren peaks any resemblance to the gentle bosom of a woman," wrote Nathaniel P. Langford on his expedition to nearby Yellowstone in 1870.

But we have no desire to enter an old argument. To us and to all who visit Grand Teton National Park today, the special appeal of the Tetons lies in the way they rise so precipitously from the lake-studded floor of the Jackson Hole valley, the tallest peak clawing the sky at nearly 14,000 feet.

Our own first glimpse of this game-rich valley in the Wyoming Rockies, back in 1934, fired us with its promise as an outdoor laboratory for wildlife research. We had fought our old Chevrolet up the dirt road from the east to Togwotee Pass. Our eyes swept the snow-flecked crests of the Teton Range. At its base shimmered broad Jackson Lake, through which flows the upper Snake River. Repeated visits to the Jackson Hole country won us completely to its sagebrush flats and timbered slopes.

From wartime service in warm oceans and hot tropical forests, we returned

**Bare of foothills, Wyoming's magnificent Tetons explode in craggy abruptness from the gentle**

**floor of Jackson Hole.**   Into this sheltered "hole," or valley, came Indians to stalk elk, and mountain men to trap beaver. Homesteaders and cattlemen followed, guided by three snowy peaks on the horizon: South, Middle, and Grand Teton. Snake River cuts the bank at far right.

to Jackson Hole and canyon roads of snow, to a dazzling whiteness scarcely toned down by forest green, to nightly subfreezing temperatures. During the following weeks the spring sun slugged it out with gray snow flurries that roared down the canyons of the Tetons and tried to spread over the valley. As if by magic a hot sun burned the snow blanket until the fence tops showed, then the tips of the sagebrush. Warm winds whipped away the evaporating moisture, while the porous glacial soil absorbed the melted snow and slowly released it to the Snake River. Almost overnight in early May, spring came to the valley, and winter slowly receded up the mountains.

Buttercups turned the first bare ground to a glistening gold. Shaggy, ill-tempered moose dragged out of the Snake River willow bottoms, waded into the unfrozen beaver ponds, and daily grew warier as they gained strength and flesh from the slimy green algae.

Grouse drummed in courtship day and night. Seldom glimpsed, Wilson's snipe performed their evening nuptial flights. Their directionless, winnowing whistles seemed to come from dead trees in the swamp, from steepled spruce trees, from the dusky sky directly above, or from low in the sedge-lined channels leading to the beaver houses. A lonesome saw-whet owl called monotonously for a mate, and there were the hoots of nesting great horned owls, the

88

**Camping** beside the Snake, John Craighead sets up bed and kitchen within arm's reach. The larder is the river, here flowing beneath Mount Teewinot. Cutthroat trout (a slash of red on both sides of the lower jaw suggested the common name) abound in its swift waters, the valley's lakes, and the ponds that beaver back up in abandoned river-channel sloughs.

Cutthroats are often greedy. When Frank Craighead opened one big fellow, he found inside, newly swallowed, a full-grown field mouse.

The rubberized nylon tent, comfortable in winter temperatures to 30 below, folds into a three-pound load. A heavier item for the packframe is Frank's "papoose," his son Charlie (right).

swirls of feeding trout, and then the aspens turning green and the willows red.

From the sagebrush of the valley and the blue waters of Jenny Lake we followed a trail over glacial moraines cloaked in lodgepole pine and climbed Cascade Canyon into the subalpine zone of fir and spruce. Above timber line on the Skyline Trail towered a tremendous stratified limestone wall contrasting with the Pre-Cambrian granite of the Teton peaks. And above the cliffs and peaks, birds of prey soared and wheeled on rising air currents while scanning the meadows below. Swainson's hawks, ferruginous roughlegs, sparrow hawks, and prairie falcons maneuvered in the rarer air at 11,000 feet, while the golden eagle soared beyond 13,000 to look down on the entire range.

We felt like staying forever up in the rock gardens above the valley. But the Tetons can be moody as well as magnificent. During one of our summer climbs lightning played among the peaks; storms that had been milling around all day fused at last in one rumbling mass of clouds and searing flashes. Thunder broke directly overhead. The air was charged, crackling. Electricity stood our hair on end, made the skin tingle. The wind came in violent gusts. Lightning struck close by, leaving a strong ozone smell in its wake.

A band of elk crossed our path, headed down. Rain and hail flailed us as we crawled into timber-line lean-tos, natural shelters where mountain sheep and elk bed down beneath the matted roofing of gnarled and ageless firs. Its force spent on the cushion of needles, rain trickled down to the dry soil below.

Thundering and mumbling, the storm moved quickly on, tagged by the sun reflected in a million water crystals adhering to the flowers. The next morning light snow covered the peaks. Clouds drifted low over the alpine gardens, letting the sun through here and there, but never for long. The mood of the mountains had changed.

Tempting but treacherous, the Tetons are not to be tackled lightly. You must not climb them alone. "Climb safely" is a basic mountaineering rule.

The elk in summer move to the high country of the Teton National Forest and the timbered and grassy vales of the Yellowstone plateau. There they fatten, raise their calves, and frolic amid the cool alpine meadows.

On clear September days, when aspens glitter golden on the hills, it is a tingling thrill to hear a bull elk bugling. Frequently we glimpse him on a hilltop

90

**Elk get a handout when winter whitens Jackson Hole**

This native deer, second largest to the moose, once ranged North America widely. As settlers slaughtered for meat and hides, the elk, or wapiti, retreated west. Like the buffalo, it barely escaped extinction.

Summering in Teton forests and Yellowstone's high glades (p. 11), these surviving bands migrate in fall to Jackson Hole. When snow buries the range they feed on hay provided by the U. S. Fish and Wildlife Service.

Adjoining Grand Teton Park, the National Elk Refuge winters a herd of 6,000 to 11,000. Licensed hunting helps keep numbers down.

Standing as high as horses, the largest males may weigh 1,000 pounds. In mating season, valleys ring with clashing antlers as rival bulls battle.

in proud pose, his many-pointed rack silhouetted against the sky. This is the season of the rut, and the bull elk is in his splendid prime.

With the first heavy snows in late October or early November, a herd estimated at 10,000 to 14,000 drifts down to winter in the lower Jackson Hole valley. During these weeks rifle fire echoes among the hills and on the flats. Legal hunting is encouraged. Wildlife research shows that even now, despite this annual check, the herd has multiplied beyond the capacity of its winter range, increasing the demands on the winter feeding program.

M ANY OF OUR sharpest memories of life in Jackson Hole focus on adventures with its mammals and birds. We always have had pets around our cabins: coyotes, ground squirrels, chipmunks, magpies, ravens, horned owls, sparrow hawks, prairie falcons, Canada geese, even white-footed mice. These pets, free to come and go as they please, can leave us completely if they wish. 91

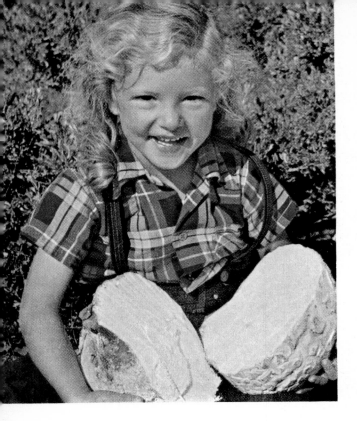

Kali, a female coyote, we raised from a pup. She played with the children, chewed up shoes, came at our call, and acted like a well-behaved dog. And like a good dog she assumed responsibilities.

One day John heard Kali barking excitedly. Between barks she was trying to pull something out of the irrigation ditch. Instantly John ran, for he saw that his year-old son Derek had crawled into the ditch. The coyote's warning probably saved the baby from drowning.

Kali later ate four of our laying hens; we merely reprimanded her.

Since our first visits, Jackson Hole has been invaded by paved roads, motels, service stations, and a swelling tide of tourist traffic, but the glorious semiwilderness back country happily remains intact. Some areas within the park are as wild as when John Colter, mountain man and trapper, set foot here in 1807.

After the trappers and hunters of last century took heavy toll of its animals, Jackson Hole relapsed into neglect. The westward trek of settlers washed around it to the Pacific, for the Hole was not farming or industrial country. Untapped by rails, the valley knew only limited lumbering. Much of Jackson

**From giant puffballs, enough to feed ten men, to tiny pine-nut morsels, the wilderness food locker**

Mountain men found food for the plucking in the Rockies. One lost explorer survived 37 days on little else but thistle roots!

Puffball mushrooms, like Karen holds above, pop out of meadows in spring or fall. Peeled, sliced, and fried in butter, they lend a banquet touch to elk steak or trout.

Onionlike camass bulbs (right) taste like potatoes when baked or boiled. They helped save Lewis and Clark explorers on Idaho's Lolo Trail. (The death camass, a similar bulb, is poisonous.)

And for dessert: pine nuts and golden currants.

**Baby scales 35 ounces.** When grown, this great horned owl may gulp seven field mice in one meal. Banding birds reveals range and life span.

Hole, therefore, still holds elk, moose, deer, and bighorn sheep. Beaver boldly cut aspen and cottonwood for their dams. Game birds abound, and rising trout ripple the lakes and streams.

Years before we found our way to Jackson Hole, the recreational value of the area and its potential as an "unfenced zoo" had been recognized. In 1897

**provides a ready menu full of zest and life.**

Resinous cones of the whitebark pine yield pine nuts.

Golden currants ripen in late summer and fall.

Teton National Forest was created. In 1921 Congress set aside land in the valley for a National Elk Refuge, and in 1929 established Grand Teton National Park. Wyoming's Game and Fish Commission has aided Federal programs to preserve the Jackson Hole country for the enjoyment of Americans forever.

Congress in 1950 tripled the park's area by including lands formerly in Jackson Hole National Monument and private holdings; 30,000 of these acres were presented to the American people by John D. Rockefeller, Jr.

"Conservation today means far more than just preserving our natural resources," said his son, Laurance S. Rockefeller, a National Geographic Trustee, at the dedication of Jackson Lake Lodge. "It means their wise use and protection so that more and more people may enjoy and benefit by them."

The $6,000,000 lodge, with its 60-foot-wide picture window, was sited by John D. Rockefeller, Jr., personally, to afford guests a magnificent view across Jackson Lake to the Tetons. Jackson Lake Lodge, its neighboring dude ranch, Jenny Lake Lodge, and the log-cabin village at Colter Bay are all managed by Jackson Hole Preserve, Inc., a nonprofit Rockefeller organization.

Colter Bay was developed as a model for park accommodations sought under the Park Service's Mission 66 program. Campgrounds, trailer sites, and scores of cabins nestle among tall evergreens. The community includes a visitor center, general store, service station, cafeteria and grill, showers, laundromat, a beach, and a marina where you can rent boats or launch your own.

W HEN YOU ARRIVE in the park, we suggest you first drive up Signal Mountain for its commanding view of the valley and range. Later you may wish to exchange the driver's seat for the saddle. Whether you elect to take a short horseback ride, join an overnight pack trip, or strike out afoot, you have 225 miles of varied trails from which to choose. A favorite is Cascade Canyon Trail, winding between crags to Lake Solitude, an 18-mile round trip. And ever beckoning the skilled climber are those inspiring cliff-hung towers of naked rock— Grand, Middle, and South Teton, Teewinot, Owen, Moran. Each craggy summit offers its special challenge.

People fall into two groups in their attitude toward the Tetons. The first somehow *must* get to the top. The second, far larger, group has this reaction: "Climb one of those things? Uh-uh! Not for me. I'll just look, thanks."

Float trips down the Snake, whispering in its gravelly bed, are a delightful way to see the park. Starting near Jackson Lake Lodge, you can join an organized float trip or launch your own rubber raft or canoe and glide silently and effortlessly through forests and meadows, then scud thrillingly through white water near the end of your 20-mile voyage to Moose.

The fast-flowing Snake stays open even through winter's coldest weather, and we have pioneered winter rafting on it to study big game and Canada geese. The

"**Come and get it!**" A ride to Emma Matilda Lake spells appetites as strong as the coffee. Rustlers and old-time posses are gone, but dude ranches and lodges carry on Jackson Hole's boot-and-saddle ways.

WILLARD R. CULVER

**Holiday riders roam the sagebrush** amid Teton splendor. Some of these guests of Jackson Lake

channel is a glassy-dark path through a lonely, glittering land. Swinging around bends, we flush geese and ducks, catch sight of mink, porcupine, and otter. Moose drag through six-foot drifts of snow, feeding on willow tips.

It was a winter float trip that showed us a rare woodland drama. We tied our raft to the bank and snowshoed up a side canyon. High above us on an open

Lodge (center) are city dwellers riding for the first time. A dam raises the lake's natural level.

slope we saw a band of mule deer, lunging forward, belly-deep in snow. They would stop, rest, plunge ahead some more. Panting with exhaustion, they reached a hard-packed snow cornice that overhung a cliff.

Hardly had they paused when a golden eagle swooped down and attacked; it struck the deer with its wings, raked their backs with its talons. Evidently the

97

**Like a figurehead on a ship,
a skier glides through the air
at Jackson, Wyoming**

Old-timers often used skis to get through the valley snow. When skiing emerged as a sport, Jackson, southern gateway to the park, found itself blessed with the right weather and terrain.

Operated for skiers in winter and sightseers in summer, the chair lift on Jackson's Snow King Mountain rises 1,571 feet in 15 minutes, giving a thrilling view of Jackson Hole and the Tetons.

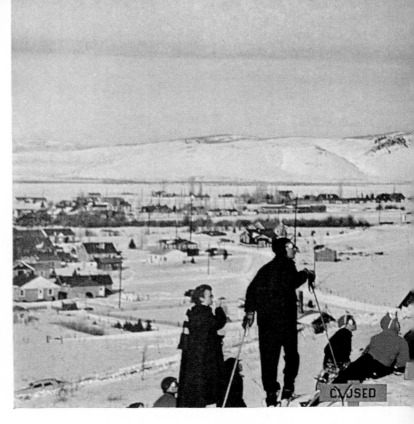

bird was trying to panic its prey into lunging over the cliff to death on the rocks below. But the deer held together, fended off attack by rising on their hind legs and flailing at the eagle with their forefeet. The air-ground combat continued until the eagle soared off to find an easier meal.

98    Even when snow crunches underfoot in Jackson Hole, and ice crystals sift

down out of a cloudless sky, everybody plays outdoors. Valley folk have a choice of skiing, cutter racing, ice fishing, and snowplane trips. Then on summer nights, from the windows of our cabins, we look across sagebrush flats at a thousand-eyed dragon writhing along beneath the Teton ramparts—the procession of automobiles carrying visitors to this enchanted landscape.

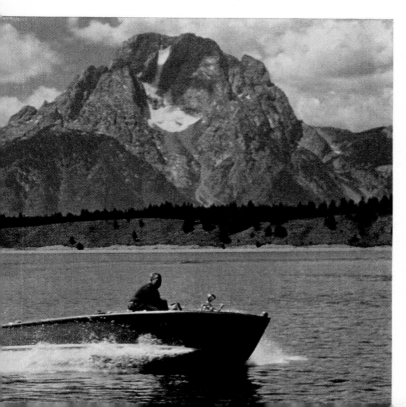

### Water skiers play on Jackson Lake

Ice Age glaciers ground out the bed of Jackson Lake, the valley's largest and deepest body of water. Retreating, they left mounds of rubble above the lake, and dark evergreens grow on them today.

Skillet Glacier rides a pocket on the side of Mount Moran (right), fourth highest Teton peak. Titanic earth forces some 60 million years ago thrust up a block 7,000 feet or more. Stream and glacier, rain and frost sculptured this high ground until mountain forms emerged. Blunt at first, the peaks grew sharp as they wore down to their hard Pre-Cambrian cores. Grand Teton, the highest, is now 13,766 feet above sea level.

WILLARD R. CULVER

**Jackson Lake Lodge** looks on splendor. Built by John D. Rockefeller, Jr., the $6,000,000 lodge can accommodate 1,100 guests in its 300 rooms. King-size window in the lounge brings the Tetons indoors.

Recently we drove to park headquarters, near Moose, to see Grand Teton's superintendent.

"Use of the park is skyrocketing," he said. "We now have a million and a half visitors each year. That's almost ten times as many as we had ten years ago. We're now fifth most visited national park."

People en masse could destroy the fragile balance of wild creatures and wild land. But, to their everlasting credit, Americans are responding to the basic idea of their national parks. The co-operation of visitors and the efforts of the Park Service and other conservation agencies ensure that Grand Teton National Park will be available to future millions in all its untouched grandeur.

Thus does the park fulfill its promise as a place of rare and rich resources where city-weary families may re-create body and spirit.

## GRAND TETON NATIONAL PARK *Northwestern Wyoming. Area 484 sq. mi.*

**Features:** Teton Range, one of world's boldest, most majestic mountain fronts, rising 7,000 feet above game-rich Jackson Hole.

**Activities:** Visitor centers at Moose, Jenny Lake, Colter Bay. Scenic drives, 225 miles of hiking and bridle trails. Pack trips. Climbing instruction at Jenny Lake. Boating, trout fishing; float trips down Snake River. Scenic flights, chair lift at Jackson.

**Season:** Road through park open year round; most activities June 15—Labor Day.

**Weather:** Warm, sunny days, cool evenings (elevation at lodges 6,500 ft.).

**What to bring:** Hiking shoes, rough-it clothing, shorts; woolens for evening. Sun lotion, camera and light meter, binoculars.

**How to get there:** Major highways intersect in park. See map at back of book. Wyo. 22 over Teton Pass steep, not for trailers. Air service to Jackson. For rail or bus write Grand Teton Lodge Co., Moran, Wyo.

**Accommodations:** Lodges at Jackson Lake, Jenny Lake; cabins at Colter Bay; write Grand Teton Lodge Co. Signal Mt. Lodge, Leek's Lodge; address, Moran, Wyo. Write park for dude ranch list. Camp and trailer grounds: first come, first served.

**Services:** Stores, garages; car rentals at Jackson or Jackson Lake Lodge. Nurse at Lodge, hospital in Jackson. Church services in park.

**Park regulations:** Camping in specified areas only. Climbers must register at Jenny Lake Ranger Station; no solo climbing. Boat permit; Wyo. fishing license. Pets on leash.

*For further information write Superintendent, Grand Teton National Park, Moose, Wyoming*

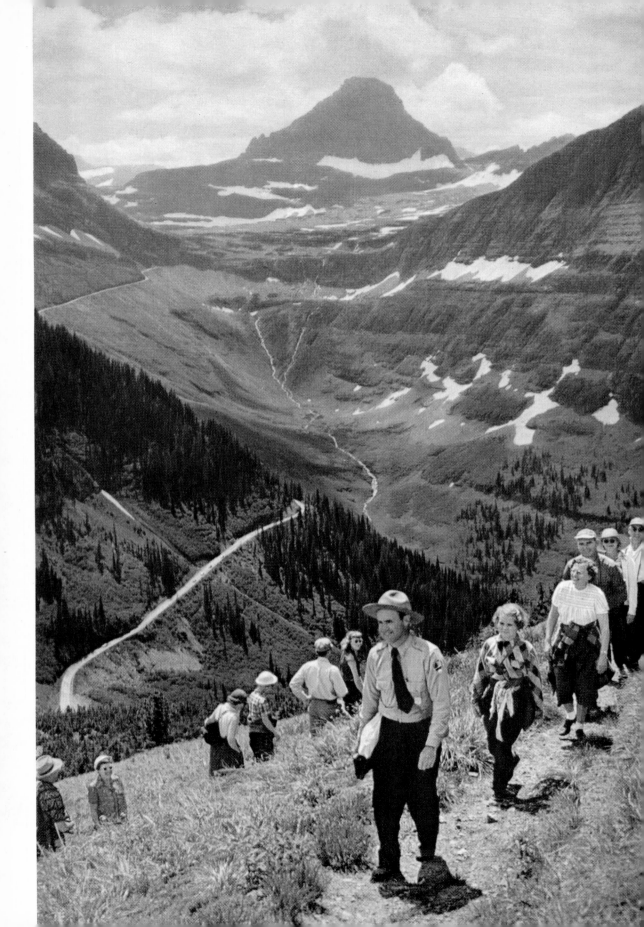

*Glacier and its Canadian twin, Waterton Lakes Park,*
*form the world's first border-straddling park,*
*symbol of friendship between neighboring nations*

# GLACIER NATIONAL PARK

*By GEORGE W. LONG, Assistant Editor, National Geographic*
*Illustrations by KATHLEEN REVIS, National Geographic Photographer*

BEFORE US loomed a colossal wall of snow-topped mountains, rising thousands of feet straight from the Montana prairies. Towering, upswept peaks marched south in shining array from Canada. Clouds wreathed the tallest pinnacles; purple shadows, creeping across stony faces, lent mystery and allure.

As we sped westward, a gap in the mountain barrier swung open and we began the climb to Marias Pass, lowest cut across the northern U. S. Rockies and southern boundary of Glacier National Park.

We arrived in West Glacier refugees from a record eastern heat wave. The bracing mountain air reminded us of a crisp October day back home, and at Lake McDonald Hotel a welcome fire crackled in the huge lobby fireplace. It was a different world, and next morning I felt frisky as a colt when I met the superintendent at park headquarters.

"Take it easy," he said. "You'll have to do plenty of hiking and riding to know Glacier. We try to

**Hikers tread a catwalk** on Glacier's Garden Wall. Below, tiny cars crawl along spectacular Going-to-the-Sun Highway to Logan Pass, under the eaves of distant Reynolds Mountain. Mule deer (right) sports velvet antlers in July.

DOUGLAS WHITESIDE

103

preserve the park's wild beauty; so there are only 70 miles of park roads compared with more than 1,000 of trails. My advice is to get out on the trails—but go easy. You've got a million acres to see."

First, to get an over-all picture of this alpine wonderland, I flew with the fire patrol in a single-motored plane. Like one of Glacier's golden eagles, we soared over lonely crags, skimmed 10,000-foot peaks, and glided over sapphire

104

**Josephine Lake mirrors** Mount Gould, banded by ancient black

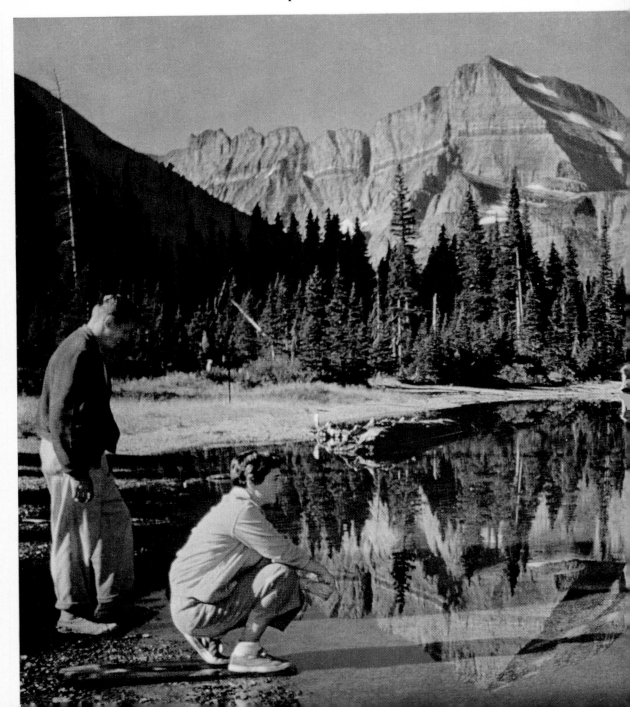

lakes. We threaded valleys green with pine forests and scudded past skyland wastes torn and scarred by the elements. We swooped into huge rock amphitheaters for close looks at some of the park's 60-odd glaciers.

I was impressed by the park's size. Compared with Montana, from which it is carved, it looks deceptively small on a map. Actually Glacier is a third again as big as Rhode Island. And how few the signs of human activity in this

105

lava 100 feet deep. The Salamander, an ice formation, suns itself on the flank of Garden Wall.

## Glacier National Park: ice-carved citadel of beauty on the Continental Divide

Awe-struck Indians from the plains of Montana looked on these mountains as rocky bones pinned to the sky. Here massed against the horizon, jagged Garden Wall seemed the world's backbone; neighboring peaks fanned out like ribs.

Carved by glaciers, the highland proved too rugged for homesteaders and too poor for miners. Its greatest wealth lay in scenery. In 1910, 1,583 square miles became Glacier National Park, now fourth largest in the Nation, after Yellowstone, Mount McKinley, and Everglades.

Soon the Great Northern Railway built Many Glacier Hotel (right), the park's biggest. Later, an annex rose beneath Allen Mountain (left). From this site, deep within the park, trails spread out into the high country like arteries from the heart (map, page 110). Some visitors ride horses on day-long trips to Iceberg Lake. Others shoulder packs and strike out for Granite Park Chalet (page 120) or a starlit campsite. Less active souls stroll easy walkways or boat on small Swiftcurrent Lake (center).

**Blackfeet** in owl and eagle feathers welcome the author's family to East Glacier Park, railroad gateway to the park. Some 3,500 Blackfeet live on a reservation, nearly as big as Delaware, abutting Glacier on the east.

gigantic preserve! Smoke hung over half a dozen far-flung campgrounds; a speedboat buzzed on Lake McDonald. Cars and buses crawled along magnificent Going-to-the-Sun Highway, which cuts across the rugged heart of glacierland; at Logan Pass, its 6,664-foot crest, sightseers waved gaily at us.

One day my family and I drove over this road-builders' miracle, one of the most spectacular 50-mile stretches in the New World. Not until 1933, when Going-to-the-Sun was completed, did a highway cross Glacier. A few years earlier a road had been blasted across Marias Pass. Before that, a motorist who wanted to cross the park had to ship his car over the pass by rail or detour some 500 miles by way of Great Falls and Missoula.

Tunneling, the road climbed high above tree-clad McDonald Valley. Near its one switchback, Ed Beatty, then chief park naturalist and our guide, pointed to rosettes etched in the rock. They looked like cross sections of cabbages.

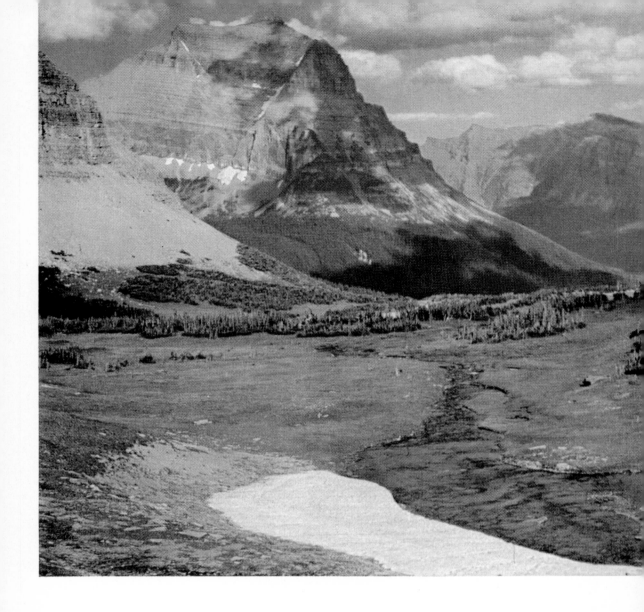

"Fossil algae," Beatty explained. "Colonies of single-celled plants that lived half a billion years ago. This is among the oldest sedimentary rock in the world —exposed when the mountains were lifted and pushed eastward. In Grand Canyon you have to go a mile deep to see rock this old."

Steadily we climbed toward timber line. Shimmering cascades dropped thousands of feet from high snow fields. For miles the jagged Garden Wall stretched above us; great chasms yawned below. Joining a tourist group at Logan Pass, on the Continental Divide, we gazed on mountains carved like Matterhorns, pyramids, Mayan temples—even a savage gorilla's head. Masses of wildflowers carpeted broad meadows nearby, aptly called the Hanging Gardens.

"More than 700,000 visitors come to Glacier every summer," a ranger told us. "Over 98 percent come by car, and most just drive through on this road.

## A legendary Indian walked to the sun above this spot

Going-to-the-Sun Mountain and the highway at its foot perpetuate the myth of Napi, Old Man of the Blackfeet, who created the rocks and forests, the animals, birds, and fishes. He molded a clay man and woman and gave them life. He taught them to hunt and to farm.

His mission ended, Napi set out for his home in the sun. He climbed the noble mountain and disappeared amid swirling snows and lightning flashes. When the sun burst forth, the Indians saw his profile engraved in rock and filled with snow. Napi's face may still be seen on the far side of the 9,604-foot peak, here looming above Logan Pass.

**Alpine blossoms** adorn glacierland's lofty meadows. Gentians (lower right) add blue to the wildflower mosaic. The hardy glacier lily will chase receding snow to the mountaintops.

I. Alleman

To Browning & Museum of the Plains Indian

Cut Bank Creek

Kiowa

Blackfeet Highway

Glacier Park Hotel

East Glacier Park

Marias Pass 5215

Great Northern Railway

St. Mary Lake

Postcard Point

Trick Falls

Two Medicine Lake

Baring Falls

Red Eagle Mt.

Mahtotopa Mt.

Triple Divide Peak 8011

CONTINENTAL DIVIDE

Goat Mt.

Hanging Gardens

9157 Reynolds Mt.

Fusillade Mt. 9552

Little Chief Mt.

Citadel Mt. 9034

Essex

Pass

Sperry Glacier

Gunsight Pass & Lake

Jackson Glacier

Mt. Stimson 10165

National Forest

8700+

Mt. Cannon

Mt. Brown

Sperry Chalet

Lake Ellen Wilson

Hungry Horse Reservoir

Going-to-the-Sun Hwy.

Avalanche Creek Campground

Lake McDonald Hotel

Glacier National Park Headquarters

Hungry Horse

Sprague Creek Campground

Lake McDonald

Apgar

West Glacier

Coram

Hungry Horse

Hungry Horse Dam

Flathead River

Columbia Falls

Flathead River

Flathead National Forest

STATUTE MILES
10
5
0

© National Geographic Map

Drawn by Irvin E. Alleman

Whitefish

**Sure-footed nanny** and her kid sidle up to a ledge above Gunsight Lake. Here in summer the mother sheds. Some 800 mountain goats, with soft-centered nonskid hoofs, make Glacier Park their home.

Fortunately not all are as hurried as one man who rushed up to me, glanced at his watch, and said, 'I've got just two hours. What can I see?' "

On our way back from St. Mary Lake (page 18) we stopped for a look at distant Jackson Glacier, once part of Blackfoot Glacier, one of the largest ice masses in the U. S. Rockies. Blackfoot shrank into several small glaciers.

"For awhile we were afraid we'd lose all our glaciers," Beatty said. "Several of the biggest disappeared, and others shrank as much as 75 percent. But since 1950 they've held their own. During recent years the park's average temperature has dropped several degrees, and the amount of rain and snow has nearly doubled. We think the world may be entering a colder, wetter cycle."

When our drive was over, my younger daughter complained, "No bears."

"They're all up in the hills eating berries," Beatty told her. "There's a big crop this year, which helps solve our bear problem. Sometimes they get too friendly and injure people without trying. Perhaps you've noticed our roadside jingle: 'Highway bears are often rude. They eat fingers as well as food.' "

In the evenings I had noticed a light hanging far above the hotel like a star. Mount Brown fire lookout, I was told. Eager to go up, I arranged to ride with

**Not-so-sure-footed girl** inches along a rocky thumb overlooking Lake Ellen Wilson. Trout in this deep-blue cup on the lip of the Continental Divide offer fishermen some of the finest sport in the park.

the lookout inspector on his next trip.

Miss Kathleen Revis, National Geographic photographer who made these splendid color photographs, went along to take pictures of mountain goats. Her tirelessness on the park's trails had surprised even the rangers.

The lookout trail, with 33 switchbacks, climbs 3,500 feet in four steep miles. Up this zigzag path mules haul the watchers' water and supplies. When I spoke of it to Jay Lytle, an old-time wrangler, he shook his head.

"Son," he chuckled, "that trail's a horse-killer on the way up and a dude-killer on the way down." But Jay, I found, had stretched the truth a mite.

Married couples, mostly college students, man the lookout towers. Honeymooning Jack and Nyla Hobbs of Chanute, Kansas, were the Mount Brown team. Their tower windows faced a sea of wild, snowcapped peaks. Mountain goats frolicked at close range.

"They're friskiest at night," Nyla smiled. "At first they kept us awake for hours, racing up and down the steps and butting the tower."

Mount Brown was my first saddle trip in the park. That evening as I tenderly lowered myself into a soft lobby chair, I recalled Irvin Cobb's quip after he took a Glacier horseback trip.

"Call that thing a saddle?" snorted the humorist. "It's a chafing dish!"

But you can have a jostling in the park without getting aboard a horse. Even motorists get their teeth rattled on Glacier's oldest road—to Kintla Lake in the remote northwest corner, an area kept almost as virgin wilderness. Big lakes lure fishermen, while frontier conditions test hardy campers and hikers.

As we drove through pine forests and skirted lush meadows, ranger Harold Estey told of winter ski patrols here, when snow drifts up to 30 feet deep.

"Great country for game," he said. "A regular zoo. We see big herds of deer, elk, moose—even wolves and mountain lions. Ever hear about the moose that

**July snowfields** lure shirt-sleeved hikers. Party above tramps a slope in sight of Mount Cannon. Rompers at right slither toward Grinnell Lake, whitened by rock powder ground beneath a glacier.

**Ranger's rope holds Boy Scouts from a crevasse's icy jaws on Grinnell Glacier,**

Creeping about 35 feet a year, Grinnell gathers a rocky harvest. Stone imbedded in the glacier's bottom acts as a massive rasp. When the frozen river meets uneven bedrock, stresses open yawning fissures.

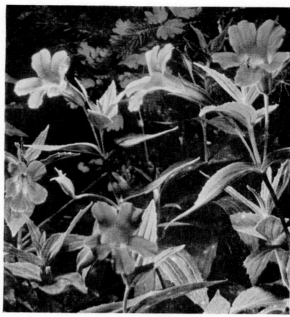

**Wildflowers blanket** rock-strewn Kootenai Pass. During the short summer, Glacier's highlands display gardens with nearly every vista. Here arnica mixes its yellow with the red of monkey flowers. Close-up above shows the latter's resemblance to a monkey's mouth. Two petals form upper lip; three the lower.

battled a bulldozer on this road? Thought it was a rival, I guess. He shook his antlers, pawed the ground, and charged head on into the 'dozer—not once, but three times. Finally staggered off. That driver sure was glad to see him go."

At Kintla Lake women were cooking lunch over open fires. Men chopped wood, hauled water, or unlimbered fishing tackle while children played. One camper strummed a guitar. We liked the easy, welcome-stranger atmosphere.

"Surprising number of people get up here," the ranger said. "We logged 2,000 camper-days last month, and many campers return year after year."

One morning I joined a group on chilly Logan Pass for a hike along the Garden Wall. The spectacular trail is strung above timber line between Going-to-the-Sun Highway and the Wall's jagged, narrow top. As we neared Granite Park Chalet the ranger-naturalist pointed to a steep path angling upward.

"In several summers here I've never climbed the Garden Wall," he said.

**Hoary marmot abandons caution** for a friendly handout. Unable to outrun natural foes—bear, coyote, and golden eagle—the marmot family posts a lookout. Sentry's whistle sends his fellows scurrying.

**Gabled roof of the continent:** clouds swirl beneath isolated Granite Park Chalet,

"It's a real stiff climb—1,500 feet up in only nine-tenths of a mile—but I hear the view up there is terrific. Any volunteers?"

To my surprise, 16 out of 24 did volunteer. We started up, while the others pushed on toward the chalet. After a hundred yards, my knees rebelled, then thought better of it. Loose shale and a rollicking wind made footing difficult. A magnificent Rocky Mountain bighorn ram bounded effortlessly ahead of us.

Finally we reached the top—9,000 feet. Before us stretched the fabulous Many Glacier region. Grinnell Glacier lay in a vast rocky cradle. Snow fields draped peaks and slopes like colossal sheets put out to dry. Beyond lakes spargoal of hikers on Garden Wall Trail. Snow fields patch the slopes of 9,004-foot Heavens Peak.

kling like scattered bits of jade we could make out the distant prairies, faint and flat. It was a full minute before anyone could speak.

I must confess to a feeling of conquest when I reached the hotel that evening. I had hiked 16 miles since morning, climbed more than 2,000 feet, and stood atop the Garden Wall! I came to earth with something of a thud when I overheard two waitresses, college girls, talking while serving dinner.

"How was your day off?" one asked the other.

"Oh, wonderful. Hiked to Canada. Thirty-two miles—up over Stoney Indian Pass to Waterton. Simply marvelous."

121

### Waterton Lake forms a path through the heart of the International Peace Park

Canada's 204-square-mile Waterton Lakes National Park begins where Glacier National Park leaves off. In 1932 the two parks were dedicated as Waterton-Glacier International Peace Park, marking a long era of good will. A 20-foot swath through forest identified the boundary; people pass freely from one side to the other.

Both parks preserve glacier-carved scenery, but, oddly enough, all remaining glaciers lie south of the border.

Here Canada looks down 7 miles of mountain-walled water into the United States. The Canadian government operates Waterton Park townsite (right) but permits private homes and stores.

Motor launch *International* leaves town on a morning run to the United States end of the lake. Hikers below await its arrival near Waterton Ranger Station in Glacier Park.

GETTING back into condition, I reveled in our almost daily hikes. I relished the picnic lunches on lofty meadows deep with flowers and the ice-cold mountain water. On the high trails there is a curious sense of being walled off from the world's turmoil. Life's pace is scaled down to a placid two miles an hour. Night brings delicious fatigue and deep, untroubled sleep.

Moving to Many Glacier, we explored the Swiftcurrent Lake region I had seen from the Garden Wall. Here, several ancient glaciers had joined forces and bulldozed their way to the plains, leaving unbelievably beautiful valleys that reached into this mountain land like the imprint of a colossal hand.

One name you hear frequently in this part of the park is Grinnell. It labels a glacier, mountain, waterfall, point, lake, and the reddish rock that colors so many formations. And little wonder. George Bird Grinnell—explorer, naturalist, and author—roamed here in the 1880's and '90's, when it was a frontier,

123

### "Giddap" is your open-sesame
### to the Canadian wilderness

The riding party organizes at Prince of Wales Hotel, a 250-guest lodge that looks like a Hänsel-and-Gretel cottage in the distance (above). At the Bosporus, a strait joining two of the three Waterton Lakes, wranglers swim the mounts (left); riders cross by boat. On the trail, horses file through rocks and stunted evergreens in sight of Bertha Peak and Mount Crandell. At journey's end, riders climb to Crypt Lake (next page).   125

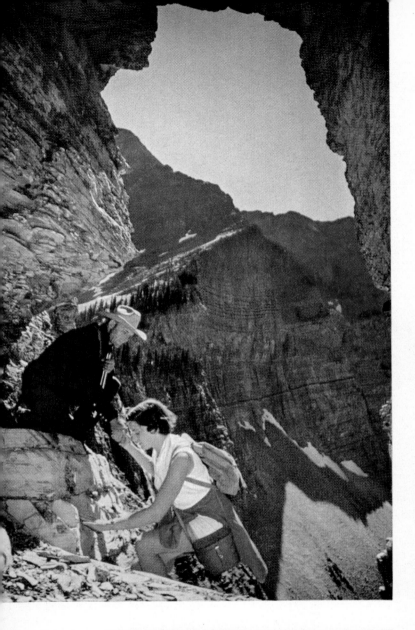

## Mountains hide Crypt Lake, a jewel cut by glaciers

To reach this Shangri-La the visitor must crawl through a 50-foot tunnel and traverse a sheer ledge into the amphitheater, or cirque, gouged by ice from crumbling sedimentary rock. The lovely tarn, whose flowered slopes lie in Canada and shadowed cliffs in the United States, drains through a cavern into Hell Roaring Canyon.

and discovered the glacier that bears his name. A tireless fighter for conservation, he urged vigorously that Glacier be made a national park. So, too, did the National Geographic in an article vividly describing the mountain fastness.

One morning, with some 50 hikers, we climbed the steep flank of Mount Grinnell to Grinnell Glacier. This huge ice lake covers an area equal to about 35 city blocks and measures 400 feet deep in places. Relentlessly it grinds forward, its melting front feeding a sparkling waterfall that drops to the valley below.

At glacier's edge the ranger tied a long rope around his waist and told everyone to grab hold. "Otherwise somebody would fall into a crevasse before you could say 'Gletschermilch,' " he observed. Like a monster snake we shuffled over the glacier, the ranger probing ahead for soft spots with an ice ax. We skirted deep crevasses and yawning holes, and explored caves of blue-white ice.

127

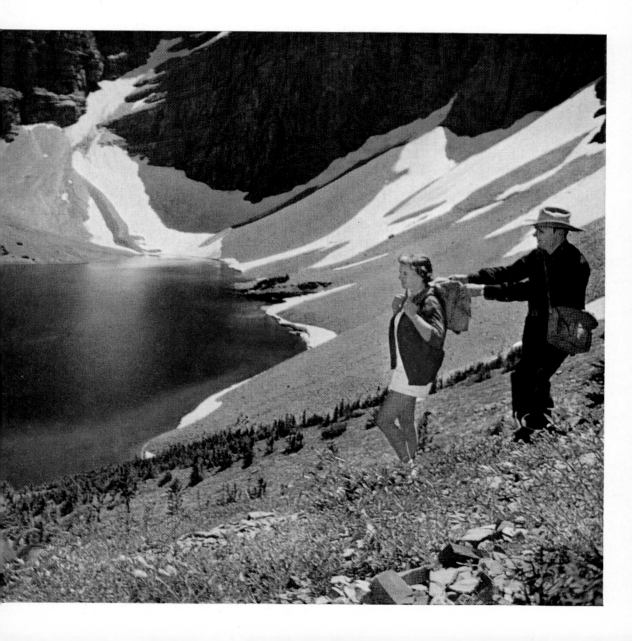

"Glacier Park doesn't get its name from the 60-odd masses of ice here now," our guide said, "but because huge Ice Age glaciers carved its rugged scenery. Half a mile deep, they covered all but the highest peaks—like the Greenland Ice-cap today. They gouged the wide valleys and rocky amphitheaters you see. They scooped out the lake bottoms and sliced some mountains thin—like the Garden Wall up there. Today's glaciers are only ice cubes by comparison. Incidentally, more than 100 feet of snow falls here at Grinnell each year."

High on many a nearby slope are strange tunnels—shafts left from old-time mining booms. Stirred by tales of rich strikes, prospectors probed the region in the early 1890's. Since the land belonged to the Blackfeet, the Great White Father paid his adopted children $1,500,000 for these mountains.

"Crowds of miners rushed in," recalled Blackie, the bearded wrangler at Many Glacier Hotel. "A boom town, Altyn, sprang up here, complete with seven saloons. Not a stick or stone remains today. Just as well, I guess. Like as not there'd be no park if the miners' hopes had really panned out."

OUR DAUGHTERS had been looking forward to visiting Canada, to crossing the "frontier" and entering a "foreign" country. At the Canadian-United States border, the customhouse of each nation flies the flags of both; no ceremony is required as you cross. In 1932 the two nations pooled their scenic treasures, creating Waterton-Glacier International Peace Park, symbol of good neighborliness. The heart of the Canadian park is Waterton Lake, a gleaming sapphire set in rugged mountains. Both countries share this jewel, for it crosses the international boundary.

Like most sightseers, we browsed about Waterton's shops, which featured British china and tweeds, Hudson's Bay blankets, Scottish woolens, and English toffee. Either country's dollars were accepted. With such goods on display, and a wife and two daughters in tow, I found both kinds disappeared like magic.

To sample Waterton's trails, we rode horseback to secluded Crypt Lake, high in a hanging valley on the international border. Many of Waterton's other beauty spots can be reached by car—places like Red Rock Canyon and lovely Cameron Lake. Swimmers sun on the beaches of this sparkling tarn while skiers glide on a snow field draped on its rocky amphitheater.

When we recrossed the border, I realized that September had crept up on us. Evenings were getting short and nights frosty. New snow had dusted the highest peaks; leaves of the mountain maple were turning crimson. We climbed from Lake McDonald's forested shores to mile-high Sperry Chalet to spend a night.

There the world's worries seemed a universe away. A harvest moon silvered the landscape; a breeze stirred, bringing a breath of chill. Soon, I mused, snow would blanket the mountains again. Man would retreat; animals would start their winter sleep or seek the sheltered valleys. For nine months the Ice Age, creator of this land of many splendors, would return to claim its own.

**A fallen cottonwood** serves young divers sporting in the crystal waters of Lake McDonald.

**GLACIER NATIONAL PARK** *Northwestern Montana. Area 1,583 sq. mi.*

**Features:** Superb glacier-carved mountain wilderness similar to central Alaska in climate, flora, and fauna. Some 60 glaciers, 200 lakes; conifer forests, flowered alpine meadows. Moose, deer, bear, coyote, bighorn sheep, mountain goat, cougar, fisher.

**Activities:** Sightseeing along 50-mi. Going-to-the-Sun Highway. 1,000 miles of trails; glaciers reached by trail only. Day and overnight saddle trips. Boating, trout fishing; wilderness camping. Campfire programs. Guided bus, launch, and trail trips. For all-expense tours write Glacier Park Co., East Glacier Park, Mont., or (Oct.–May) 218 Great Northern Bldg., St. Paul, Minn.

**Season:** Normally June 15–Sept. 10.

**Weather:** Bracing; occasional rain squalls (elevation at hotels 4,500 ft. or under).

**What to bring:** Hiking shoes and rough-it clothing; woolens for evening. Raincoat, camera, binoculars.

**How to get there:** From east or west, US 2. South, US 93 or 89. See map at back of book. Great Northern Railway. Buses from Missoula, Shelby, or Great Falls, Mont. Northwest-Orient and Western Airlines serve nearby cities; surface connections to park.

**Accommodations:** Hotels: Glacier Park, Many Glacier, Lake McDonald; write Glacier Park Co. for reservations. Chalets: Granite Park and Sperry reached by trail, write B. Ross Luding, Martin City, Mont. Cabins at Rising Sun and Many Glacier. Trailer and campgrounds at Sprague Creek, Rising Sun, Many Glacier, Two Medicine, Apgar Village; eight remote campgrounds.

**Services:** Cafeterias, stores, garages; car rentals at East Glacier Park and Whitefish. Religious services in park.

**Park regulations:** Fishing by rod in hand only; no license required; no live bait. Camping in specified areas only; wilderness camping by permit. No molesting wildlife. Pets allowed on leash, but not on trails.

*For further information write Superintendent, Glacier National Park, Montana*

**Thirsty sightseers split a watermelon along the Continental Divide**

Indians tracking game blazed a trail amid these snowy peaks. Today Trail Ridge Road follows that path through Colorado's Rocky Mountain National Park. For 11 of its miles, motorists ride above the 11,000-foot timber line. Flower-flecked alpine meadows invite a pause, an impromptu pic-

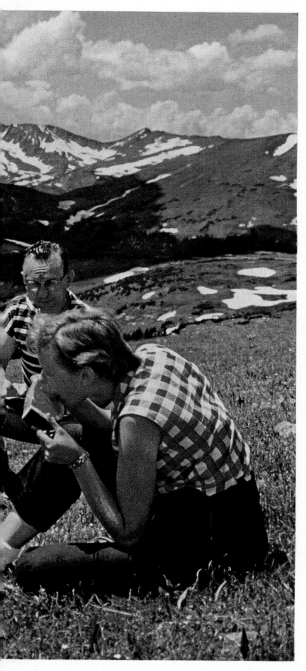

nic. Looking west one gazes on a loop of the Continental Divide; one segment follows ridges in the middle distance, another the white horizon of the Neversummer Mountains.

Snows usually block the route, part of transcontinental US 34, from the middle of October to June.

# ROCKY MOUNTAIN
## NATIONAL PARK

*By KATHLEEN REVIS*
*National Geographic Staff*
*Photographs by the author*

EVEN RESTLESS KIT CARSON felt the pull of this scenery, and in the 1850's built a cabin in these parts. But you need not be a rugged trapper to come under the Rocky Mountain spell. Though formidable to look at, these Colorado peaks are friendly and easy to enjoy.

The casual tourist can motor along cloud-drifted Trail Ridge Road, one of the Nation's highest. From 12,000 feet he looks down on seas of wild flowers—and up toward 42 still higher peaks. One-third of the park lies above the timber line.

Whether he goes by car, astride a horse, or on his own two feet, he has a world of sights to see: the works of today's beavers and of ancient vanished glaciers . . . the bounding bighorn ram . . . the swift grace of deer and elk in the afternoon light . . . the grandeur of perpetual snows . . . the petal perfection of moss campion.

To me, this area between Estes Park and Grand Lake makes the best introduction to mountain fun. High point of the park is 14,255-foot Longs Peak.

In 1864, after failing to climb it, one man wrote, "We are quite sure that no living creature, unless it had wings to

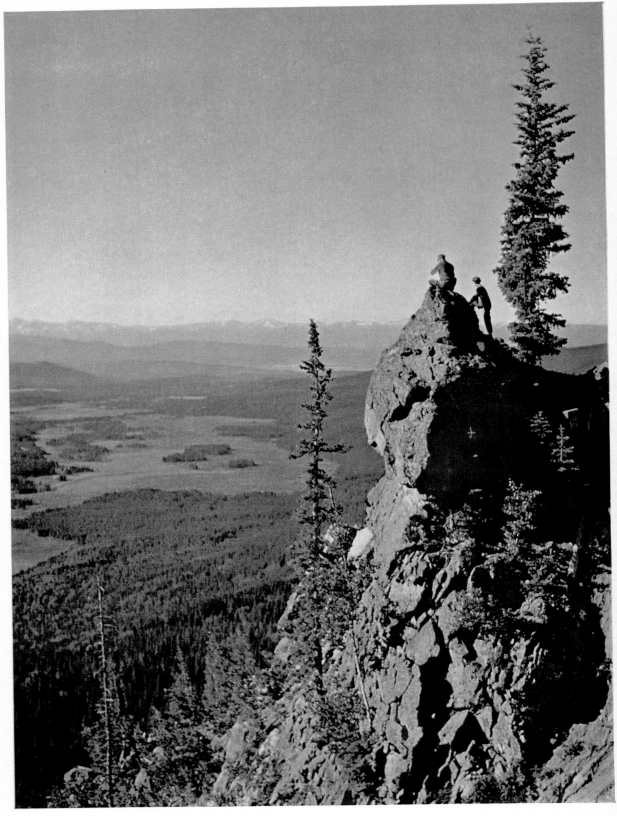

132    **Mountaineers' reward:**    From a pinnacle as sharp as a conifer, hikers survey the headwaters
    **a view and a victory**    of the Colorado River. At right, a party returns from Longs Peak
    through the glacier-gouged Trough, on the Keyhole climbing route.

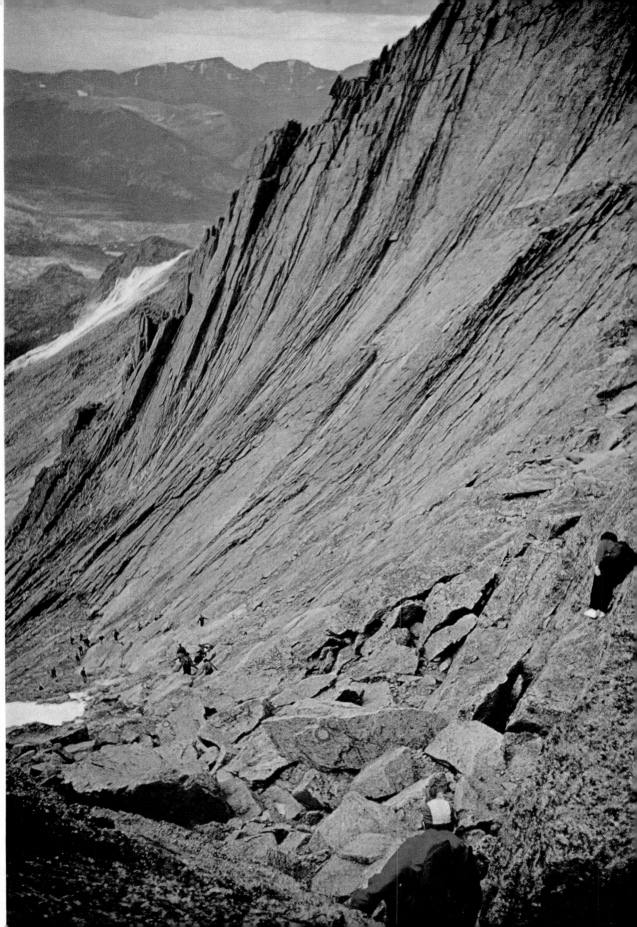

**A youthful posse
dodges a highland shower
in Beaver Meadow**

Rocky Mountain National Park, distinguished by its glacial meadows, evergreen forests, and the raw beauty of the great Front Range of the Rockies, was established in 1915. But neighboring ranches date from homesteading days in the 1860's. Today many throw open their gates to dude guests. Together these ranches and local stables maintain the largest concentration of trail horses in the United States.

Mounts for these vacationing youngsters come from Stead's Ranch. Glacier-formed Beaver Meadow through which they ride is a favorite haunt for deer.

Below, a junior cowgirl dons a slicker in a summer shower.

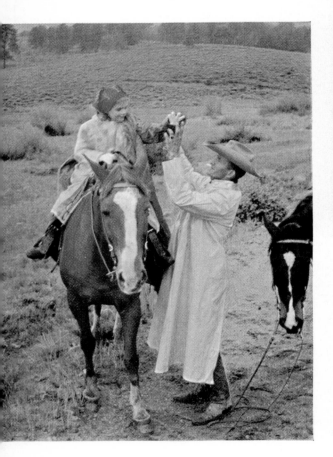

fly, was ever upon its summit . . . that no man will ever be." But four years later a party climbed to the top.

A few generations later, as a novice, I tried the peak myself. Longs Peak by then had been scaled by hundreds young and old, and I took encouragement from that.

I set out at 6:30 one August morning, weighted by an unfamiliar pack. Two thousand feet above camp we passed timber line, where century-old trees grow only waist-high. The trail topped a glacial moraine; we caught our first full view of the dizzying cliff that rope-climbers ascend. But we took the easier cable route that lay to the north.

As we climbed over boulders, my lungs seemed about to burst. Once "above burro line," as one climber put it, I got my second wind. Gripping the cable anchored to sheer rock, I pulled myself up. After six and a half exhausting hours I stood on top. Naturalist Enos A. Mills, veteran of some 300 Longs Peak climbs and father of the park, considered this summit "an area sufficient for a baseball game." But to me, baseball held less allure than the superb view, a victorious downward hike—and a night of solid rest.

**Fording Big Thompson River,** a wrangler brings in horses from mountain pasture. Ice once filled this valley. A row of trees at upper right grows atop the moraine that marks the ancient glacier's edge.

**Ground squirrel** snacks with a friend.

## ROCKY MOUNTAIN NATIONAL PARK

**Features:** Colorado wonderland encompassing 65 peaks above 10,000 feet in its 395 square miles. Moraines, lakes, conifer forests, some 700 wild-flower species, bighorn sheep. Adjoins Shadow Mountain National Recreation Area.

**Activities:** Moraine Park Visitor Center, scenic drives, riding, hiking, climbing, trout fishing. Nature walks, campfire programs. Winter sports.

**Season:** Chiefly June—Sept. Park open year round.

**Weather:** Crisp (elevation 7,800 to 14,255 ft.)

**Clothing:** Hiking togs and woolens.

**How to get there:** From east or west, US 34. See map at back of book. Air, rail, bus via Denver.

**Accommodations:** Hotels, lodges, camps (write park for franchise list; or chamber of commerce at Estes Park or Grand Lake for out-of-park spots). Free campgrounds, trailer sites.

**Park regulations:** Fires, camping in campgrounds only. Colorado fishing license. No pets on trails.

*For further information write Superintendent, Rocky Mountain National Park, Estes Park, Colo.*

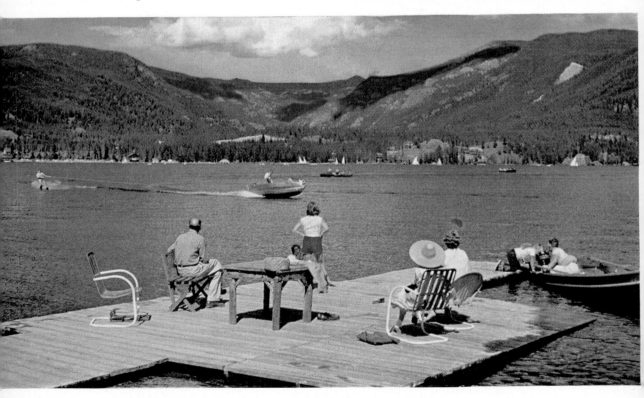

**Grand Lake,** adjacent to the park, brims with water sports and boasts the "highest yacht club in the United States."

**Chill waters of Chasm Falls crash down a granite flume in Fall River Canyon.**

# DEVILS TOWER

You come upon it in the northeastern corner of Wyoming where the Black Hills dwindle into plains. Suddenly the rolling land is rent by a solitary, massive tower of rock, almost shocking in its impact. Devils Tower, a weird volcanic pillar, thrusts like a nubbin of the underworld through the gentle soil. In 1906 President Theodore Roosevelt declared the Wyoming wonder our first national monument, one of nature's legacies to be protected by law.

Devils Tower, soaring 852 feet above the parking circle, rises 1,278 feet above the Belle Fourche River, flowing nearby. Geologists debate its origin. Most agree that molten rock welling up within the earth intruded surface layers, possibly 50 million years ago. Erosion washed away the enfolding soil, leaving the monolith to stand alone. Encircled by majestic stands of ponderosa pine, Devils Tower seems itself like the petrified stump of some gigantic prehistoric tree. The spectacular flutings on its flanks resulted from crack patterns that shot through the buried magma as it cooled and shrank.

Prairie falcons nest among these columns that average ten feet across, while chipmunks scurry through the sage on the flat acre-and-a-half top. At its base, a colony of prairie dogs entertains visitors—some 100,000 each year.

# THEODORE ROOSEVELT
## NATIONAL MEMORIAL PARK

Darkness hid the Badlands of western North Dakota as the transcontinental train panted to a stop. A bespectacled easterner stepped to the platform of Little Missouri depot and gathered his hunting gear. Theodore Roosevelt, not yet 25, planned to shoot a buffalo in this frontierland of 1883.

He got his buffalo. But the starkly eroded, freakishly painted hills and the rugged ways of a ranch captured him for life. Within 20 days of his arrival, T. R. bought land. Thus began his love affair with the American West. He remained a champion of the wilderness, a guardian of its resources.

Teddy Roosevelt would have been "dee-lighted" to know that his Elkhorn Ranch and two huge neighboring areas now form a national memorial park. In these three tracts, totaling 110 square miles, visitors camp and hike among weird buttes, sagebrush plains, grassy bottom lands, cottonwood groves, and scatterings of petrified wood. They walk on reddish clay turned into bricklike rock by the heat of smoldering lignite beneath the surface.

Buffalo were disappearing when Roosevelt came to hunt them. Now, in the protection of his park, they thrive along with antelope and deer.

140    **Devils Tower** stands like the stump of a monster tree, talus strewn at its base like chips from Paul Bunyan's ax. Sioux Indians claimed a giant grizzly clawed the formation, causing its fluting. In 1941 a parachutist reached the summit the "easy" way. Unable to descend, he shivered a week until rescue climbers helped him down.

BATES LITTLEHALES, NATIONAL GEOGRAPHIC PHOTOGRAPHER

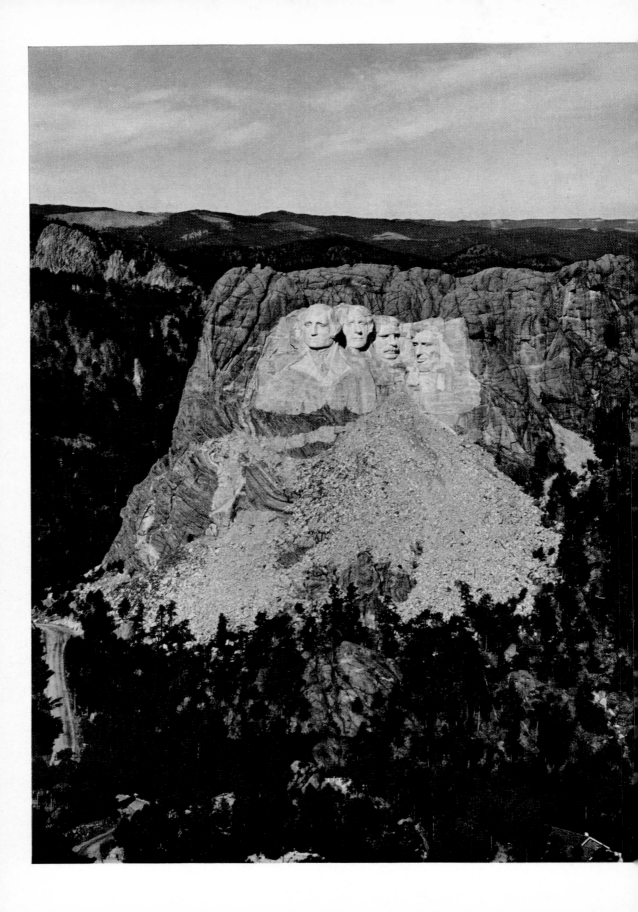

# MOUNT RUSHMORE

*By BART McDOWELL, National Geographic Staff*

THE PRESIDENT placed a drill in the hands of a stocky, energetic man. The tool bit deep into granite. Thus in 1927 did Calvin Coolidge, self-conscious in a ten-gallon hat, launch the work of sculptor Gutzon Borglum upon the face of Mount Rushmore in South Dakota.

For 14 summers mountain foliage—pine, spruce, silver birch, aspen—shuddered to the blast of dynamite, the chatter of jackhammer. When the last stone fragment tumbled from the mountain, stillness settled over the valley. Carved from this Western Gibraltar stood the world's most heroic sculpture.

"Trained but not tamed," men said of Idaho-born Borglum. A famed disciple of Rodin in Paris, he was a man of many enthusiasms—writer, engineer, an impatient patriot. "There is not a monument in the country as big as a snuff box," he said in 1916. America demanded "an enlarged dimension—a new scale."

Borglum found that scale, and a challenge for all his talents, when historian Doane Robinson suggested a monumental sculpture in the Black Hills. Near the town of Keystone the sculptor examined an exposed granite core. The southeastern face of 5,725-foot Mount Rushmore offered greatest promise. Private funds, then Federal appropriations got the job underway.

Borglum fashioned plaster models, measured them, then dropped proportionate plumb lines from the mountaintop. Faces would be 60 feet tall—as high as a five-story building. Dynamite shots probed reliable rock beneath the deeply fissured surface. Nine times Borglum remade his models to conform to solid stone. He climbed scaffolds training miners to help him; he darted about the canyon to test the effect of shadow upon a cheek or chin.

First face to be completed was, appropriately, George Washington's. Next emerged Thomas Jefferson, eyes fixed on the horizon his Louisiana Purchase had assured. Brow-first, Abraham Lincoln took shape, melancholy in his mission to keep America intact. Last, with a square jaw apt in granite, Theodore

**Giants of history**—George Washington, Thomas Jefferson, Theodore Roosevelt, and Abraham Lincoln—keep vigil in the Black Hills of South Dakota. The national memorial stands visible for 60 miles.

**Stone eyes look on eternity.** When sculptor Borglum learned that this granite erodes perhaps an inch in 100,000 years, he added a foot to Washington's nose. "It will give him another million years!"

Roosevelt's image evoked the vigor of 20th century America. But Gutzon Borglum did not live to see his masterpiece complete; he died at 74, leaving seven months' work to the son he had named for Lincoln.

"I don't intend that it shall be just a three-day tourist wonder," Borglum once said. Tourists themselves, a million a year, testify to his success. They stop in hotels and motor courts in Rapid City and Keystone, South Dakota. In holiday mood they picnic in nearby Black Hills National Forest or feast in the attractive restaurant at the Rushmore site itself.

They come not to gaze at a giant curiosity, but to observe a monument as large and permanent as the dream these four men made real. Some return time and again to watch morning sunlight move across the faces, to see the figures backed by a Western sunset, to attend the nightly summer ceremony in the amphitheater as floodlights whiten the granite against a black sky.

At whatever time of day, the setting inspires an inward awe. Frank Lloyd Wright left aside all his brilliant barbs when he saw Rushmore: "The noble countenances emerge as though the spirit of the mountain heard a human plan and itself became a human countenance." Vacationers, freshly conscious of the meaning of citizenship, say even more by their reflective silence.

**Lincoln's quartz-seamed face** dwarfs an inspection team. Eye pupil is four feet across, mouth 22 feet long, head twice as high as that of Egypt's Sphinx. If carved full figure, he would stand 465 feet tall.

BATES LITTLEHALES, NATIONAL GEOGRAPHIC PHOTOGRAPHER

**Delicate calcite veins** lace the limestone chambers of Wind Cave, 46 road miles south of Mount Rushmore.

Millions of years ago a sea that covered this region deposited limestone layers. Pressure from below warped the earth's crust into the Black Hills dome and fractured these ancient beds. Percolating limy waters mortared the cracks with calcite. When subterranean streams dissolved out Wind Cave's chambers, the resistant veins remained as projecting fins and boxes.

"Like the work of a mad set designer for a horror movie," one tourist described the grotesque passages, the frostwork ledges, the pigeonholes on the rust-red walls. Boxwork formations are found in only a few of the world's caverns.

# WIND CAVE

TUCKED IN A GULLY on the southeast flank of South Dakota's Black Hills lies a whistling barometer. This rare phenomenon is a hole in the ground, ten inches across, opening to a cave below. As atmospheric pressure changes, air sucks into or blows out from its rocky throat, sometimes with bush-rattling force.

A Black Hills pioneer, Tom Bingham, discovered the mysterious cleft in 1881. But Indians probably knew of it long before, for Sioux legends tell of a sacred cave of the winds through which their forefathers entered the West.

Today hundreds of palefaces daily step into this happy hunting ground of geology—Wind Cave's honeycombed walls and ceilings, in soft, warm hues, are the world's finest known boxwork formations. Electricity lights 3½ of the 10 miles of explored passageways that descend some 240 feet. April through October ranger-led tours examine the North Room, Post Office, Rookery, Queen's Drawing Room, and Cathedral. In the Fairgrounds, ultraviolet light sets aglow the calcite fantasies of a frostwork ledge. When the elevator surfaces with visitors, sweatered against the cave's 47° chill, the warm hills seem charged with blues and greens to eyes attuned to reds and browns.

You needn't be a spelunker to savor the cave's setting. The rolling plains, laced with ponderosa pine, forge a treasured link with the sea of grass that once stretched a thousand miles. Then came cattle to overgraze it, plows to break the virgin sod. Wind Cave National Park preserves a lingering segment of the Great Plains where buffalo roam, knee-deep in wind-rippled grass.

A buffalo once charged into a bus in the park. Simply ornery—or perhaps he was stirred by ancestral memories of days when thundering herds stopped transcontinental trains for hours. A century ago more than 50,000,000 roved the heart of America. Wanton slaughter cut their numbers to less than 1,000. Now some 5,000 of the exiled monarchs live in U. S. preserves.

About 350 Great Plains buffalo graze peacefully and freely on the rolling prairie land of Wind Cave's 44-square-mile fenced-in range. In winter they swing massive heads from side to side, battering through deep snow to find forage. They share their domain with elk, deer, pronghorn—and thousands of prairie dogs. These bustling rodents maintain more than a dozen colonies here. Each hummocky town is clear of long grass, for the little fellows combine appetite with a shrewd insistence on a clear view around. A nonvegetarian coyote on the outskirts sends them diving for their burrows.

While observing buffalo, take a tip from Mr. Prairie Dog: be ready to duck for cover. A buffalo is no domestic animal. He can weigh a ton, run 30 miles an hour, and turn on a buffalo nickel. And he's unpredictable. The park highway usually provides a close enough view of the great shaggy beasts.

Open all year, the park has a visitor center, refreshments, gift shop, and campground. Nearby Hot Springs and Custer provide accommodations.

# JEWEL CAVE

JEWEL CAVE APPEALS to those who like their caves primitive but safe, unadorned with graded walkways, elevators, and electric lights. Ladders join various levels where the hand lantern lights dazzling displays of dogtooth calcite. Like nearby Wind Cave, Jewel Cave was carved when underground streams invaded fractured Black Hills limestone. Then seepage, saturated with calcium carbonate, spangled the chambers with crystals. With infinite leisure these grew, faceted, glittering, curved like canine teeth.

May through September a park ranger guides hourly tours through this little gem of a national monument, set amid the virgin ponderosa pines off US 16.

147

**The prairie dog,** a species of ground squirrel, is named for his barking call.

# BADLANDS

A THREE-TOED HORSE once roamed swampy grasslands east of the Black Hills and there he met his death. Perhaps a saber-toothed cat killed him. Or he had a fracas with a rhinoceros, or simply got mired. Layers of silt and volcanic ash covered his bones, which petrified and rested there some 25,000,000 years. Climates changed. The region dried up. Rare but violent rains cut deep into the earth, and ancient sediments again were on the move.

Finally a thunderstorm washed the last bit of clay from a leg bone, and it rattled into the gully below. In the summer of 1958 a man wandering among the Badlands rills spied the fossil bone. He picked it up, mused a bit at the wonder of this ancient world, and, heeding park regulations, put it down where he got it—next to the tooth of an extinct giant pig, near the rib fragment of a tiny deer, not far from two huge turtle fossils.

These relics of the past litter the gullies of South Dakota's Badlands National

Monument, a broad 40-mile strip of eroding clays between the White River and the high plains to the north.

"A no man's land of unimaginable desolation," a journalist once characterized this terrain, and so it seems at first. Tortured pinnacles crowd the highway. Parking turnouts survey a marching sea of buttes, battlements, haystack hills. Fancy sees in them the Pyramids, Great Wall of China, Kremlin, Taj Mahal, and Aztec and Maya temples. Through them all runs a fugue of color: pastel blues, pinks, greens, and tan compose banded rhythms along the edges of table-flat layers. Kaleidoscopic patterns shift as evening shadows crawl across the crumbling wilderness. In cool moonlight, black shadows lace the luminous ridges and spires; the region's stark beauty almost persuades the observer he has been whisked to another planet.

But all is not desolation. On high ground, prairie dog, cottontail, and coyote scurry through grass that crowds erosion's sharp edge. White-tailed deer and pronghorn sprint through lowland meadows. In spring, wildflowers abound.

Nearly a million people a year travel US 16A through the Badlands on their

way west, to the Black Hills and national parks beyond. Most content themselves with stops at the Cedar Pass visitor center and scenic overlooks along the 30-mile park highway. Many time their visits for early morning or evening to avoid midday's heat and glare. Children work off energy scampering over ridges and ledges. Parents stretch their legs in fossil-rich ravines that have lured the world's scientists for more than a hundred years.

Some stay in the lodge or campground at Cedar Pass, or in one of two primitive campgrounds. Often the next stop is the South Dakota School of Mines in Rapid City, where an impressive museum display brings to life long-gone Badlands beasts.

**In this weird land of long ago** scientists hunt big game from Oligocene times. Erosion uncovers rich fossil finds. Here the clay mounds are cracked into millions of inch-square chunks by the hot, dry air; hikers become dehydrated too. Dakota Indians called the area *mako sica*—bad land.
STEWART ANDERSON

149

## PART TWO

# THE GREAT PLATEAU

THIS IS THE LAND of juniper and sandstone. It is a dry and thirsty land, yet water made it what it is.

Water formed its rocks in the beds of ancient seas. Water sculptured the rocks when they rose mile-high. Water gnawed its gorges, carved its square-cut buttes. Water stripped away its flesh, leaving a bright and jumbled skeleton.

Today incredible ribs of stone arch from slickrock walls of hidden chasms. Painted pinnacles raise bony fingers beside red cliffs that mothered them.

"Ours has been the first, and will doubtless be the last, party to visit this profitless locality," one explorer said. But now, a century later, more than a million people each year stand on Grand Canyon's rims. Another million enjoy parks farther north.

Still it remains a remote, sparsely settled land, of tremendous distances and violent contrasts. Black storm clouds invade the clear air with the clamor of thunder, the quick stab of lightning. Dusty gullies become raging torrents. Then sunset paints the innocent dome of sky in colors which defy the artist's imagination.

One can only gaze in awe at these wonders and hope to return again and again to this stark and lonely land.

151

0    150
STATUTE MILES
© N.G.S.
Irvin E. Alleman

*In the mile-deep chasm of the Colorado,*
*one of the world's greatest wonders,*
*rocks reveal nature's story of creation*

# GRAND CANYON

*By LOUIS SCHELLBACH, former Chief Naturalist, Grand Canyon National Park*
*Photographs by JUSTIN LOCKE*

I HAVE LISTENED to thousands of exclamations from awed visitors when first they laid eyes on Grand Canyon. But in my 22 years with this national park I never heard of a more apt comment than that of a cowboy who emerged from a forest to find the colossal abyss yawning before him. "Wow! Something sure happened!"

Averaging eight miles in width throughout its 217-mile length, the incredible mile-deep chasm staggers human senses. Its colors shift like a kaleidoscope as the sun spotlights a different spectacle every hour. Dawn gilds its sculptured pinnacles but leaves the depths in blue shadow. Noon exposes a pitiless desert. Evening sets rock spires afire with alpenglow. Moonlight tints the gorge with mystery, and morning's fog fills it with a river of cotton.

"Something sure happened" to create Grand Canyon. Many visitors want to know just *what* happened. "Did the earth crack open? Did glaciers cut it?"

Not many million years ago northern Arizona stood barely above sea level, and through it ran a sluggish river. Then the region started to rise into an immense plateau. But the ground rose so slowly that it did not change the river's course. Using silt, sand, gravel, and boulders as abrasives, the Colorado scoured its bed. Though the land rose a mile and more, the river held more

**Perched on the brink of eternity,** a young couple peers into the dark-walled Inner Gorge. Fixed glasses at nearby Yavapai Point (right) pinpoint the canyon's features.

154    **The hungry Colorado River** has gnawed Grand Canyon down to earth's primeval rock. Surveyed from Desert View Watchtower, lofty North Rim shows geology's layer cake of sediments laid down eons ago. Rains, frost,

and thaw, and the probing roots of plants have widened the canyon as much as 18 miles. Here the midday sun paints erosion's face in searing reds. The following pages reveal contrasts in Grand Canyon's ever-changing moods.

155

**Etched by morning's cool shadows,** white-throned temples of Deva, Brahma, and Zoroaster guard a crumbling wasteland. Bright Angel Point (left) looks down its namesake canyon to South Rim's banded wall.

**Alpenglow at sundown** bathes the canyon's heights. The Battleship, foreground, sails on

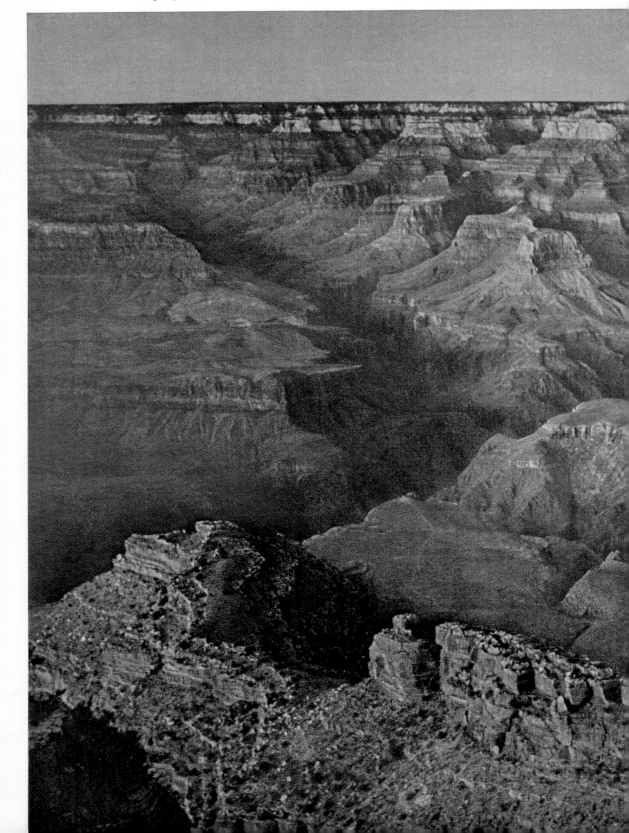

a blue-shadowed sea below South Rim's Hopi Point. Bright Angel Canyon joins the Colorado's gorge on the left.

or less its original level. If we liken the earth's crust to a layer cake, then the river, by analogy, becomes a cake knife. But instead of the knife's slicing downward, the cake rose against the blade.

Erosion ate away the chasm walls. Wind carved caves in soft cliffs. Pelting rains washed away soil. Water ran into cracks, froze, and split off fragments. Water undercut ledges, which eventually tumbled down. Rain on the plateau to the north runs into the canyon. As a result the North Rim has been cut back 2½ times as far as the South, where water drains away from the rim.

RECENTLY I JOINED some tenderfoot riders on a mule trip into the canyon. "Keep the reins in your hands at all times," our guide counseled. "Keep your feet in the stirrups, your mind in the middle. Never dismount unless I am at your side. Obey those rules and your mule will take care of you."

With these words we rode off the brink of the South Rim and down Bright Angel Trail toward the Inner Gorge, almost a mile below (page 14). Our party was taking a ride back through the ages that were required to form the earth's crust. But at this moment they were indifferent to geology; they thought only of mules and heights. Most had never ridden a mule in their lives.

160

## "Earth's history from the beginning lies exposed before you," says the ranger-naturalist

At Yavapai Lookout on South Rim, visitors learn of their planet's violent, convulsive past, laid bare by the relentless gouging of the Colorado River. Exposed rock layers reveal a story of mighty, age-long cataclysms: of mountains buckling skyward and wearing away; of molten rock welling up; of seas sweeping over the land and laying down vast deposits, then disappearing.

Trail riders read geology's open book closer at hand. Returning from the canyon floor, they mount the ladder of the ages. Here in a gigantic cross section of the earth's crust (below), nature has written the story of life's development and illustrated it with fossils of extinct animals.

Older Pre-Cambrian walls of the Inner Gorge, formed some 1,500,000,000 years ago, show no trace of life. But primitive algae left their mark in Younger Pre-Cambrian rocks. Climbing past layers that tell of life's growing complexity in the Paleozoic Era, riders see fossil remains of trilobites, then, higher up, tracks left by amphibians as they ventured from ancient seas.

The record of the Age of Reptiles has washed away. It would have towered far above the present rim. Our own Age of Mammals has left no sedimentary deposits here.

North

7250 feet
7000

6000

5000

MARINE DEPOSITS
Fossil shells, coral, and sponges.

DUNE SANDS. Fossil tracks of primitive reptiles and amphibians.

Coconino Plateau

FRESH-WATER DEPOSITS. Amphibian and reptile footprints, fossil ferns, and insect wings.

Yaki Point
7250 feet

Kaibab limestone [gray-white]

FLOOD PLAIN DEPOSITS. Amphibian and primitive reptile tracks, imprints of fernlike plants.

Coconino sandstone [buff]

Hermit shale [red]

SEA DEPOSITS. Fossil shells and corals. Base is the decomposition products from old erosion surface.

O'Neill Butte

Supai formation [red]

MARINE ORIGIN

OFFSHORE DEPOSITS
Fossil trilobites, crablike animals.

Redwall limestone [blue-gray, stained red]

Erosion Surface

BEACH DEPOSIT. Preserved ripple marks, seaweeds, and primitive shells.

Muav limestone [buff]

Bright Angel shale [green-gray]

Tonto Platform

Tonto Platform

Tapeats sandstone [brown]

Tonto group

Erosion Surface [Great Unconformity]

Inner Gorge [Granite Gorge]

Grand Canyon Series [Chuar group]

Vishnu schist [dark gray]

Vishnu schist

Granite [pink or white]
Molten rock which intruded older schist.

Kaibab Suspension Bridge

Colorado River

Fault

Fault

Dark limestones contain earliest traces of life on this continent; red shales, quartzites, and brown sandstones.

Record lost by erosion

CARBONIFEROUS

DEVONIAN

CAMBRIAN

PALEOZOIC

PRE-CAMBRIAN

GEOLOGIC CROSS SECTION
OF THE
GRAND CANYON
From Yaki Point to Suspension Bridge

0          4000
Horizontal scale in feet

© National Geographic Society

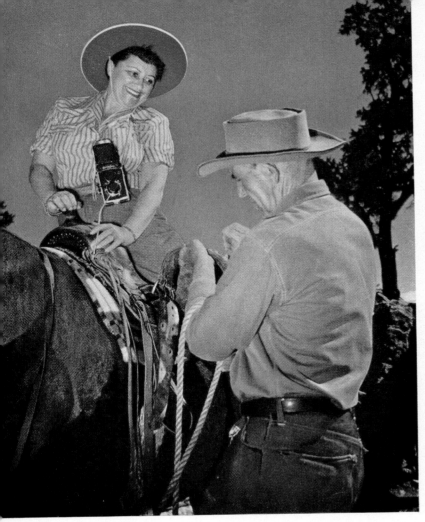

Banter prevails on the South Rim every morning as visitors saddle up for a swing down the switchbacks. "Don't fall into the canyon," nonriding friends counsel.

The quaking tenderfoot shrugs off the joshing with an air of bravado. But the moment his mule ambles to the canyon's lip and steps off into space, he clutches the saddle horn, leans away from the abyss, and lets the animal take charge.

Chosen over horses because of strength and stability, the trail mule gets weeks of rigid training before passengers are entrusted to his broad back. Trainers get on and off the wrong side, clap hats over the mule's ears, bang cameras against his flank, and otherwise imitate tenderfoot ways. The result is a mount esteemed for his patience, endurance, sagacity.

A rider should not weigh more than 200 pounds, nor be under 12 or "too advanced in age." Veterans of the trip swear they wouldn't have missed it for anything.

As long as the mules headed straight down, the trail seemed a comfortable four feet wide. Newcomers got their first shock when we halted for the traditional group picture. Each mule did as he was trained: he put his tail to the wall and let his head hang out over space. Nothing but mule intervened between rider and thin air. Frightened tenderfeet clutched saddle horns and leaned back toward the rock.

"Wish I'd written my will," muttered one.

Riders were scarcely adjusted to saddles when the caravan abruptly entered a dizzy series of switchbacks cut into sheer cliffs. Approaching a turn, the mules leaned so far over the precipice it seemed they intended to step off into the abyss. Then, so slowly that to novices the fateful seconds lasted forever, our mounts pivoted, one foot after another.

Appearances to the contrary, the animal is not bent on suicide. In more than 50 years, Grand Canyon mules have yet to lose a customer to accident.

"The first few hundred yards always seem the worst," our guide told us. "A

**Snaking down Jacob's Ladder,** mules give dudes' nerves a test on Bright Angel Trail. Tonto Plateau lies beyond green clumps of Indian Garden.

woman may get scared or her husband may decide he has 'heart trouble.' They can dismount and hike to the rim, but very few do."

Riders turned in their saddles to see the fault line that Bright Angel Trail follows; the broken and shifted rocks on one side stand 180 feet above matching strata on the other. Some of our party observed that they had journeyed a thousand feet below the canyon's rim. Confidence partly restored, they began to enjoy the marvelous view. Earth's strata changed colors before their eyes. The gray-white top layer of sea-formed limestone gave way to buff-colored sandstone, hardened wind-blown dunes of an ancient desert landscape.

At last we entered the 550-foot Redwall, a magnificent pink façade whose blue-gray limestone had been stained red by iron oxides. The trail down this cliff follows Jacob's Ladder, another series of switchbacks. Our mules chose this alarming stretch to display their appetites. For any clump of green they stuck their heads way out over the trail's edge.

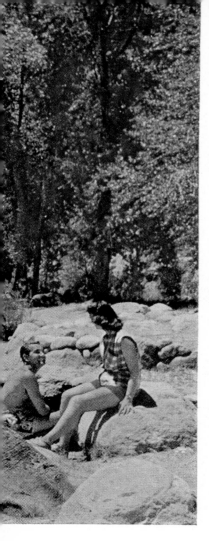

**A pocket of luxury within the canyon wilderness,
Phantom Ranch offers trail-weary riders
a refreshing dip and a good night's sleep**

Wildlife trespassers wander freely among rustic cabins and
central lodge in this oasis watered by Bright Angel Creek.
Here the air is 20 degrees warmer than on the South Rim,
towering nearly 4,400 feet above. Maj. John Wesley Powell
camped near here on his epic 1869 journey down the muddy
Colorado through what he named the Grand Canyon.

"Hold your reins tight; yank his head up," advised
our guide. "If you let him, your mule will eat anything—sticks, straw hats, old ropes."

We stopped for lunch and to stretch numbed legs
at Indian Garden, a cottonwood oasis on the Tonto
Platform, a wide plateau two-thirds of the distance
from rim to river. Long ago the Havasupai Indians
irrigated their farm plots from springs here. Today
those springs supply all the water used by Grand
Canyon community, park headquarters on the South
Rim. Pumps lift the sparkling load three-fifths of a
mile.

Leaving the platform, we followed another zigzag
trail cut into the rocks of Inner or Granite Gorge to
the Colorado River, 7.8 trail miles from our starting
point. Here we stood 4,500 feet below the South
Rim and 5,700 below the North Rim. Manhattan
Island could be tucked into a 13-mile stretch of the
canyon. If the 1,472-foot Empire State Building were set down on the river bed,
only its television tower would stick out of the Inner Gorge.

Held between sheer walls only 300 feet apart, the river roared in fury as boulders in its grip crashed against one another and bedrock. When the wind is right
its mighty voice can be heard as far as the South Rim. Living up to its Spanish
name, *colorado* (red), the river seemed more mud than water. Half a million
tons of soil a day were moving before our eyes. "Too thick to drink and too thin
to plow," is the way old-timers describe the Colorado's water.

Conqueror of the Colorado was Maj. John Wesley Powell, one-armed Civil
War veteran and geologist. Undeterred by frightening tales of underground
channels, he left Green River, Wyoming, on May 24, 1869 with nine men and
four boats to explore and chart the river.

Mile after mile the boats twisted through whirlpools and crashed against
rocks. Day after day the men endured skimpy rations, damp clothing, and weary

165

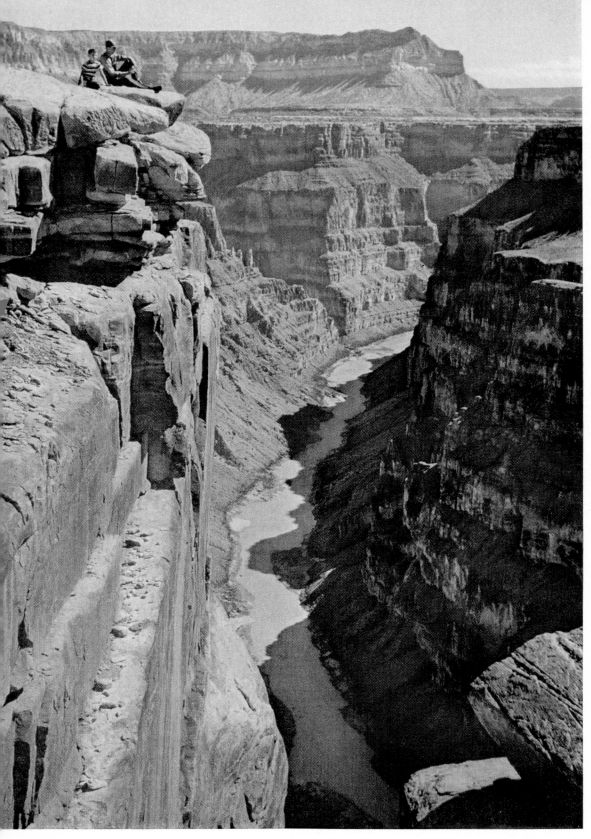

166 **From Toroweap Overlook** a cliff plunges 2,802 feet into the Colorado in Grand Canyon National Monument, a wilderness area adjoining the park.

portages. Early in August the voyagers entered the Grand Canyon. On the 28th of that month three men gave up rather than face further perils. Making their farewells, each party felt sure the other had chosen certain death.

Powell and his five boatmen triumphantly emerged from the canyon the very next day. The three who quit were killed by Indians.

As highways of commerce, many rivers are servants to man. But the 1,450-mile-long Colorado with its hundreds of dangerous rapids posed a threat even to the most experienced boatmen until a few years ago. Today the river is so well charted and its caprices known that many organized parties have boated and rafted in relative safety through the maelstrom of the Grand Canyon itself.

KAIBAB SUSPENSION BRIDGE, just wide enough for a pack mule, led us to the north bank and on to Phantom Ranch, only resort in the canyon, for a cool dip in the pool, dinner, and relaxing sleep in a guest cabin. Bright Angel Creek, as clear as the Colorado is muddy, made the ranch an oasis.

We were in another climate—20 degrees warmer than on the South Rim. It can be snowing on North Rim, raining on South Rim, and merely misting at Phantom Ranch. Daylight is shortened by canyon walls rising high on every side.

**"River rats"** slam through Granite Rapids. Once only the hardiest of oarsmen braved the canyon's 15-foot waves. Then in 1949 Otis Marston made a motor run through. Many persons have done so since.

WILLIAM BELKNAP, JR.

"The man who works only from sunup to sunset wouldn't have much of a job here," said the manager of Phantom Ranch. "During a busy summer week we have to pack in 3,500 pounds of supplies. Dirty laundry goes out, fresh linen, food, fuel oil—even mail—comes in by mule express.

"This is a sanctuary for wild animals," he continued, "and they know it. My wife found a bull snake in the house the other day and had to carry it by the tail out to the rocks. We drove a beaver away because he was felling our trees, two a night. A bobcat used to promenade past the ranch house every evening. Deer steal the mules' hay and ring-tailed cats prowl for garbage."

As our party rode on from Phantom Ranch to the North Rim we climbed through four life zones—all in 14 miles. To pass through these zones at sea level would take us from Mexico's Sonora Desert to southern Canada. Snows close the North Rim in winter. The South Rim, 1,000 to 2,000 feet lower, is open all year.

### Canyon cliffs rim Supai, home of the Havasupais

Havasu Creek, born of gushing springs, nurtures the remote valley settlement of Supai, a true "fortress built by Nature" at the western end of Grand Canyon National Park. Diversion ditches water fruit orchards, farms, and pastures, turning some 175 acres into a green paradise amid an inferno of sun-blistered buttes and savage gorges.

Cheerful Havasupai Indians woo the tourist dollar, even appoint a tribal tourist manager to greet guests. They arrive down eight-mile Hualpai Trail on horseback along with mail and supplies, for no wheels roll into this hideaway Eden.

The marked climatic differences in the canyon make it a barrier to many small animals. Those on one rim are now of different species or subspecies from their relatives on the other. Classic examples are the Kaibab squirrel, found only on the North Rim, and its South Rim counterpart, the Abert squirrel. Both have tufted ears and a chestnut stripe down the back. But the Kaibab has a white tail and black belly; the Abert, white belly and gray tail.

Grand Canyon's barrier deflects north-south highway and rail traffic too. By muleback, the 10 air miles from rim to rim take two days and 28 trail miles. By automobile via Navajo Bridge is a day faster but some 200 miles longer.

S HELTERED in a side canyon of the park is the most isolated Indian reservation in the United States. Here live some 200 Havasupais. Havasupais are not celebrated as warriors, philosophers, dancers, or artists, but they know a good    169 thing when they see it, and that is Supai, the tribe's adopted home. In a green valley surrounded by red stone walls, Supai is a lotus-eaters' land where no one worries much about H-bombs or anything else. Avoiding the heat of the day, the Havasupais till their farms no more than they have to, but they work hard at having a good time. Rodeos, card games, sweat baths, and idle talk fill their days. They seem to suffer just two indignities: youngsters must go to school and their fathers must buy licenses to hunt.

Many Hopis, Havasupais, Walpais, and Navajos work in Grand Canyon community. The Fred Harvey Company retains scores of Hopis, mostly as

170

### Havasupai boys lead a life Huck Finn would envy

Around the age of two, young braves learn to ride by hanging on to Dad. Football, baseball, and Wild West movies later absorb them. Restrictions are few, discipline practically nonexistent, since parents believe harsh words shrivel young souls.

Every day finds boys swimming in Havasu Creek or shouting against the roar of 220-foot Mooney Falls (right). From the color of the pools the tribe takes its name—Havasupai, the Blue-green Water People.

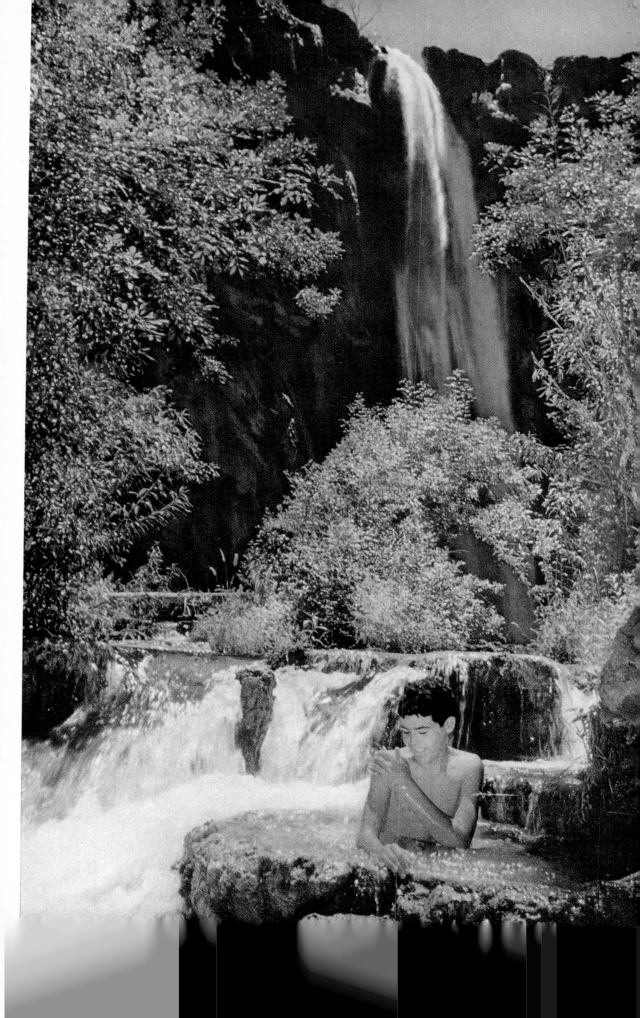

bellboys, maids, and kitchen help. Guests at El Tovar Hotel gape at the Hopi bellboy in blue velveteen jacket and bright headband running a vacuum cleaner across the lobby carpet. And evenings they watch Hopis from the reservation perform their feather dance on the canyon rim or inside Hopi House.

Hopis guided Don García López de Cárdenas and his 12 Spanish followers to the South Rim in 1540, sixty-seven years before Englishmen settled Jamestown, Virginia. Instead of finding the fabled golden Seven Cities of Cíbola, López, a lieutenant of Coronado, found a mighty canyon that barred further progress.

Before retreating, some of his soldiers ventured into the gorge. The Spanish chronicle records that those who went down discovered that the rocks which had seemed "about as tall as a man" when viewed from the rim were actually "bigger than the great tower of Seville."

Like many visitors today, the Spaniards did not appreciate the canyon's size until they descended into it. Gazing toward the North Rim across miles of clear Arizona air, one feels he can reach out and touch Wotan's Throne, Deva, Brahma, and other formations named for Old World deities.

As I look upon this incredible chasm I experience an uplifting of the spirit and a deep sense of humility. Like all who savor Grand Canyon's majesty, I find endless freshness in what naturalist John Burroughs called "the world's most wonderful spectacle, ever-changing, alive with a million moods."

**GRAND CANYON NATIONAL PARK**  *Northern Arizona. Area 1,052 sq. mi.*

**Features:** World's mightiest gorge, cut by the Colorado River. Finest open record of earth's history. Varying color moods. Desert wildlife. Four distinct climatic and plant-life zones from canyon bottom to North Rim. **Activities:** *South Rim.* Visitor center at Grand Canyon Village, interpretive talks at Yavapai Point. Rim drives, mule and horse trips, bus tours, scenic flights. Campfire programs, Hopi dances. *North Rim.* Bus and saddle trips, nature walks, evening programs. **Season:** South Rim open all year. North Rim, about May 15–Oct. 15. **Weather:** South Rim (elev. 6,900 ft.) bright, warm days, pleasant nights. North Rim (elev. 8,100 ft.) cooler; snow in winter. Canyon floor 20 degrees warmer than South Rim. **What to bring:** Cottons, hat, hiking shoes. Rough-it clothing, long-sleeve shirt for trail trips. Sun-glasses, sun lotion, binoculars, camera and light meter. **How to get there:** See map at back of book. *South Rim.* Ariz. 64 from US 89 or 66. Santa Fe Ry. from Williams, Ariz., direct to park in summer. Frontier Airlines to Flagstaff. Buses from Williams, Flagstaff. *North Rim.* Ariz. 67 from US 89. Union Pacific RR, Western Airlines to Cedar City, Utah. Bus to park. **Accommodations:** *South Rim.* El Tovar Hotel, Bright Angel Lodge, Phantom Ranch in canyon (all open year round); Yavapai Lodge, auto lodge (both summer only); write Fred Harvey, Grand Canyon, Ariz. Free campgrounds, trailer parks. *North Rim.* Grand Canyon Lodge (June–Sept.), auto camp (May–Oct.); write Utah Parks Co., Cedar City. Camp and trailer ground at Bright Angel Point. **Services:** Hospital at South Rim, nurse at lodge at North Rim. Restaurants, stores, garages at both rims. Church services in park. **Park regulations:** Camping, fires in designated areas only. Hiking on trails only. *Don't overestimate your endurance; the hike up-trail from the canyon floor is strenuous.* Pets allowed on leash, not in canyon.

*For further information write Supt., Grand Canyon National Park, Grand Canyon, Arizona*

**Swirling and stamping,** Indians pirouette like gaudy birds on the plaza outside South Rim's Hopi House. Hopis stage their evening dances all year round. Young palefaces in the tree get a grandstand view.

173

# LAKE MEAD

LEGENDS OF DESERT MIRAGES pale before the startling reality of Lake Mead and Lake Mohave. Walled by the painted mesas of Arizona and Nevada, they lie deep, blue, and inviting beneath the brazen summer sun.

Formed by 726-foot-high Hoover Dam, itself a wonder of the modern world, Lake Mead stretches 115 miles up the Colorado River into Grand Canyon's western end. Downstream 67 miles from Hoover Dam's spillways, Davis Dam backs up the long, bent finger of Lake Mohave.

These huge man-made lakes are the heart of a 3,000-square-mile oasis, Lake Mead National Recreation Area, enjoyed all year by holidayers, many arriving via nearby Las Vegas. Boats and water skiers crisscross the lakes, hundreds of feet above the old river channel explorer John Wesley Powell braved in 1869. Yet the gaunt shore's scene remains little changed. Bighorns bound down from lava cliffs for a drink in waters where large-mouth black bass swim.

You can fish year round, hunt game birds and animals in season, hike and explore in fall's crisp weather, or delight in desert floral displays February to June. Though summer temperatures soar, nights usually call for a blanket.

WILLIAM BELKNAP, JR.

174      **Beaches and marinas** that now ring Lakes Mead and Mohave would have made old-time rivermen rub their eyes. Though the stark shores lack trees, campers harvest driftwood, often too decorative to burn.

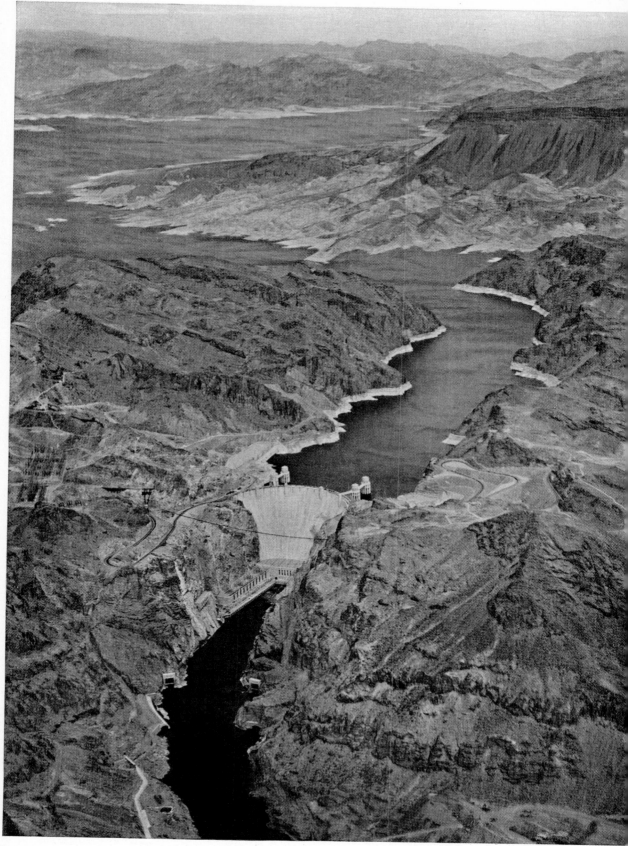

**Hoover Dam,** linking Nevada (left) and Arizona, impounds a desert sea that lures vacationists and wildlife.

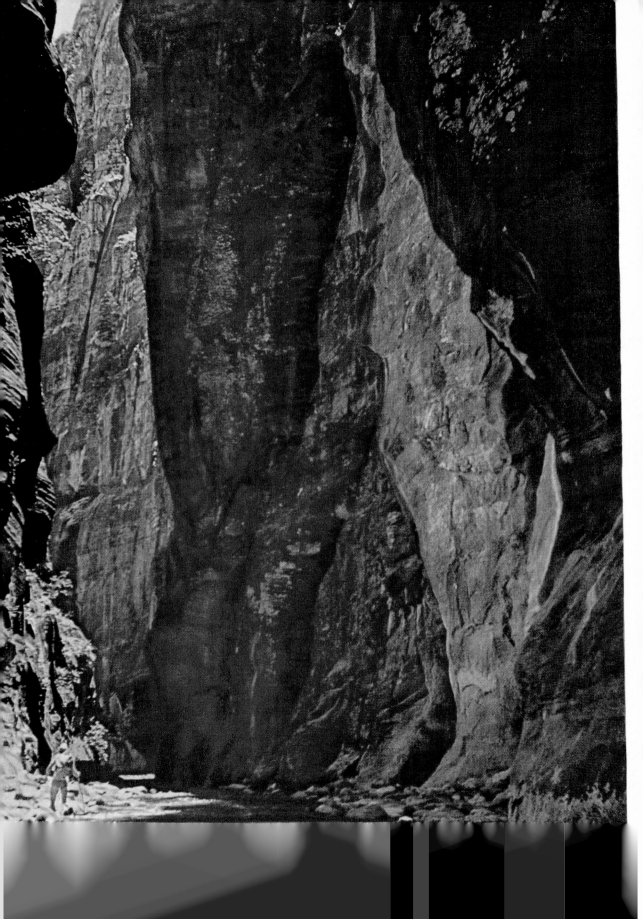

# ZION NATIONAL PARK

*By LEWIS F. CLARK*
*Photographs by JUSTIN LOCKE*

**M**Y BROTHER'S LETTER breathed enthusiasm. "Let's go through the
Virgin River Narrows this summer," he wrote. We had long
dreamed of such a trip into the wilds of southwestern Utah's
Zion National Park. Here the North Fork of the Virgin River
has carved one of America's greatest stone miracles. Like an endless belt of
sandpaper, grit-bearing water has scoured through layer after layer of sandstone
to create fantastic Zion Canyon.

Great monoliths, blazing with color, guard the course of the Virgin as it tumbles southward along Zion's green floor. From the park's south entrance a highway skims past eight miles of these rock sentinels—Bridge Mountain, the Altar
of Sacrifice with its white summit streaked with crimson, Mountain of the Sun,
Lady Mountain, the Great White Throne, a dozen others—to the Temple of
Sinawava. Alcoves, broad amphitheaters, magnificent arches indent these majestic cliffs. Slender pilasters stand everywhere.

A mile north of road's end the canyon shrivels to a writhing gorge; in places
only a few feet separate walls half a mile high. Here the Virgin has a fall of 90
feet to a mile, 10 times that of the Colorado in Grand Canyon. Though more
than half a million visit Zion each year, only a few have penetrated this chasm.
Perhaps the first was Grove Karl Gilbert, geologist, map maker, and early Trustee of the National Geographic Society, who explored the North Fork in 1872
and named these twisting miles the Narrows.

Zion's chief ranger was dubious when we registered for our unconventional
two-day hike early in July. "Our flash floods come between now and the end of
August," he told us. "Thunderstorms could start any day." But trusting our ex-

**Like Wall Street skyscrapers,** cliffs of the Narrows soar above the
Virgin River's flood-scoured bed; they sometimes hide the sky. In
one side canyon in Zion the author could touch both walls at once.

177

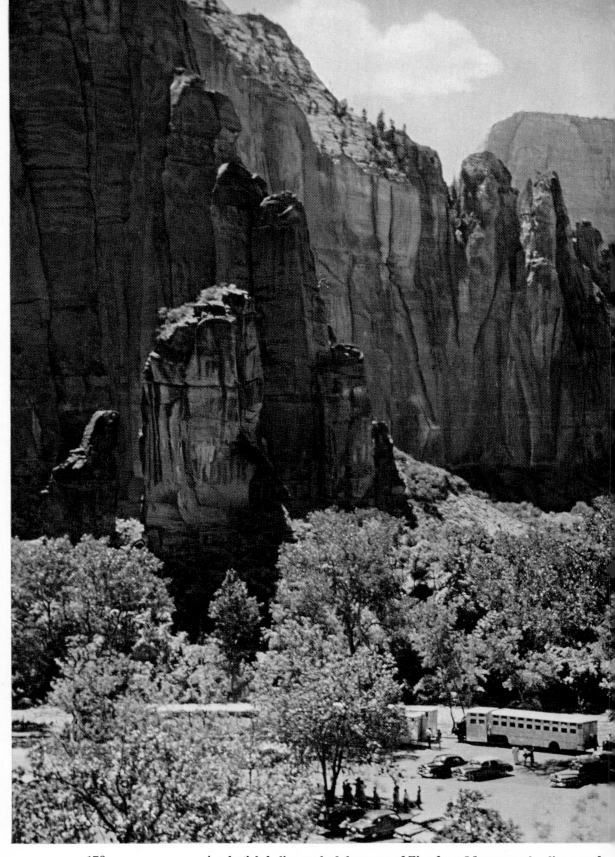

**A celestial skyline evoked the name of Zion from Mormons who discovered**

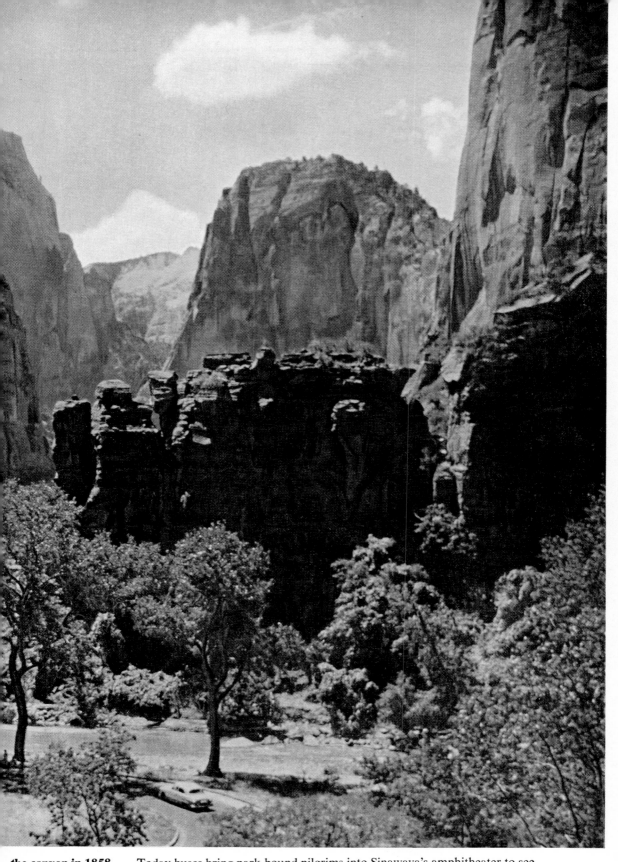

**the canyon in 1858.** Today buses bring park-bound pilgrims into Sinawava's amphitheater to see its "towering temples of stone." The Great White Throne rises at center.

**On the track of nature,** a ranger leads visitors to the mouth of the Virgin River Narrows. Thousands hike the easy mile north from road's end in the Temple of Sinawava. Ferns and flowers soften the canyon floor. Even in the Narrows vegetation thrives on the sun's brief daily penetration.

Three-toed dinosaurs roamed the Zion of yesteryear. Cougars still lurk here, and golden eagles rest on its crags and pinnacles.

perience and equipment, he granted permission. We would camp on the plateau above the gorge that night. If skies were clear in the morning, the three girls in the party would drive back to Zion Canyon and meet us late the following afternoon at the south end of the Narrows. We nine men would try the river.

We took the Mount Carmel Highway to the park's east gate. From the canyon floor, six great switchbacks climb in easy grades some 800 feet in three miles— all contained in an area of less than one-third square mile! Then the highway plunges into the north wall of Bridge Mountain and through a 5,607-foot tunnel continues its climb to the summit of Zion Canyon's east wall. Six galleries gouged

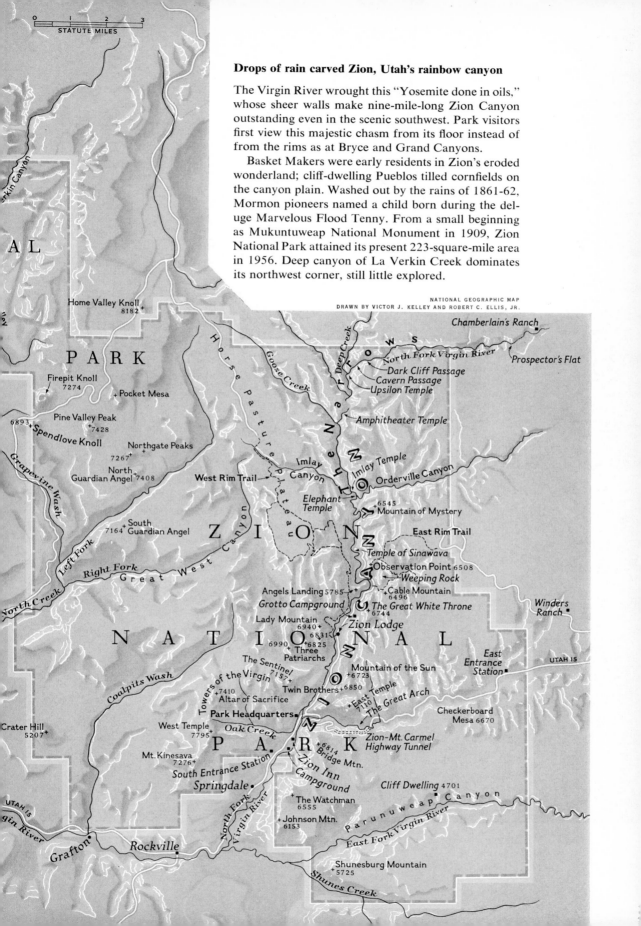

**Drops of rain carved Zion, Utah's rainbow canyon**

The Virgin River wrought this "Yosemite done in oils," whose sheer walls make nine-mile-long Zion Canyon outstanding even in the scenic southwest. Park visitors first view this majestic chasm from its floor instead of from the rims as at Bryce and Grand Canyons.

Basket Makers were early residents in Zion's eroded wonderland; cliff-dwelling Pueblos tilled cornfields on the canyon plain. Washed out by the rains of 1861-62, Mormon pioneers named a child born during the deluge Marvelous Flood Tenny. From a small beginning as Mukuntuweap National Monument in 1909, Zion National Park attained its present 223-square-mile area in 1956. Deep canyon of La Verkin Creek dominates its northwest corner, still little explored.

NATIONAL GEOGRAPHIC MAP
DRAWN BY VICTOR J. KELLEY AND ROBERT C. ELLIS, JR.

STATUTE MILES
0 1 2 3

AL

PARK

Home Valley Knoll 8182

Firepit Knoll 7274

Pocket Mesa

Pine Valley Peak 7428

6893 Spendlove Knoll

Northgate Peaks 7267

North Guardian Angel 7408

West Rim Trail

Grapevine Wash

South Guardian Angel 7164

ZION

Horse Pasture Plateau

Goose Creek

Deep Creek

Narrows

North Fork Virgin River

Chamberlain's Ranch

Prospector's Flat

Dark Cliff Passage
Cavern Passage
Upsilon Temple

Amphitheater Temple

Imlay Canyon

Imlay Temple

Orderville Canyon

Elephant Temple

6545
Mountain of Mystery

East Rim Trail

Temple of Sinawava
Observation Point 6508
Weeping Rock

Great West Canyon

Left Fork

Right Fork

North Creek

Angels Landing 5785
Grotto Campground

Lady Mountain 6940

6990 6831
6825
Three Patriarchs

The Sentinel 7157

Towers of the Virgin
7410
Altar of Sacrifice

Park Headquarters

West Temple 7795

Oak Creek

Mt. Kinesava 7276

South Entrance Station

Springdale

Crater Hill 5207

Coalpits Wash

NATIONAL

Cable Mountain 6496
The Great White Throne 6744

Zion Lodge

Mountain of the Sun 6723

Twin Brothers 6850
East Temple 7110
The Great Arch

PARK

Winders Ranch

East Entrance Station

UTAH 15

Checkerboard Mesa 6670

Zion-Mt. Carmel Highway Tunnel

6814
Bridge Mtn.

Zion Inn Campground

The Watchman 6555

Johnson Mtn. 6153

Cliff Dwelling 4701

Parunuweap Canyon

East Fork Virgin River

North Fork Virgin River

UTAH 15
Virgin River

Grafton

Rockville

Shunesburg Mountain 5725

Shunes Creek

182     **A pony's step from thin air,** East Rim trail-riders skirt Navajo sandstone cliffs on the climb to canyon top. The seven-mile round trip takes about five hours. Longer, more strenuous West Rim Trail spells a full day in the saddle. Riders pack food and water.

in the rock enable travelers to view such scenic wonders as the Great Arch of Zion, one of the largest natural arches in the world.

To see anything more dramatic one must take to the park's many trails. From East Rim Trail the climber has an eye-popping view the full length of Zion Canyon. No less spectacular is the longer trail to the west rim. One of its steeper stretches—"Walter's Wiggles"—was built by custodian Walter Ruesch in 1919, the year Zion became a national park. Twenty-one switchbacks in 600 feet of canyonside trail mount to a shelf on the cliff. "It's the only place in the world a horse is going two ways all the time," one rider remarked.

Symbol of Zion Canyon is the Great White Throne, rising 2,450 feet above the Virgin River foaming at its base. In two days we would see this stupendous flat-topped rock—if all went well.

We camped outside park boundaries, not far from the top of the Narrows. Light clouds in the west made a beautiful sunset. Next morning there were no clouds—a good omen. We forded a stream, followed a tortuous road, and two miles east of the park boundary we took our leave of the girls. To their shouts of "Good luck!" we strode off toward the river. Our map showed 12 miles of water-grade route between us and our goal. This would take us through the gradually deepening upper gorge and between the towering walls of the Narrows to the Temple of Sinawava—the end of the canyon road.

The creek bed dropped steadily before us. The defile tightened around us. We watched for possible escape ledges where we could climb beyond the high-water mark. We recalled rumors of gorge waters rising 100 feet in 10 minutes, stories of the musty downdraft that precedes a flood, photographs of a wall of water plunging down like a wave crest. The thought that we could be trapped never left our minds.

In Dark Cliff Passage the walls rose sheer and smooth, like the hull of a ship in dry dock. Cavern Passage was evidently cut through harder rock, overhanging and twisted. As we looked up, no sky at all was visible.

**Thirsty mounts drink** from La Verkin Creek in Zion's wild northwestern ell. Hurricane Fault's 2,500-foot cliffs jut nearby.

Abruptly the cavern opened into a hall which looked deceptively simple. But on the shallow side of the stream we stepped onto soft footing.

"Quicksand!" someone warned. We waded noisily into deeper water and found firm bottom. Farther on the walls parted again and we passed into a natural temple. Sculptured cliffs of many hues rose above us.

Z ION NATIONAL PARK once lay under fathoms of water. Water pressure and chemical action changed layers of gravel, sand, and lava ash into solid rock, cemented and colored by iron oxides and lime. Embedded in this slowly upthrust rock are fossilized fish, shells, and plant life; here are found the bones and tracks of dinosaurs which disappeared 60 million years ago.

184    Formations of six geologic epochs are prominently displayed in the park.

Youngest, and therefore the uppermost, is the Carmel limestone which caps the East Temple, West Temple, and the Altar of Sacrifice. This 200- to 300-foot layer was the floor of the shallow sea, perhaps 120 million years ago. Beneath is the Navajo sandstone, more than 2,000 feet thick. From these mighty beds Zion's rainbow canyon has been carved.

The lower sandstone walls, predominantly red, run a full range of purples, blues, and browns in changing light. Higher up, the spectrum pales through pinks, lilacs, and buffs to the limestone's gray-white. Above all a cap of green forest touches the brilliant blue sky.

Such scenic riches inspired one Mormon, Isaac Behunin, to reason: "These great mountains are natural temples of God. We can worship here as well as in the man-made temples in Zion. Let us call it Little Zion."

So it came to be known. But Brigham Young was not satisfied. "It is not Zion," said he. Some of the faithful thereafter called it "Not Zion."

Mormon pioneers sent to live in the canyon protested the lack of timber for construction. "Lumber will soar down from the cliffs like an eagle," Brigham Young is said to have told them.

Some 30 years later the prophecy came true. In 1900 David Flanigan hit upon the idea of a 2,600-foot cable from canyon rim to floor to bring down the fine yellow-pine timber that stood above the cliff. Today's visitor can see the upper tower of Flanigan's cable, still perched atop Cable Mountain, northeast of the Great White Throne.

There is no evidence that Escalante, the Franciscan Father, or Jedediah Smith, the fur trader, ever saw Zion Canyon, though Escalante crossed the Virgin River in 1776 and Smith traversed La Verkin Canyon in 1826.

Nephi Johnson, a young Mormon missionary and interpreter among the Paiute Indians, was probably the first white man to see its depths. Called by

**Lunching on tableland,** a trail party gets an eye-level view of 6,744-foot Great White Throne (left), long a challenge to climbers. Zion Canyon's west wall rises on right.

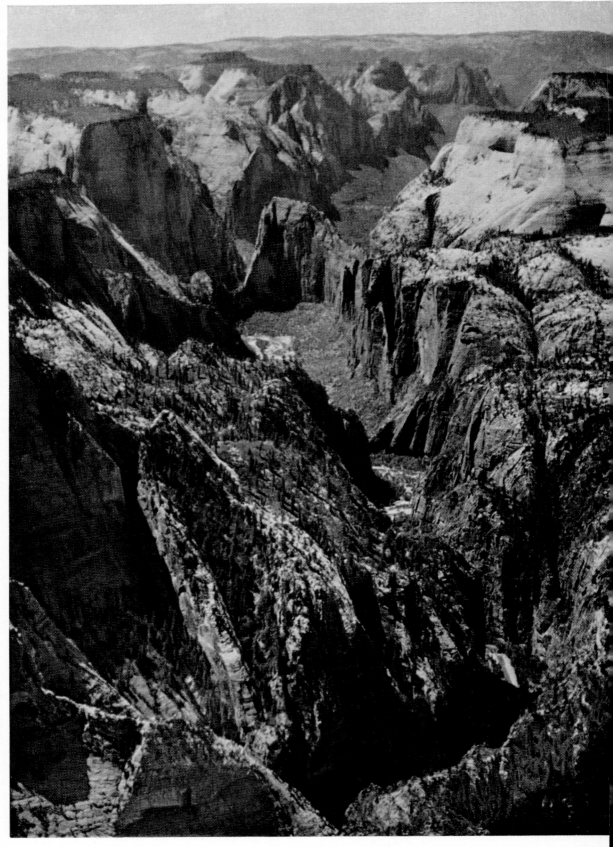

**Zion: "The most wonderful defile it has been my fortune to behold," said explorer Grove Karl Gilbert.**

Brigham Young in the fall of 1858 to explore the upper Virgin River, he persuaded the Paiutes to guide him over the rugged escarpment of the Hurricane Cliffs and up the Virgin River as far as the Narrows. His Indian guide refused to go any farther than Oak Creek because Wai-no-pits, the Evil One, might lurk in the shadows of the narrow canyon.

That night, camped on a rocky bar in Deep Creek, I almost agreed with the Paiutes. From a sandy couch I gazed at the darkening sky. To the north, stars disappeared behind thin clouds. Could it be raining in Cedar Breaks? I heard a roaring sound like distant thunder or a great waterfall. Then I saw winking lights—a plane. Relaxed now, I watched moonlight outline the chasm walls. Then I dozed.

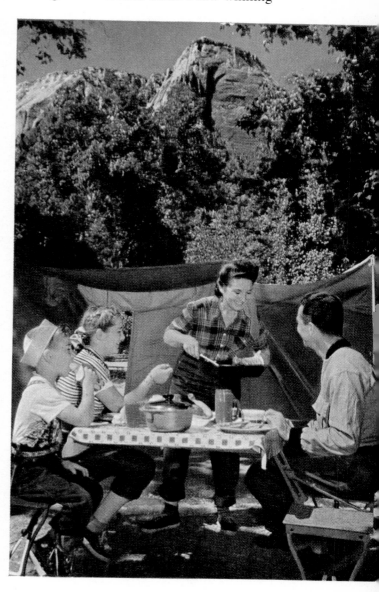

The next time my eyes opened the sky was paling. A fire blazed and the doubts of the night had fled. The canyon that had looked so forbidding in evening shadow now beckoned with the sunrise.

We climbed over the debris of a fresh-looking avalanche. Tons of rock had poured through a notch high in the cliff. The hurtling boulders had torn branches from canyon pines. Over all lay a blanket of fine rock dust.

We passed hanging valleys where intermittent tributaries poured their waters into the canyon in cascades and clear falls. We walked through Amphitheater Temple, a beautiful meadow filled with grasses and wildflowers. Tall pines stood against the cliffs that enclosed it.

As we rounded a turn, the walls closed in. Water filled the gorge from side to side. Often the walls overhung the stream. In places we couldn't see even a patch of sky to judge if the weather was still favorable. We

The Virgin River tumbles from the Narrows (foreground), named by Gilbert, dodges Angel's Landing, and rolls on between giant altars of stone. Each year it gnaws away 300,000 tons of rock. Eventually erosion will wash away the cliffs one elderly lady found so magnificent—"but they do shut off the view!" Right: Appetites are keen at Grotto Campground.

187

seemed to be splashing through high, vaulted tunnels. For 40 or 50 minutes at a stretch we saw no possibility of climbing up if the waters should rise. Eerie walls echoed and re-echoed our voices. With the help of walking sticks, we found fairly secure footing on the round stones that covered the riverbed.

At one point I heard a low gurgling—mysterious and ominous. After a search, I found its source, a spring higher than my head, pouring into a dark pool. The chasm widened, but each side was blocked by immense rocks fallen from the heights. The only way was through the pool, which was too deep to wade. Putting cameras and wrist watches into plastic bags, we plunged into the water and swam across, towing our buoyant packs.

We were surprised to find several water ouzels, seemingly unconcerned at our approach. Whether through fear or lack of it, one of these small slate-gray birds sat quietly on a branch while we petted it. Another we gently picked up and carried a quarter of a mile. Rather than frightened, it seemed merely curious when we placed it on the limb of a tree.

Again the walls closed in. The water became deeper, the course more winding. Then, at an almost closed horseshoe bend we glimpsed the Mountain of Mystery jutting skyward. We knew that not far from this 6,545-foot peak lie well-known park landmarks: Weeping Rock, Angel's Landing, and Cable Mountain, all easily reached from Zion Lodge and Grotto Campground.

The canyon widened, and on the gravelly shore we saw horseshoe tracks and a gum wrapper. Civilization was near. At last, seven great bends beyond Orderville Canyon, we heard voices. Across the river were the girls. They had walked up from the Temple of Sinawava.

As we emerged dripping from the river at the trail's end, a group of park visitors looked toward the Narrows behind us as a ranger told of its hazards.

That night it rained lightly.

Several weeks later we heard that a flash flood had inundated the upper canyon. The river had increased its volume 50 times, mostly within 15 minutes.

---

**ZION NATIONAL PARK** *Southwestern Utah. Area 223 sq. mi.*

**Features:** Vertical Zion Canyon, cut from forested tableland by Virgin River. Eroded back country. Desert wildlife. Indian ruins.
**Activities:** Visitor center at park headquarters. Scenic drives; 155 mi. of hiking, climbing, riding trails. Nature talks.
**Season:** Open all year. Roads snowfree.
**Weather:** Summer days hot, nights cool.
**What to bring:** Hiking shoes, rough-it togs, cottons, light jacket. Sunglasses, camera.
**How to get there:** US 89 or 91 to Utah 15.

Union Pacific RR or Western Airlines to Cedar City, Utah; bus connections to park.
**Accommodations:** Zion Lodge (June 15–Sept. 10), Zion Inn (May 15–Oct. 1); write Utah Parks Co., Cedar City. Camp and trailer ground open all year. Motels in Springdale.
**Services:** Restaurants, stores, garages in park. Nurse, church services at Zion Lodge.
**Park regulations:** Camping and fires outside campgrounds by permit only. Stay on trails; no hiking or climbing alone. Pets on leash.

*For further information write Superintendent, Zion National Park, Springdale, Utah*

**Planed by the floods of time,** cliffs of Zion's remote Hop Creek Valley rival the Narrows.

**Enchanted castles of Bryce Canyon** were carved by the artful fingers of frost and rain. Northeast from Sunset Point the visitor views a spectrum ranging from flaming yellow to the purple of Utah's distant Table Cliffs. Park's mile-and-a-half elevation cools the dry air.

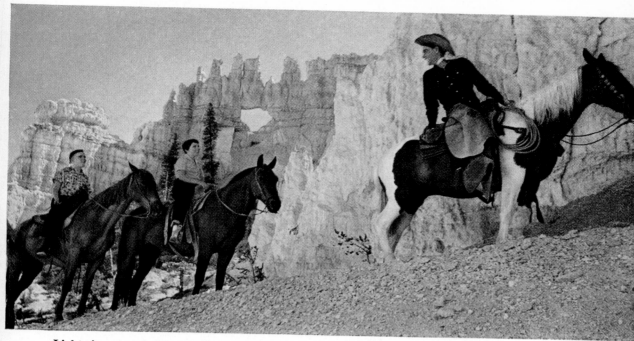

**Light pierces a window** of Oastler Castle, whose battlements flank Campbell Canyon Trail.

# BRYCE CANYON

*Photographs by WILLIAM BELKNAP, JR.*

O N A THAWING SPRING DAY, visitors can actually hear erosion: the trickle of water, the tumbling of rocks, the rattle of gravel. In the 56 square miles of Bryce Canyon National Park, geology is as current as a newspaper, and far more sensational. For the traveler planning an easy three-park vacation—Grand Canyon, Zion, and Bryce—geologists promise a cross-section history of the planet earth. Rocks deep in Grand Canyon, formed some 1.5 billion years ago, are perhaps twice as old as life itself; the Canyon's youngest stones are still about 180 million years old. Zion continues from there with the Age of Reptiles. Bryce belongs to the timely Age of Mammals, the last 60 million years.

These iron-stained rocks, hardened from ocean sediment and desert drift, were once lifted two miles above sea level. The mass cracked, so that on the faulted eastern side of a plateau in southern Utah water and ice could pry into crevices and carve what Paiute Indians called "red rocks standing like men in a bowl-shaped canyon."

Capt. George M. Wheeler, an early surveyor, found the bewildering landscape "a work of genii now chained up in a spell of enchantment while their

192 **Javanese spires rise from a silent city:** the view from Inspiration Point. Bryce is not a true canyon but the cracked eastern face of a green plateau. "A cavern with the roof stripped away," some describe it. Varying tints come from iron and manganese oxides in the rock.

**Hikers thread Navajo Loop Trail** into a magic world of temples, palaces, and sculptured figures. Paiutes believed these were creatures who fell into evil ways and were turned to stone. Science calls it erosion.

structures fall in ruins." Imaginations run riot as visitors today delight in naming thousands of these eroded fantasies. Perhaps the only person to escape Bryce Canyon's spell was the Mormon homesteader who gave the place his name. Ebenezer Bryce called it "a hell of a place to lose a cow."

Some 300,000 travelers a year judge Bryce a wonderful proof that nature is still an artist, and still at work on the Great Plateau. After feasting on its magnificent scenery, one lady said: "Zion was the fruit cocktail, and Grand Canyon the main course. But I had to come to Bryce to get my dessert!"

**Queen Victoria** (left and right) serenely surveys her garden of stone. The Three Wise Men (above) eternally seek the road to Bethlehem. One teen-ager imagined them guided missiles, all set to blast off. Hikers below rest in the depths of Wall Street, a chasm that seldom gets direct sunlight. Faces reflect the glow of flaming rock.

**Nature's giants** dwarf puny mortals pressing for a look from Bryce Point. Colors in the canyon range from red and pink to gold and frosty white, with touches of blue and lavender. Throughout the day patterns and hues shift constantly with the moving sun. Some rocks seem to glow as if lit by internal fires. By moonlight they appear almost phosphorescent.

## BRYCE CANYON NATIONAL PARK

**Features:** Some of world's most fanciful and richly colored formations, carved from 20 miles of southwestern Utah's Pink Cliffs. Bryce Canyon itself is the most spectacular of a dozen basins, or amphitheaters, in the 56-sq.-mi. park.

**Activities:** Visitor center. 17 mi. Rim Drive (go first to Rainbow Point, stop at Bryce, Inspiration, Sunset, Sunrise, and other overlooks on way back). 61 mi. of hiking and riding trails. Guided walks on Navajo Loop Trail. Illustrated talks.

**Season:** Visitor center open all year. Rainbow Point road, April—Dec.

**Weather:** Summer days warm, dry; nights nippy. (Rim elev. 8,000 to 9,100 ft.) Winters cold, snow (p. 50).

**What to bring:** Hiking shoes, rough-it clothing; woolens for evening. Sunglasses, camera, binoculars.

**How to get there:** US 89 to Panguitch, east on Utah 12. (Zion National Park is 85 mi. southwest, Grand Canyon's North Rim 160 mi. south.) Union Pacific RR, Bonanza Airlines to Cedar City; bus to park.

**Accommodations:** Lodge (June 15—Sept. 6), Inn (May 15—Oct. 12); write Utah Parks Co., Cedar City. Free camp and trailer ground.

**Services:** Restaurants, stores, garage. Nurse at lodge, hospital in Panguitch. Church services in park.

**Park regulations:** Camping and picnicking in campground only. Do not disturb formations or wildlife. Stay on trails. *Don't overdo: you are at high altitude.* No pets on trails.

*For further information write Supt., Bryce Canyon National Park, Utah*

# CEDAR BREAKS

Between Bryce Canyon and Cedar City, drivers can pull up at a two-mile-high overlook in Cedar Breaks National Monument and get a hawk's-eye view of formations even more colorful than Bryce offers close up.

In this huge amphitheater, cut from Utah's Pink Cliffs, mineral-stained ridges radiate toward the cliff arc like painted spokes of a circus wagon wheel.

A lodge (write Utah Parks Co., Cedar City), a campground, and often a committee of deer welcome summer travelers. Rangers answer the inevitable question: Cedar Breaks was named by Mormon settlers who thought junipers were cedars. "Breaks" are cliffs at a mesa's edge.

# CAPITOL REEF

A bare century ago westbound wagons were halted in south central Utah by a sudden escarpment. The cliff—layered in chocolate, green, and ivory—ran about 150 miles; horsemen could cross it in only three places. This was the famous Waterpocket Fold.

Polygamists took refuge here and bequeathed a name to Cohab Canyon. Even after 61 square miles were set aside as Capitol Reef National Monument in 1937, the area remained incompletely explored.

Motorists with a zest for untamed country can put in at Capitol Reef Lodge, a motel, or local ranches, or camp near the monument's eroded domes, cliffs, pinnacles, and petrified forests. Around them stirs the "night life" of these sheer-walled canyons—the distant, sad song of the coyote, the nearby bustle of the "trade" rat who is said to leave an offering for every item of camp gear he steals.

Superintendent: Torrey, Utah.

200

Sparrow hawk eats mice and grasshoppers.

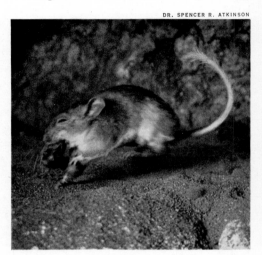

Pack or trade rat gives baby a ride.

Jack rabbit needs little water.

**Indestructible coyote, the West's commonest predator, brings home a jack rabbit.**

## Wildlife on a Thirsty Plateau

"What could possibly live here?" the parks visitor asks, gazing at the stark canyons that scar the Great Plateau. The answer: everything from the cougar stalking a mule deer among the rocks to a tiny chipmunk bravely raiding picnic crumbs.

For wherever water gathers—along canyon floors, in desert potholes, amid the plants atop mesas—wilderness creatures enact their drama. Bobcats prowl the piñon forest for ground squirrels and cottontails. Foxes and coyotes roam the sagebrush for jack rabbits. Soaring overhead, hawks, owls, ravens, and eagles search for marmots and mice.

Lizards scamper over rocks where an occasional rattlesnake suns itself. The skunk parades in lonely majesty, and a yellow-haired porcupine waddles into an empty tent to chew on the salty handle of a hatchet.

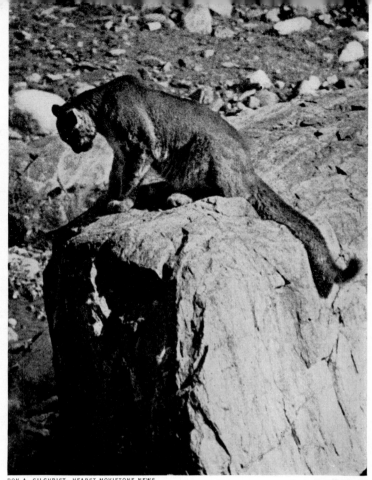

**Protected in parks,** mountain lion helps keep nature in balance.

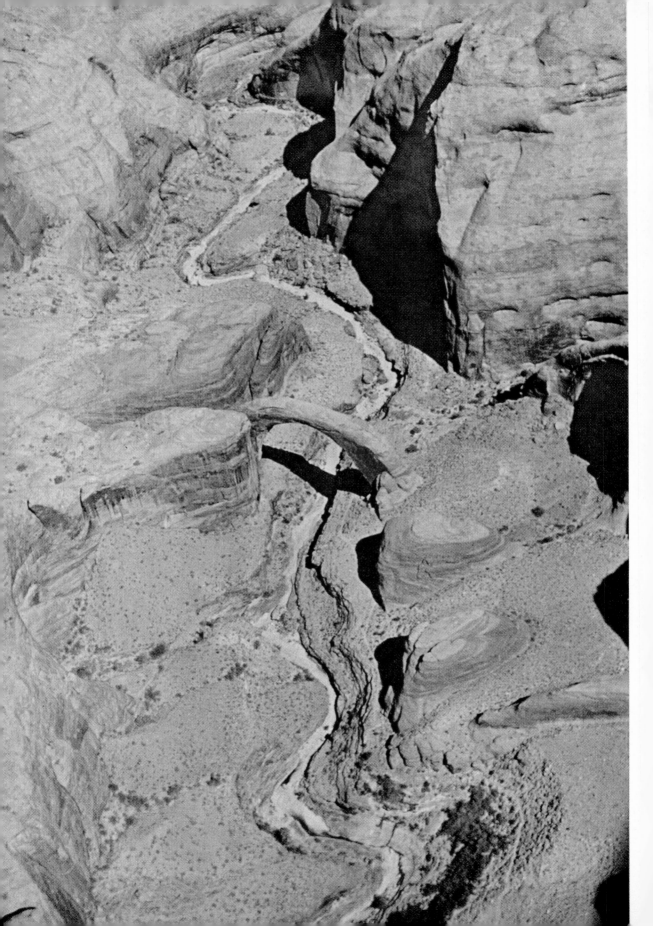

# RAINBOW BRIDGE

*By RALPH GRAY, National Geographic Staff*
*Photographs by the author*

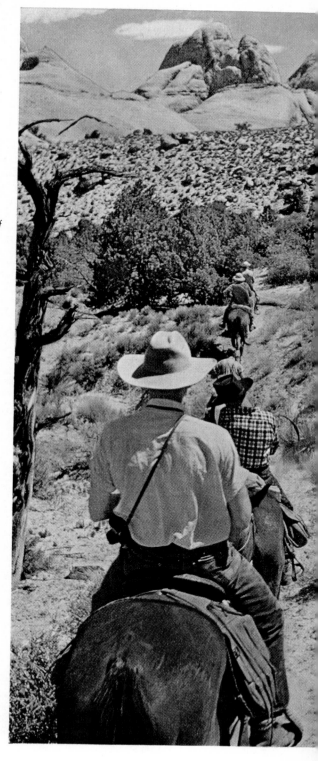

AMID A JUMBLE of slickrock canyons that crease the Utah-Arizona border rises Rainbow Bridge, one of the world's wonders. Colorado River boats churn to within a few miles of this hidden gem. Planes fly over to give sightseers a view of it, like half a butterscotch Life Saver lodged in a crevice. I saw it the old way—from the back of a tired pony after 14 jarring miles.

I saddled up with a party of riders near Navajo Mountain Trading Post. All day our sweating mounts picked their way across the northern ridges of Navajo Mountain, the whale-backed landmark of the state boundary. We saw water only three times, at the bottom of great gulches down whose sides our blowing horses lurched. On the heights again, their shod feet slid on polished sandstone.

Shadows had cooled Bridge Canyon by the time we reached it. We clopped over a shoulder of talus, then drew rein to stare. Ahead, partly hidden by an intervening cliff, an incredible arch of stone gracefully curved across the evening sky.

**Rainbow's arch of stone** spans the dusty creek that carved it. Ages ago, digging its channel in southern Utah's desert, Bridge Creek cut into necks of sandstone. The stream wore away other formations, but this one it penetrated, leaving a great rib of rock in air.

**Thousands of tons of sandstone soar gracefully across the sky**

The world's largest natural bridge spans 278 feet and arches 309 feet above Bridge Creek. Seen from below, it reveals its immensity. But from the rim of Bridge Canyon, the span is dwarfed by the wilderness around it. In 1909, spurred by Indian rumors about *Nonnezoshi* (Stone Rainbow), a party first saw it after days of parched travel through red rock and yellow sand. Presented in the *National Geographic* by Byron Cummings, one of its discoverers, Rainbow Bridge was made a national monument by President Taft in 1910.

**Roping down** onto the bridge from its western abutment, Geographic staffman Ted Park lashes onto a spike driven into the rock.

Rainbow Bridge! Seeing it, I felt that lifeless matter had been caught in dramatic action. From high on one canyon wall the solid rock seems to stream up, out, and down in fluid motion.

Nature has fashioned hundreds of arches and bridges in Utah and Arizona; new ones are found almost every year. Yet Rainbow overshadows them all. It spans 278 feet and rises 309 feet—large enough, lacking inches, to frame the United States Capitol.

The job of making camp barred me from closer acquaintance until next morning. Then, joined by two companions, I hiked down the canyon and stood under the vaulting rock. In its shadow we found the registry book, kept since earliest days for the visitors who have reached Rainbow, among them Theodore Roosevelt and Zane Grey. I became signer number 10,741. That's less than the number of people who visit Grand Canyon on two summer days. I read scribbled reactions of awe, relief, frivolity. One girl claimed

RAINBOW BRIDGE WOULD TOP THE U.S. CAPITOL

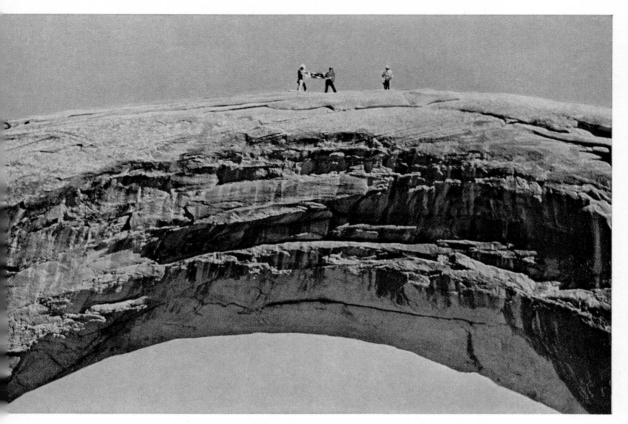

**Blustery wind** greets author's party atop Rainbow. "It seemed crowded with just us three."

to be "first to sleep all night on the bridge." Farther along, in the "Method of Transportation" column, a man wrote, "hands and knees."

With full canteens and a 40-foot rope, three of us set out to climb Rainbow Bridge, something few attempt. Clinging to toe holds, we inched up the canyon's west wall and reached the great shoulder that rises almost level with the rounded top of the bridge. From this abutment we roped down to the arch—slender looking from afar, but actually 42 feet thick at its top, and as wide as a high-crowned country road. We felt the thrill of achievement as we stepped to the apex of the Rainbow. We exchanged triumphant handshakes, spread a National Geographic Society flag to the gusty breeze, then walked to the edge and peered down. Cutting far beneath our feet, the canyon floor looked no wider than a footpath. Instinctively, we recoiled from gaping emptiness.

Certainly we had conquered Rainbow Bridge. But as we huddled on that age-old, weathered crest, surrounded by the austere cliffs of its hideaway, we felt puny and uncertain—like trespassers in a world of giants.

**A new door to Rainbow** will open when Colorado waters fill behind Glen Canyon Dam. Visitors will skim over the lake to within shouting distance of the bridge instead of hiking in from the river.

# NATURAL BRIDGES

EVERY SUMMER a few uranium hunters wander into Natural Bridges National Monument, geiger counters in hand. A ranger soon sets them straight—prospecting is forbidden on park lands. Some linger to see what our Nation values more than radioactive ore: three huge bridges, hewn from buff sandstone, all within four square miles of southeastern Utah's tangled canyons.

Each spotlights a different phase in nature's leisurely bridge-building. Kachina, youngest of the trio, seems at first glance to block its stream bed like a 206-foot dam. The waters that ate away its flank broke through only in comparatively recent times. Winter's frosts and thaws are still slenderizing the 93-foot-thick span. Springtime visitors taking the ladder trail to Kachina usually find fresh flakings of stone scattered beneath it.

From Kachina, hikers follow a two-mile trail to the largest and most perfect bridge, a flat-topped spur of rimrock leaping its gorge in a 268-foot stride. So gracefully arched is its underside that it was named Sipapu after the Pueblo's sacred entrance to the underworld.

Close by monument headquarters and campground, a tendril of rock, Owachomo Bridge, soars 180 feet. Oldest of the three, its span has weathered to a mere nine feet in thickness. Zeke Johnson, an early custodian, recalled that a geologist pronounced Owachomo ten million years old. "That was July, 1926," Zeke said, "so if he's right, it will be 10,000,040 years old in July, 1966."

# ARCHES NATIONAL MONUMENT

*By PAUL JENSEN, National Geographic Staff*

WHAT'S THE DIFFERENCE between a natural bridge and an arch? Bates Wilson, superintendent of Arches, gave me the answer. "Simple," he said. "A bridge bridges a watercourse and an arch doesn't.

"Anywhere in Utah's redrock country a canyon stream might cut itself a bridge. But all 88 arches here are on high ground away from streams. All were cut just by weather from stone fins."

"Fins?" I asked. We had driven up the new road from the visitor center on US 160, and stopped at Courthouse Towers. Park Avenue's sandstone skyscrapers stretched before us—only the doormen and poodles were missing. Beyond sprawled The Windows, a reef rising in turrets, spires, and balanced rocks.

"Fins," said Bates and pointed to a fresh crease in my fender. The paint had

**Like a viaduct for some forgotten city,** Sipapu strides 220 feet above its cottonwood-crowded gorge. Cass Hite, a prospector, discovered the bridges in 1883, but not until 1904 were they fully reported—in the *National Geographic*. Natural Bridges became a monument in 1908.

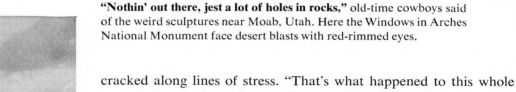

**"Nothin' out there, jest a lot of holes in rocks,"** old-time cowboys said of the weird sculptures near Moab, Utah. Here the Windows in Arches National Monument face desert blasts with red-rimmed eyes.

cracked along lines of stress. "That's what happened to this whole area. Only here the 'paint' is a 300-foot-thick layer of Entrada sandstone. The earth humped and the Entrada cracked clear to the bottom in regular rows ten to twenty feet wide. Over in Devil's Garden you'll see miles of packed fins."

"And these isolated rocks?" I looked down Courthouse Wash.

"Flukes of erosion," said Bates. "Over millions of years the elements have worn most of the fins away, leaving solitary formations like the Organ, Sheep Rock, the Three Gossips. Then there's Delicate Arch, which is unique. But that's one you'll want to see alone. Some things are better without people talking all the time."

The West abounds in marvels of nature: the world's grandest canyon, its biggest trees. But Delicate Arch is not the world's biggest anything. It doesn't have to be. Alone, it would be lovely. Combined with its setting, it was incomparably beautiful to me.

Michelangelo said of the sculptor's art: "The more the marble wastes, the more the statue grows." Here nature's hand has chiseled a great amphitheater and on its rim left standing a spraddle-legged colossus. I saw not a speck of dust or even a lichen clinging to this pink stone arc or to the coliseum it embellishes, whose polished sides plummet to the valley. Beyond the gorge of the Colorado River rise the snow-capped La Sal Mountains.

The sun went down and an eerie pall fell over the lifeless scene.

**Delicate Arch,** star of the 53-square-mile preserve, stands 85 feet high    211
and 65 wide on the lip of a slickrock bowl. Wind and rain carved
it from a sandstone reef. Cowboys called it "Old maid's bloomers."

JACK BREED AND (ABOVE) U. S. AIR FORCE

**Landscape Arch's** ribbon of stone leaps nimbly over crude boulders it shucked off. The 291-foot span, longest of its kind in the world, is a show-window example of arch-making. Winter rain, penetrating cracks in a high reef or fin, pried relentlessly as it froze. Block after block broke away until a tiny window opened. Wind-driven sand helped file it into an arch. Now only this fragile strip of rock stands in air. Tomorrow—or in a few centuries—another slab may crack off and carry the whole arch away, leaving only stubs like those beyond the man.

Wisps of a breeze hissed across the grainy surface. Swept by a sudden chill of loneliness, I hurried down the trail to the car and to my motel in bustling Moab.

Whereas Delicate Arch impressed me with its weird beauty, Landscape Arch, carved from an enormous fin in the middle of Devil's Garden, struck me as just plain impossible. Coming up the trail, I didn't see it at first, for it blended into the high wall behind. Then suddenly it seemed to snap into place—a 291-foot band of black and red stone, the world's longest natural span. Of all things, I found myself thinking of a bee.

An aeronautical engineer once "proved" that a bumblebee can't fly. It doesn't have enough wing area, is poorly streamlined, and has no control surfaces whatever. Well, mathematically speaking, Landscape Arch can't stay up. Any structural engineer can prove it's all wrong—far too long, far too flat. One end is only six feet thick, while in the center the arch humps its back, spreads 20 feet wide, and weighs thousands of tons. But there it stands.

Bates Wilson, who feels about his arches as a gardener does his petunias, worries over the cracks that pierce Landscape. When it falls, as surely it must, it will be a black day for him.

Go see it soon, and while you are at Arches spend a little time; there are a dozen other marvels to inspect. Ask the ranger to take you through the Fiery Furnace, where slender fins, blazing red in sunset's glow, tower 200 feet above a labyrinth. The going is rough, but deep within the Furnace fresh water awaits in potholes and there are cool coves where the sun never penetrates.

# BLACK CANYON
# OF THE GUNNISON

ANGLERS SEEKING RAINBOW TROUT in the gorge of the Gunnison River have reported that in full daylight they could see stars gleaming in the strip of sky overhead. Rangers label this a fish story—but do confirm that, except at midday, an eerie twilight shrouds the depths between the sheer walls.

Knifing through a plateau in the San Juan Mountains region of western Colorado, the Gunnison has cut as deep as 2,700 feet through base rock. Black Canyon of the Gunnison National Monument, established in 1933, includes the deepest 10-mile stretch of this stupendous chasm. And black is the word for the canyon. Cliff bottoms reveal ebonylike schist, millions of years old. Overhangs cast long shadows on frowning walls banded by coarse gneiss and granite ranging from somber gray to pink.

To stand at the lip of the abyss and peer straight down at the tiny, writhing river is enough to raise the hackles on summer sightseers.

Small trees crowd the plateau, among them piñon patriarchs whose 700-odd years are chronicled in the rings of their gnarled trunks. Vacationers who pitch tents at the north and south rim campgrounds may glimpse the rare Rocky Mountain bighorn. Elk often winter in the 21-square-mile sanctuary.

# COLORADO NATIONAL MONUMENT

DRAMATIC RED SANDSTONE FORMATIONS unfold before visitors to this western Colorado preserve. A 22-mile scenic drive, open all year, skims the edges of canyons that cut deeply into the escarpment above the Colorado River near the cities of Grand Junction and Fruita. Overlooks and self-guiding trails give motorists and campers close acquaintance with Window Rock and the pot-bellied "coke ovens" of Monument Canyon, the arrow-straight vista down Red Canyon, and such columns and spires as 500-foot-tall Independence Rock.

Juniper, piñon, and flowering plants dot the red-rocked land. Formed during the Age of Reptiles, the red strata lie directly on black granite dating from earth's nearly lifeless infancy. No vein of stone exists here between the two layers to record the passage of a half-billion years. Rangers call this strange geological missing link the great hiatus.

Where brontosaurus, the "thunder lizard," once shook the ground with his tread, a small herd of bison now grazes within the monument's 28 square miles.

**"Place of high rocks and much water,"** Ute Indians described the gorge of the Gunnison. Scenic drives parallel north and south rims.

EDWARDS PARK, NATIONAL GEOGRAPHIC STAFF

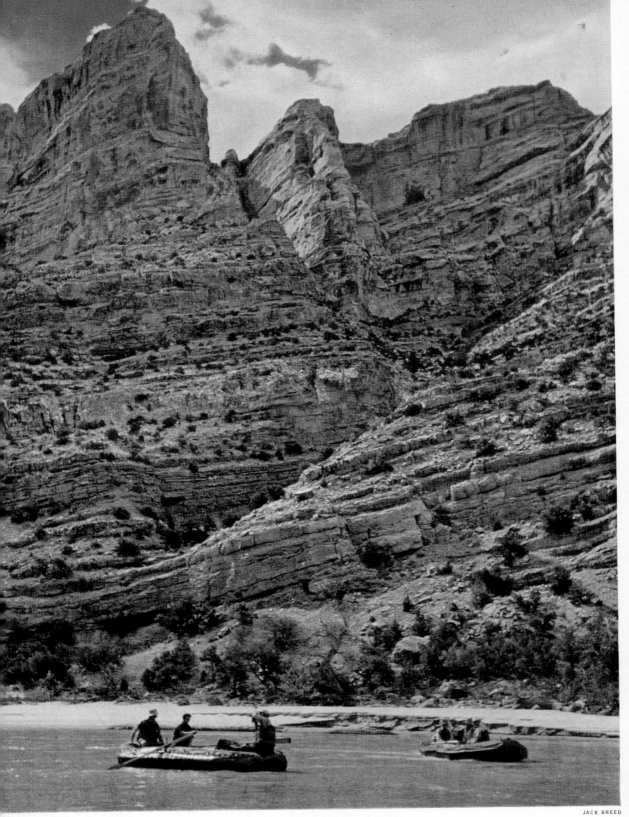

JACK BREED

**High cliffs and high adventure** mark the 75-mile raft run down the Yampa and Green Rivers across the monument. Many of Dinosaur's most spectacular sights are known only to those who ride its rivers.

*Daring "river rats" shoot the rapids through Colorado-Utah*
*borderlands where monstrous reptiles met a mysterious end*

# DINOSAUR NATIONAL MONUMENT

*By JACK BREED*

T HIS RIVER IS STRICTLY A ONE-WAY STREET," said Bus Hatch. "Once we enter the canyon of the Yampa, there's no turning back. So if any of you fellows want to reconsider. . . ."

His glance traveled deliberately over each member of the little group. Our three rubber life rafts, loaded with camp equipment, were drawn up on the muddy shore near Lily Park, Colorado. Ahead lay 75 miles of white water twisting into Utah through some of the West's most spectacular gorges, the bright-hued cliffs of Dinosaur National Monument. We grinned back at Bus.

"Well, don't say I didn't warn you," he said. "Let's shove off."

I clambered aboard Bus's raft. This jolly, plump contractor from Vernal, Utah, and his son Don were "river rats" of no mean skill. The rest of us—Conrad Wirth and four Park Service colleagues, a local rancher, and I—made up in high spirits what we might have lacked in experience.

Our boats looked ugly but dependable. Navy craft designed to hold 10 men each, their rubbery buoyancy gave them an obvious advantage over wooden skiffs. Our 4½-day trip downriver would take us to the Dinosaur Quarry, where paleontologists unearthed more than two dozen complete dinosaur skeletons.

For the first few miles of our journey down the Yampa we had leisure to study the country. Here the river, yellow and brown with

**Indian warrior** has guarded Dinosaur's cliffs 1,000 years or more. The monument is rich in such petroglyphs.

**In reptilian coils, two rivers course through Dinosaur land**

Carrying Colorado's silt toward Utah, the slender Yampa (right) joins the Green River for a promenade around 700-foot-high

Steamboat Rock. In this cliff-barricaded meadow a hermit, Pat Lynch, took refuge for 50 years; oldtimers called the site Pats Hole. Today a road enters from US 40. Echo Park, in shadow at right, is named for Steamboat's resonance. Spanish explored region in 1776.

silt, was a sluggish stream less than a foot deep; we used oars more than out-board motors. But our placid drifting drew to a close with the distant roar of white water ahead. We tipped up the propellers to avoid concealed rocks; the canyon walls converged. It looked as if the river were turning into a broad stair-case, each step capped by curling spray.

I flinched as the first ripple glistened ahead. But nothing happened. Our rub-ber boat simply buckled, folding itself over rocks like a caterpillar.

On a sandbar beneath Yampa Canyon's walls we ate a typical river rat's lunch of bean stew and sandwiches. No one needed to tell us how the Yampa had earned its title, "River of no return." We could not possibly have climbed its 1,400-foot cliffs or hiked back upstream. I was glad I had no appendix.

Back on the river, we saw Canada geese placidly swimming. Beavers moved close to the banks; deer occasionally bounded up the talus slopes. "You can see why early trappers liked this country," Bus said. "Mountain men camped here in the 1830's and '40's. We'd better pick a spot ourselves."

It was only 5 p.m., but the sun sets early and rises late in narrow canyons. We pitched camp on a grassy slope in Starvation Valley, at the head of Big Joe Rapids. Soon steaks were sizzling and we were ready for sleeping bags.

In the morning we made a recon-naissance of the rapids below. The water raged with whirlpools and waves 8 and 10 feet high. Don tossed in sev-eral logs. We watched one swirl past— and disappear into a foaming caldron.

"Stay clear of that one!" yelled Bus.

He took his raft first. Standing in the stern, Bus gunned his engine and pointed the bow toward midriver, seeming to head for the worst waves of all. He shot into them—and vanished.

He reappeared skimming the crest of a wave, his raft bending around a stubborn rock. Spume drenched him, but he never took his eyes from the river. In an instant he had cleared the rapids. Cheers from all hands.

220   **Storm clouds threaten** as raftsmen pit their skill against Green River rapids in Split Mountain Canyon. Channels change day to day as the rampaging stream shifts boulders.

JACK BREED

The rest of us followed. Now the river widened and we entered the amphitheater called Harding Hole. From here the Yampa threads white sandstone cliffs. Drifting, we lounged and looked up at the blue ribbon of sky.

"Steamboat round the bend!" Tom Vint sang out, and we saw massive Steamboat Rock, marking the Yampa's wedding with the Green. We camped here in the meadow of Pats Hole and next day rode the Green River through Whirlpool Canyon. Rock slides strewed the banks; juniper and scrub pine clung to crevices.

On our final day, Bus cautioned us. "I've run boats through Grand Canyon, the San Juan, the Snake. None has worse stretches than you'll find in Split Mountain Canyon today." And indeed we had close calls. Once Bus lost control; in a wooden craft, we would have cracked up. Then the canyon opened up, and twilight found the river more peaceful. We were at voyage end: Dinosaur Quarry.

I tried to imagine this country when dinosaurs roamed it, back in the Jurassic

**"Where can we see the dinosaurs?"** eager visitors ask. "You're about 120 million years late," rangers reply. "But our new visitor center tells about ones that used to live here." Bones of this 70-foot-long diplodocus at the National Museum in Washington came from Dinosaur.

GIANT DINOSAUR

**New roof for an ancient wall,** the visitor center at Dinosaur Quarry, open all year, encloses the fossil-filled cliff. The 328-square-mile monument has summer campgrounds, trails, wilderness roads. Lodgings, supplies at Vernal, Utah, on US 40. Superintendent: Box 621, Vernal.

period. No Rocky Mountains, no canyons; just tropical marshland from central Utah to the Mississippi, with a fringe of volcanoes showering ash and dust. Several kinds of dinosaurs lived here—some no bigger than a turkey; others, like the brontosaurus, 80 feet long. All were a bit stupid, averaging one pound of brain to 40 tons of bulk.

What killed these dinosaurs? Perhaps a blizzard of volcanic ash or a bacterial plague. Rivers washed their carcasses against a great sandbank where they were covered by sand and silt. Silica impregnated their bones. Sand and bone became stone. In 1909 Dr. Earl Douglas, of Pittsburgh's Carnegie Museum, discovered the paleontological treasure trove, one of the world's richest.

Today this cliff makes an exhibit unique in our national parks. From a balcony within glass walls visitors view fossil bones as they were uncovered and glimpse vistas of life history more exciting even than canyons and rapids.

223

# LEHMAN CAVES

SOMETIMES YOU WONDER if there's a cave in the West that wasn't discovered by a cowboy and his horse tumbling through the roof. That's how homesteader Ab Lehman gave his name to an intimate, exquisite cavern system on the flank of 13,063-foot Wheeler Peak near Baker, in eastern Nevada. One-hour tours, all year, lead past "bacon-strip" draperies, past stalactite clusters that have wrenched free of the ceiling and look like parachutes. In spring and summer the wild and scenic square-mile monument offers cabins and refreshments. Campers pitch their tents amid the aspens along trout streams nearby.

# TIMPANOGOS CAVE

LEAVE HIGH-HEELED SHOES in the car when you visit Timpanogos. The cave lies at the end of a mile-and-a-half trail that switchbacks up the side of American Fork Canyon in Utah's scenic Wasatch Mountains. Don't forget a sweater, for cave temperature hovers around 42°. But the delights of these little chambers outweigh the chill. Stalactites are jeweled with drops of water, for this is a living cave, its formations still growing. Pale colors tinge coral-like helictites, fragile structures whose crystals grow every which way. Only 35 miles from Salt Lake City, the 250-acre monument closes in winter.

# CRATERS OF THE MOON

YOUNGSTERS EXPECT MOON MEN in pressurized suits and fishbowl helmets. Instead they find in this 75-square-mile national monument in southern Idaho one of the world's most complete displays of volcanism. Here the earth's crust was weak, and for thousands of years lava bubbled from wounds along the Great Rift. Hot magma lapped around living trees, turned them to torches, and left molds of their burned-out trunks. Molten blobs, hurled from spatter cones, hardened in mid-air to the teardrop shape of bombs.

Today all is black desolation with an austere beauty of its own. Rivers of rock seem still to flow around cinder cones and lava domes. Visitors tentatively touch ropy lava to see if it's still warm. They enjoy playing Superman, hoisting overhead fantastically heavy-looking chunks of volcanic froth.

A loop road and trails explore these pockmarked wonders. Campers pitch tents on the cinders and slake 110° thirst on cold spring water piped from mountains to the north. In winter skiers sport on the cinder slopes.

**To explore Boy Scout Cave** at Craters, youngsters lug a sled through midsummer heat (above), then pull themselves across the cave's watery ice with prospector's picks. Hard hats guard against jagged lava that insulates this once-molten tube, keeping temperatures near freezing.

WILLIAM BELKNAP, JR.

Denver

40

85

COLORADO
KANSAS

o Pueblo

*Arkansas River*

287

o Walsenburg

Raton o

**Capulin Mountain**
NATIONAL MONUMENT

OKLAHOMA
TEXAS

87

*Amarillo* o

66

*Pecos River*

NEW MEXICO
TEXAS

o Roswell

o Carlsbad

**Carlsbad Caverns**
NATIONAL PARK

80

o Alpine

90

**Big Bend**
NATIONAL PARK

*Rio Grande*

*San Antonio* o

---

## PART THREE

---

# THE SOUTHWEST

---

IN THE PAINTED DESERT a silent ocean of mesas and buttes rolls to the horizon. Sunwashed colors play on their wrinkled skins, setting afire chunks of petrified wood. Amid the gesturing saguaros of Arizona, the sweeping range lands and vast caverns of New Mexico, there is the same grandness—and seeming emptiness. It is as though this broad Southwest heard no voice but the dry whisper of its winds, saw nothing but the glare of its sun. It is as though man had never intruded on this communion of land and sky.

Yet for thousands of years men have come, one migration elbowing aside its predecessor. In forgotten canyons stand crumbling villages that once rang with life. On cliff walls Indian sketches show helmeted conquistadors astride monstrous horses. Each age has left its mark on this dry and sunny land where nothing seems to perish.

Descendants of early pit-dwellers live in adobe pueblos and sell pottery to Spanish-American ranchers—and "Anglo" tourists. Singing a high-pitched dirge, the Navajo trots home to his hogan. Serenely unconcerned with humans, the Southwest has absorbed them all, preserved their cultures, and thus enriched itself.

---

227

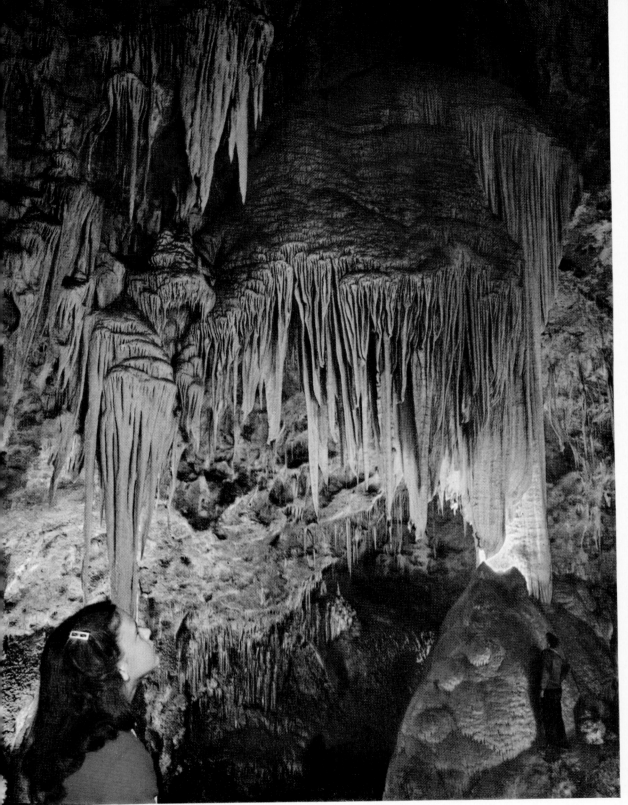

228 **Limestone cascades in a frozen Niagara;** stone parachutes hang motionless in Carlsbad's Big Room. Dripping water patiently fashioned these translucent stalactites. Tubular, they resound like bells if struck, but, since knuckles may break them, the practice is forbidden.

*Beneath sunbaked cactus lands where conquistadors marched
and outlaws ambushed wagon trains of California gold,
Carlsbad's cool caverns reveal a vast and gleaming fairyland*

# CARLSBAD CAVERNS

*By MASON SUTHERLAND, Assistant Editor, National Geographic
Photographs by E. "TEX" HELM*

N EW MEXICO RANCHERS in the
1880's noticed sky-darkening
flights of bats that spiraled like a
tornado funnel from a cave in the
foothills of the Guadalupe Mountains. But not
until 1901 did a young cowboy, James Larkin
White, light a kerosene torch to explore deeper
recesses of the bats' home.

White descended into a world of hidden
wonders, a network of corridors and vaulted
chambers, ornate with magical formations.
From then on he made Carlsbad Caverns his
life's work and hobby. He found with each trip
a new fantasy that had been wrought through
ages of darkness by drops of water. Fragile
chandeliers, folds of mineral drapery, pillars,
domes, make-believe birds, fanciful flowers
lurked wherever his torchlight fell.

Yet this enchanted underworld remained

**Queen's Draperies** burst into flame as a torch
shines through them. Absorbing light, they
glow for seconds after it has been doused.

230     **"You are entering the world's most spectacular caverns,"** announces the tour leader at the start of the three-mile hike. Elevators await those who can't make it. At summer twilight bats stream out entrance.

relatively obscure until 1924 and 1925 when the National Geographic Society put it on the map. Backed by a grant from The Society and guided by Jim White, Dr. Willis T. Lee of the United States Geological Survey explored and mapped portions of the caverns, which he described in two *National Geographic* articles. "The most spectacular underground wonder in America," Lee wrote. "For spacious chambers, for variety and beauty, [the cave] is king of its kind."

Thus Carlsbad Caverns achieved their first nationwide publicity. They were established as a national park in 1930.

In the days when Dr. Lee was supervising the recently explored caverns, yearly visitors were counted in the hundreds. Within 30 years annual attendance soared above the half-million mark. Today rangers lead four-hour trips along three miles of paved trails. For my tour I had the company of Col. Thomas Boles, the park's first superintendent, who served 19 years at the caverns. "I have made 5,071 complete trips and enjoyed every one," he told me.

FOR A MOMENT we paused at the caverns' natural mouth. The ranger leading our tour told how Carlsbad Caverns were hollowed out of a 1,600-foot-thick limestone formation called the Capitan, deposited in a shallow sea some 200 million years ago. When the Rockies started growing, about 60 million years ago, the Carlsbad area was uplifted. Between that era and the Pleistocene, a million years ago, ground water entered fissures and dissolved the less resistant stone. Collapse hastened water's work. Finally the water table fell and air filled the cavities.

Then the decorative phase of cavern building set in. Rain water, seeping from the surface, picked up limestone. Wherever drip was slow enough, evaporation squeezed out the water and deposited minerals which, layer by layer, formed stalactites and stalagmites. Nature sought to fill the chambers she took so long to hollow out.

Starting down the switchbacks, a series of winding ramps descending 829 feet, the height of an 80-story building, we passed the entrance to Bat Cave. No place in the caverns is gloomier than this unlighted passage, seldom shown to visitors. As many as eight million bats at a time have slept by day on Bat Cave's ceiling, hanging head down. At night they feed on insects outside. Leaving at the rate of 300 a second, they may take four hours to clear the exit, filling the evening air with their sweet and musky odor.

"I recall one morning," said Boles, "when a party got caught in the bats' return flight. Women screamed and raised skirts above their heads."

Beyond Bat Cave we entered the Main Corridor, a cathedral-like hall a mile long that descends deep into the earth. We saw natural sculptures such as the American Eagle, with a 12-foot wingspread; the Whale's Mouth; the Three Little Monkeys, perched high above the trail; and the Baby Hippo. My attention was drawn to millions of tons of material which had fallen from the ceiling.

231

"Don't be alarmed," said Boles. "You couldn't be in a safer place. No collapse has taken place in thousands of years." One spectacular collapse has been named the Iceberg. Despite its 100,000 tons, the Iceberg slipped so gently that its stalactites received no injury.

"Remember you can destroy in an instant what nature took centuries to build," tour leaders counsel. "Please don't touch the formations. Stay on the trail at all times and make your trip quietly."

I heard the silence rule broken at the Iceberg. Snapping off the lights to give us a taste of the utter blackness in which the caverns grew, our guide asked us not to speak lest we destroy the illusion. A creepy interval followed. Then some man pinched his wife, she giggled, and the crowd roared.

In the Green Lake Room, first of the scenic rooms on the first half of the tour, floodlights threw the Veiled Statue into relief. This shrouded column resulted when stalactite met stalagmite. Nearby the Frozen Waterfall spilled out of a tunnel, and a small enchanted pond explained the room's name. It turned reflected light an emerald green.

232

We entered the King's Palace, perhaps the caverns' most ornate chamber, where the trail leveled off under thousands of stalactites, glittering like chandeliers. Each of these downward-hanging stone lances was formed by water seeping from the ceiling and leaving a mineral trail in tubular form. One seven-foot pendant as slender as a soda straw is known as the King's Bellcord.

Generally, when droplets roll off a stalactite and hit the floor, they build a stalagmite. But few of these reach upward in the King's Palace. One stalagmite, however, comes within a knife's blade of kissing its corresponding stalactite. Doomed never to touch, since no water now drops between them, they are called the Frustrated Lovers. These two guard a keyhole entrance to the Queen's Chamber. There we found the famous draperies, masses of stalactites grown together like curtains. We saw no sign of the Queen herself, but the King's Boots hung in her chamber.

Baby of the royal chambers is the Papoose Room, its low ceiling gleaming with porcupine-quill stalactites. No one has described them better than the little girl who said, "That's just how my foot feels when it goes to sleep."

At one time Colonel Boles used to halt touring parties in the scenic rooms for lunch. They would drink pure, cold drip water caught on the spot. Now Carlsbad's guests break their tours for lunch before tackling the mile-and-a-quarter trail around the Big Room. We mounted Appetite Hill, 80 feet of rugged switchbacks, walked past the Boneyard, where partly dissolved rocks illustrate the first stages of the caverns' formation, and took a passage to the huge subterranean lunchroom where we bought coffee and sandwiches and sat at a picnic table.

**Nature fills its cavities** with limestone marvels. Shapes vary from swirling stone portieres at the Dome Room entrance (opposite page) to the tiny forest of stalactites and stalagmites that crams the Dolls' Theater (right). Little of this ornamentation can exceed 100,000 years, for most rest on fossils of that age.

Some pillars, gleaming like candle wax, are wet—still growing. "Popcorn" studding them shows they were immersed in water. Broken stubs bear witness to the Park Service rule: "Don't touch the formations!"

**Temple of the Sun** (right) has never seen its namesake's light. Tinged with delicate hues by iron oxides, decorative formations turn the ceiling into an inverted pincushion. Taffylike in appearance, stalactites can gash anyone blundering off the trail. Some visitors nose into side passages, but when guides switch off lights "explorers" quickly return, rather than face alone the inky blackness that reigned here millions of years.

Though hikers can sit for a moment along the trail, this 40-minute rest was welcome. Reminiscing, Boles spoke of the Rat Hole trip that parties used to take before tours grew too unwieldy.

"That narrow tunnel made an interesting detour," he said. "Everybody had a laugh when fat men got stuck in a tight gap. One guide used to save an old starched collar for the occasion. Just as the visitor's trousers grew taut under the strain, the guide would rip the collar. It sounded like the seams giving way!"

At last we hiked to the Big Room, the world's largest known underground chamber. Like a vast, richly ornamented cathedral, the Big Room has the ground plan of a cross, one arm measuring some 2,000 feet, the crosspiece stretching 1,100. The ceiling at its highest point rises 285 feet.

We caught a distant view of the Rock of Ages, one of the caverns' most famed formations. At this monumental stalagmite, Colonel Boles used to stop tour parties and call the roll of states. He saved the Texans until the last, because, "cheering the mention of their state, they made further roll call impossible."

We marched past Crystal Spring Dome, fastest growing formation in the

235

North

G u a d a l u p e

Parking Terrace,
capacity 600 automobiles

Natural Entrance

Bat Cave

Feet below elevator building

-100
-200
-300
-400
-500
-600
-700
-800
-900

Elevator building with three-
story observation tower, 4406
feet above sea level.

Auditorium

Devil's Spring

Whale's Mouth

The

Natural Bridge

Carlsbad, 27 miles

Devil's Den
Tunnel blasted to bypass
exhausting climb over rubble pile.

Main

American
Eagle

Baby Hippo

Corridor

Three Little
Monkeys

Feet below elevator building

-100
-200
-300
-400
-500
-600
-700
-750

Passage to the lunch room,
elevators, and Left Hand Tunnel

Iceberg

Appetite Hill

Boneyard

D
R

Veiled
Statue

Bashful
Elephant

King's Pala

-750
-800

Frustrated L

King's
Bellcord
Frozen Waterfall
Green Lake Room

To the
New Mexico Room

Queen's
Chambers

Que
Drape

-800

Pap
Ro

-900

**Carlsbad Caverns unroofed: a depth map reveals the cave's enormity**

In contrast to National Geographic explorers who clambered over loose rocks and collapsed formations, today's visitors follow a paved trail. After walking a mile down the Main Corridor without seeing many striking formations, some begin to wonder. But skepticism turns to awe when they enter Green Lake Room, first of the decorated chambers, 80 stories underground. Eyes are dazzled by myriad glittering stone icicles. Appetite Hill readies hikers for the lunchroom, halfway point of tours. The second half is spent circling the Big Room. Elevators then return parties to New Mexico's sunlight.

Of Carlsbad's 23 miles of explored passages only the three paved miles are shown. Some narrow tunnels have never been entered. Deepest pit probes 1,100 feet below surface.

CAVERN SURVEY BY WALTER MORRISON, NATIONAL GEOGRAPHIC CARTOGRAPHER

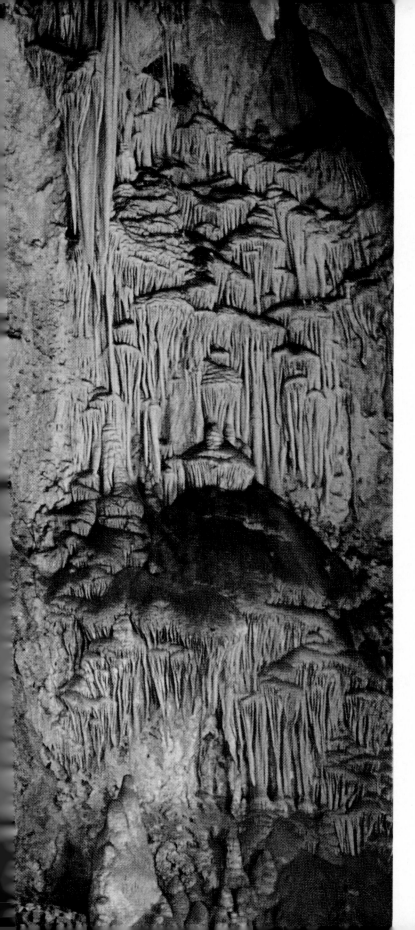

## For a mile and a quarter hikers wind beneath Big Room's bearded ceiling

So vast is the Big Room and so twisting the trail that most visitors fail to recognize it as a single chamber. Its stalactites resemble ribbons, soda straws, atomic clouds. One, poised over the path, is aptly named the Sword of Damocles. Stalagmites of every shape grope upward from the floor. Most celebrated of all, huge Rock of Ages occupies a niche in the dark central window.

Sometimes stalactite and stalagmite meet and merge into a pillar or column. Most of Carlsbad's formations have stopped growing, reflecting climatic changes overhead in semiarid New Mexico.

Other caverns may be more vividly colored than Carlsbad, but none matches the immensity of its spectacle. The Park Service shuns colored floodlights, insists on showing the formations in their natural state.

To take these pictures, photographer Tex Helm used multiple-flash gear and a bank of 13 mounted cameras, each set at a slightly different lens opening. Bulbs and reflectors bathed the caverns in a blinding, crucible glow for one-thirtieth of a second.

Helm's over-all shot of the Big Room (page 40) took 2,400 huge bulbs and bombarded the great sanctum with light four times as intense as New Mexico's sun.

239

**Cave pearls** grew in a stone nest. Drops of water rolled grains of sand, gradually coating them with lustrous minerals.

**The Society's 1924 expedition captured these flash-powder shots of cave wonders**

Probing the caverns for the National Geographic, Dr. Willis T. Lee and his men were lowered into Bat Cave in a guano bucket. They struggled down unknown tunnels, into yawning pits, and over jagged blocks of fallen limestone "like a train of ants making its way through a brickpile." Feeble torches were almost helpful since they lit "only one difficulty at a time."

Lee returned (right) to photograph formations like the popcorn-coated stalactite that reminded him of a cave man's club.

caverns. Though some 95 percent of the formations are dry, and hence dormant, here the eye easily picks out splashing drops of water that spread a thin coat of limestone paint. The Dome is accumulating about 2½ cubic inches of mineral a year. A small pool, Crystal Spring, collects at its foot.

We peered down the Bottomless Pit, whose bottom actually can be seen by flashlight, 138 feet below the trail. Here the ceiling of the Big Room reaches its apex, so the vertical drop from ceiling to pit bottom covers 423 feet—largest in the caverns.

The trail skirted Mirror Lake, which correctly reflects its own inverted signpost. The Totem Pole, tallest of several skinny stalagmites, lacks a parental stalactite because water dripped too fast to deposit a big growth overhead. Passing the pastel-hued Temple of the

**Algae** growing under lights tint stone grapes green. Cave fungi thrive in dark. Carlsbad would make a good mushroom garden.

Sun, we walked through the Hall of Giants where the Onyx Draperies hung above the trail and three huge domes rose beside it, the largest reaching 62 feet above us to stage the Big Room's smashing climax.

In 1924 Dr. Lee and his aides explored and mapped Lower Cave. Actually no deeper than the scenic rooms, it may be seen 90 to 100 feet below the main trail in the Big Room. Two abysses look down into it. One is the Jumping-off Place (no one has jumped yet), the other, the site of a rusting ladder used by the 1924 National Geographic expedition. Today's guides know five other ways of entering Lower Cave.

In the caverns' dim lighting one loses all sense of time. Passing a park ranger, I said "Good night." His answering laugh sent me to my watch:

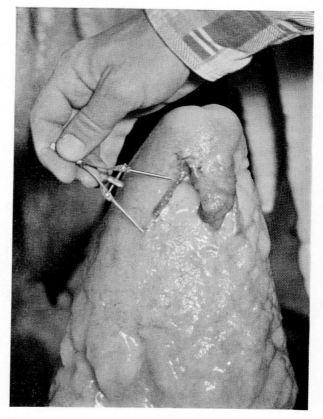

**Unlucky bat** tumbled on a growing stalagmite; now it's a fossil. As many as 300 bats roost head down on a square foot of Bat Cave's ceiling. Guano miners took 100,000 tons of fertilizer from the floor.

241

2:30 in the afternoon. Floodlights give many areas a fairly even illumination, and skillful lighting accents big formations. But I took equal pleasure in some lesser sculptures that had to be picked out with a flashlight.

I saw a stone hen that had sat on her nest for thousands of years without laying an egg. The Statue of Liberty held a torch in her left hand. Abraham Lincoln brooded with furrowed brow and bearded chin; and a life-sized Santa Claus, complete with stocking cap, perched atop a totem pole.

I was enchanted by a miniature city with Gothic cathedrals and castles standing on a bluff beside the Big Room trail. Long stone faces recalled Easter Island sculptures. There were stalagmites that looked like fire hydrants, giant candlesticks with melted wax running down their sides, and tombstones in a Moslem cemetery. I even spotted a stalactite growing from the girder of an elevator.

**Hungry hikers** welcome a 40-minute rest in the domed lunchroom, 754 feet below the surface. Box

And like every tired sightseer, I felt grateful for those elevators that waited near the lunchroom to whisk us to the surface.

Though all attention is usually focused on the caverns, the national park embraces 77 square miles of semidesert near the Texas border. Some of the thousand mule deer that roam this sanctuary have been spotted apparently reading a sign, "U. S. park boundary. No hunting allowed." My car's headlights picked up glow from the eyes of deer idling in the park highway.

About 30 known caverns lie within the park. A guide showed me one, New Cave, or Slaughter Cave. It cannot match the size or beauty of Carlsbad Caverns, but boasts such gigantic formations as a 100-foot pillar, 18 feet in diameter, decorated by fluted draperies that resound like organ pipes. If Carlsbad continues to grow in popularity, new wonders may be opened to the public. 243

lunches feed 2,000 an hour. Elevators are nearby.

**CARLSBAD CAVERNS NATIONAL PARK**
*Southeastern New Mexico. Area 77 sq. mi.*

**Features:** World's most spectacular limestone caverns; colorful stalactite-stalagmite formations in fanciful shapes. Big Room is world's largest known underground chamber.
**Activities:** Visitor center. Four-hour cavern trips start in morning all year; extra afternoon trips in summer. Elevator service down to lunchroom and second half of tour, to surface at tour's end. Special photographic tours. Naturalist talk on bats each summer evening.
**Season:** Park open year round.
**Weather:** Surface temperature varies from near zero in winter to above 100° in summer. Cave is a constant 56°. Elevation at entrance 4,350 ft.
**What to bring:** Light sweater or jacket for cave; low-heeled shoes with rubber soles or heels. Camera for flash or time exposures on photo tour.
**How to get there:** US 62-180 and 285 (see map at back of book). Continental Airlines, Sante Fe Rwy. to Carlsbad, New Mex. Major air and rail service to El Paso, Tex. Carlsbad Cavern Coaches from Carlsbad and El Paso to park.
**Accommodations:** None in park. Hotels, motels, trailer parks in Carlsbad and nearby towns.
**Services:** Restaurant, curio shop, nursery, kennel adjoin visitor center. Lunchroom in caverns. Garages, car rentals, hospital, church services in Carlsbad, 27 mi. NE.
**Park regulations:** No camping or fires; lunching in designated places only. Walking sticks in caverns by permit. Pets on leash, none inside.

*For further information write Superintendent, Box 111, Carlsbad, New Mexico*

# BIG BEND

*By BART McDOWELL, National Geographic Staff*

TEXANS HAVE A large superlative for the park they gave to the Nation. "It's not the biggest or newest," said a gun-toting U. S. marshal from San Angelo. "But it is the *wildest* national park in the U. S. A."

Texans make a flamboyant case for their claim. Even today parts of Big Bend National Park are unexplored. Law and order are still uneasy newcomers; on some risky patrols, park rangers are carefully dispatched in pairs. Yet for comfort-loving travelers, Big Bend offers safe and varied action, shirtsleeve weather in the dead of winter, and blanketed beds on summer nights.

This authentic wilderness owes its unspoiled state to freaks of geology. Mountains here are turned upside down, and the Rio Grande has dug itself a formidable system of moats. Spanish conquistadors, even after their triumphs in the Andes, never succeeded in exploring the Rio Grande around its great U-shaped bend. Later men also failed—U. S. boundary surveyors, Texas Rangers, everyone until Robert T. Hill came in 1899. Paddling 10 hours a day, six men in Geological Survey boats bested the canyons. "Every stone," wrote Hill, "was closely scanned for men in ambush."

Violent men indeed took refuge behind the Big Bend barricades. Comanche warriors trailed through Persimmon Gap (where motorists from Marathon now enter the park) going to and from their raids in Mexico. Train robbers, smugglers, revolutionaries, bandit gangs all hid in the Chisos Mountains. A gold mine lost, a damsel kidnaped, a rancher

**Cool cottages,** at an elevation of 5,400 feet, offer pleasant summers in the Chisos Mountains Basin.

**Big Bend National Park,** established in 1944, hugs the Mexican border where the Rio Grande makes a sweeping 100-mile turn. Here in Boquillas Canyon the river courses between Texas (right) and Mexico.

WILLIAM A. BARDSLEY AND (RIGHT) W. RAY SCOTT

245

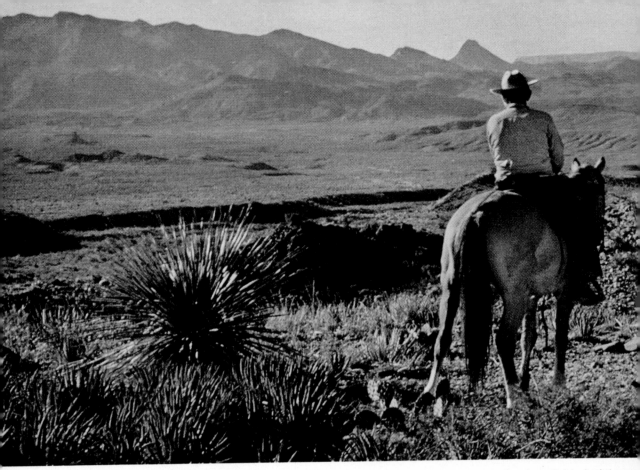

**Big Bend bigness sprawls northward** from Burro Mesa. Pioneers said every plant here "either sticks,

slain—such events are still recalled by local folk. Crusty Judge Roy Bean, "the law west of the Pecos," claimed dominion over this land. Pancho Villa's guerrillas invaded U. S. territory here at Boquillas as late as 1916.

Times change, and the real violence is now mainly confined to the struggle of river against rock and to the colors of high desert. Here nature is balanced upon contrasts. The great river waters a warm, fertile strip along its banks; beneath cottonwoods, park visitors run trotlines for 10-pound catfish and sometimes wade abroad into Mexico. Nearby, lunarlike mesas display the austere beauty of classic desert. Beyond, the 7,800-foot Chisos Mountains stand abruptly cool and green.

Campsites in each environment give Big Bend a year-round use. Roads and trails lead to the habitats of whitetail and mule deer, the cranky javelina or peccary, the pronghorn, mountain lion, beaver, and to the only known U. S. nesting place of the lyric-voiced Colima warbler. With horse and guide or on marked hiking trails, the visitor can share the same Southwestern vistas seen by the earliest explorers—and perhaps find spots untrod before.

246      **Cliffs of two countries,** pried apart by the Rio Grande, face each other at Santa Elena Canyon. This shaded picnic spot is 94 miles south of Alpine, Texas, served by Trans-Texas Airways and Southern Pacific Railroad. For information write Superintendent, Big Bend National Park, Texas.

stings, or stinks." But today's city-weary vacationists find the 1,107-square-mile park a feast.

# WHITE
# SANDS

*By WILLIAM BELKNAP, JR.*

*Photographs by the author*

**Slat sails** set to the desert breeze, a family embarks on picnic delights.

**S**TAY ON THE ROAD, folks. Watch our speed limits," said the ranger as he handed us our permit, "and have fun!"

We had turned off US 70 at the monument visitor center, and the country looked flat and unpromising. Have fun doing what? I began to wonder if there would even be anything to photograph. My family, like most others, had come little suspecting the surprises in store.

As we drove along White Sands Drive, my disappointment quickly faded. Shimmering white dunes loomed ahead. Our son Buzz, 12, and our daughter Loie, 10, called a halt at the first drifts and shot from the car as if spring-ejected. They scampered up a slope, dropped to their knees, and scooped up great handfuls. Then the magic hit Fran and me as we ran our fingers through the incredibly soft stuff, cool and delightful. Off came our shoes and we raced up a snowy mound.

"I had no idea it could be this lovely," Fran said. "It's like fairyland!"

Enchantment, disbelief, puzzlement—ours were typical reactions to White Sands. We strolled along the roadside dunes, fascinated by the way desert plants —yuccas, sumacs, and even cottonwoods—fought to keep their heads above the sugary tide. Just sand? Not quite. It was like nothing we had ever seen, great rolling waves of it, white and fresh as a wilderness snowfall.

**Children have a three-ring circus in New Mexico's 140,000-acre sandbox.**

**At sunset,** shadow islands float on an amethyst sea. After a day busy with people and loud with

Like three million visitors before us, we began to appreciate White Sands' uniqueness. Later, at the museum, we learned it is the world's largest known surface deposit of gypsum sand. Utah and Australia have some, but neither deposit rivals New Mexico's 275-square-mile display. Dunes at White Sands are not only the largest in area; they move faster, pile steeper, look whiter, and are just plain more fun than any others.

How does pulverized gypsum differ from ordinary beach sand? If you heat quartz sand, it melts into glass, but gypsum bakes into pure plaster of Paris. Also, gypsum is much softer and, being white, stays cooler in the sun. It rubs to powder between your fingers, and its wind-driven crystals will not pit the play, peace comes to the desert.

finish of your car. You can even taste the difference. Unlike sand, gypsum dissolves in water and has a definite flavor—mineral and unpleasant.

Late on our first day a windstorm arose, and we saw nature's construction force at work building the gypsum dunes. Fran and Loie stayed snug in the car, but curiosity sent Buzz and me struggling up a powdery hillside.

Amazingly, once on top we walked through the storm without getting sand in our eyes. The heavy gypsum traveled as "bed load," rolling, skipping, and bouncing, instead of flying. Braced against the blast, with heavy particles peppering our legs, we saw White Sands come to life. Wind undermined our shoes when we stood still, letting us sink slowly. Air turbulence started small dunes as we watched. Feet first, we slid down the steep dune—and got sandblasted as our faces passed the crest.

The chief ranger has his hands full. His job is an odd combination of protecting a natural wonder and running an amusement park.

"Traffic is our number one problem," he explained. "People like to race and cut corners on the Loop Drive. Some ignore the no-dune-driving signs; they don't realize the danger. If they don't bog down near the road, the bigger dunes beckon. Usually they leave the car imbedded and hitchhike for help."

Perhaps the busiest Park Service man is the road man, who puts in endless hours aboard a grader. The more the wind blows the harder he works. Often he's hard at it by dawn, using his grader like a snowplow.

"We used to fight the sand," he said. "Now we cooperate with it. If a dune wants to cover the road, we bulldoze another route around the dune."

White Sands National Monument occupies part of New Mexico's Tularosa Basin. Because of its relative isolation, natural barriers, and clear atmosphere, this 100-mile-long valley was used as a practice bombing range during World War II. Fifteen miles from monument headquarters lies the fast-growing city of Alamogordo, a name that still rings a bell the Nation over for its connection with the first atomic bomb. The historic blast was set off in a wasteland nearby. Between Alamogordo and White Sands is Holloman Air Force Base, home of the Air Force Missile Development Center. The Army, Air Force,

251

### An automobile threads dunes
### like a mouse in a monstrous maze

Swinging around the Heart of Sands, the monument's recreation center, a car rides the Loop Drive, a track graded wherever fickle nature directs. Dunes constantly lope over it and change its course.

Shallow ditch gouged at center shows how near ground water is to the surface. High mineral content makes it too strong to drink, but it supports more than 100 plant species that have adapted to Tularosa Basin's arid and alkaline life.

Cloudbursts and melting snows dissolve gypsum beds in the distant mountains. Runoff collects in marshy Lake Lucero (mid-distance), for the basin has no outlet. Evaporation leaves transparent selenite crystals (below). Wind pulverizes and whirls them into gleaming patterns. Drifts rise in slopes before the wind, drop off as cliffs to the lee.

An odd adaptation to this snow-white wilderness is the bleached earless lizard (right). Its *Holbrookia* clan is normally brown. But for centuries only lighter members blending with the sands escaped enemies, and a white race arose. Only other dunes dweller is the Apache pocket mouse. It wears a white coat too.

254        **A billowing sea of dunes,** bound by shores of the San Andres Mountains,

washes over a patch of stunted yucca. Restless as the winds that whip them, dunes rise 50 feet.

and Navy use the Tularosa Basin range to test missiles and research rockets.

Missiles have long been associated with White Sands. Several fluted stone projectile points—spearheads used by Folsom man some 10,000 years ago—have been found in the area. Campsites, arrowheads, and implements of later nomadic Indians show up along its margins. But modern missiles seldom affect visitors at White Sands. Proving grounds officers may restrict traffic along the highway during important "shoots," purely as an ultra precaution. The rockets land many miles away and are almost never seen from the road.

Recreational hub of White Sands is the picnic area. We thought the palette-

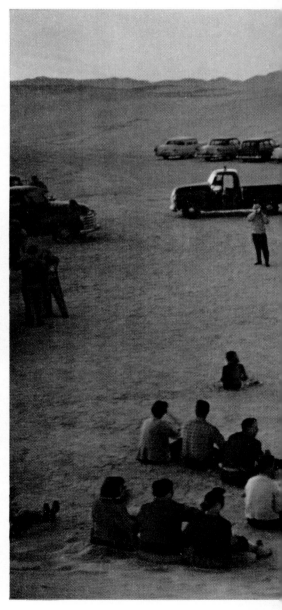

**White Sands'** feathery dunes play host to more than 300,000 visitors each year. The national monument, proclaimed by President Hoover in 1933, encompasses one-third of the dunes area in the world's largest gypsum desert. Remoteness deters commercial development of the gypsum.

Proudly calling itself "The Rocket City," nearby Alamogordo takes its name from the Spanish for "fat cottonwood."

Every spring, people come from all over to celebrate Play Day, "world's largest picnic." Dusk throws a blue shroud over a group (right) relaxing after the frolic.

shaped arena had been carved by bulldozers, but these creamy flats are natural. Their moist floors are surprisingly solid. Shelters and grills await picnickers, but wood and water are strictly bring-'em-yourself. There's no camping.

Unlike most other parks, recreation is stressed more than conservation. What damage can anyone do? The moving sands bury more plants in a month than visitors could pick in a year. Even litterbugs can't mar their beauty for long.

"We don't condone breaking regulations," the superintendent explained. " 'Take only pictures, leave only tracks' is as good a rule here as anywhere. But our feature attraction, being in motion, is just about indestructible."

**Spiny symbol** of the southwestern desert, the saguaro may top 50 feet and wave 40 oddly curved arms. Yet early growth is slow. It takes 30 years to stand a yard tall and 75 years for the first branch to sprout. The cactus may live two centuries.

# SAGUARO NATIONAL MONUMENT

A STRANGE ARMY of towering, gesturing figures stands rooted to the southern Arizona soil 16 miles east of Tucson. Stately ranks of saguaros, mightiest cacti in the United States, raise bristled arms above the 99-square-mile national monument that bears their name.

These green giants belie the image many have of the Sonoran desert as a lifeless, dun-colored waste. Visitors picnic in the cactus forest at the foot of the Tanque Verde Mountains amid a pastel preserve abounding in wildlife.

Saguaros live off moisture stored in spongelike tissue. After rain, their broad, shallow root systems may suck up a ton of water. The plant's ribs widen like accordion pleats, its tough skin distends and sometimes bursts. Indians harvest its scarlet fruit. The creamy blossom is Arizona's State flower.

# ORGAN PIPE CACTUS

THE DESERT PULSES with life as spring touches Arizona's Organ Pipe Cactus National Monument. Wild flowers parade their colors all through this 516-square-mile preserve along the Mexican border. Lavender-tinged petals open during night's coolness at the ends of the 20-foot organ pipes, some 30 stalks clustering in a single plant. Blossoms tip fluted saguaro columns. Barrel cacti tilt to greet the sun.

Antelope, kangaroo rats, and peccaries forage amid this untouched desert. The gilded flicker drills a nest in the moist cactus fiber while the elf owl roosts among its spines. Coyotes yodel—and campers feel that beyond the hiss of their cookstoves civilization has slipped 10,000 years away.

# CHIRICAHUA

RISING ABRUPTLY from southeastern Arizona's yellow desert, the Chiricahua Mountains look misplaced. Their purple crests and green forested flanks recall New England; their tortuous canyons and grotesque rock sculptures seem to belong on the moon. Layers of ancient lava, cracked and eroded, form Punch and Judy, China Boy, and other likenesses in the 17-square-mile monument.

Campers, hikers, and trail riders from nearby ranches see Arizona white-tailed deer and coatimundis roaming deep gorges that once sheltered the Chiricahua Apaches. From these mountains, Geronimo swept down with his warriors and Big Foot Massai staged one-man raids. Cochise Head, a mountaintop profile nearby, honors the wily chief who held off Fort Bowie's troopers a dozen years.

# PETRIFIED FOREST

*By EDWARDS PARK*
*National Geographic Staff*

AS THOUGH DROPPED by a negligent giant, thousands of jewel-like logs lie scattered across the blistered, mile-high desert in northeastern Arizona. In the Triassic Age, these were living trees. But 160 million years saw their wood turn to stone, glowing with rainbow colors. The world's biggest, brightest collection of petrified wood now clusters within the 147 square miles of Petrified Forest.

US 66, "Main Street of America," slices across the forest's northern section, tempting travelers to swing off the highway for a look at one of nature's strangest revelations. I followed their lead. Like many visitors (nearly a million come each year), I planned to spend an hour or two but ended up staying all day.

Like broken jackstraws, the shattered stone trees lie clumped in six distinct areas.

WILLIAM BELKNAP, JR.

**Polished cross sections** reveal beauty locked in stony hearts of primal trees.

261

**Colors come alive as a petrified slab gets its face doused.**

**Erosion gnaws at Chinle, age-old mud that swallowed a log jam**

Rain and wind nibbling at the claylike earth of Blue Mesa leave some petrified logs stranded on slender pedestals. Each stone chunk acts as a cap and slows further erosion of its support. But eventually it will crash, as thousands have before it, and roll into the gully to join them in magnificent clutter. Here banded pyramids and cones clearly show the ancient marsh layers.

Paved roads lead to five of these forests, each with its special features. At Rainbow Forest visitors wind through a garden of tumbled 160-foot trunks to snap pictures of Old Faithful, a sprawling forest monster that looks as if it crashed to the ground perhaps a dozen years ago. Actually, its huge gnarled trunk belongs to no familiar species—none but a dinosaur would recognize it. At Crystal Forest, short logs seem to have been left for pulpwood. But no woodsman cut these glittering chunks. Petrified wood is harder than steel.

"The only trees we don't have are upright ones, though we have found a few stumps," a ranger told me as I gazed at Jasper Forest's prostrate trees. He explained that they probably grew along a wide, primeval river. Most were a long-extinct type of pine. Falling from natural causes, they were swept off by

264

**Onyx Bridge,** a lone tree amid shattered stone logs,

WILLIAM BELKNAP, JR.

**Agate House's** fire insurance rates are low. Centuries ago, Indians built this dwelling entirely of petrified wood chunks. Partly restored, it overlooks Rainbow Forest.

floods and grounded here, in what was then a marshy area. "These petrified trees have lost their branches and most of their bark," he continued. "This supports the theory that they tumbled downstream and came to rest battered and stripped of boughs." The stranded trunks were buried by layers of marshy sediments that geologists call the Chinle Formation. The land sank. Then an upheaval, some 60 million years ago, produced the Rocky Mountains—and raised the 400-foot-thick Chinle to the surface, exposing it to erosion. Gradually some of the trees were laid bare. But now they were stone.

The magic was performed by silica and other water-carried minerals that filled each wood cell, duplicating its structure like plaster in a cast. Over the centuries, every detail of the original wood was retained. Traces of iron, manga-

spans its dry wash in the Painted Desert's Black Forest, a roadless section north of US 66.

**Broken Bridge** is a prehistoric pine. Mineralized eons ago, it braced itself like a keystone arch when a gully opened beneath.

nese oxide, and carbon added their colors. At Rainbow Forest Museum I had seen polished cross sections of agatized logs that glowed with all of Arizona's brilliance: the deep reds and orange of sunrise, the purple of a thunderstorm, the blazing blue of the desert sky.

Where plain silica infiltrated the cells the logs look exactly like yellowed trunks lying half-shattered and rotting. The scattered chips surely flew from an ax only yesterday. The grain stands out; splinters protrude. I picked up a sliver, expecting the spongy feel of old wood. But what I touched was cold stone —heavy, brittle, dry. Weathering and earthquakes caused the chipping, and the fracturing that makes many long trunks look as if they had been sawed.

At Blue Mesa, rain has sculptured the Chinle into miniature buttes and mesas, banded with mineral colors. I saw petrified logs jutting from hummocks like guns from a turret, exposed as the enfolding earth washed away.

Although geologists foresee more agate wood cropping up as the Chinle wears down, the law imposes severe penalties for removing any of our present heritage of petrified wood. Rangers told me why. If each visitor should pick up just one piece and lug it home, there would be no Petrified Forest left for our grandchildren to see. But you needn't go away empty-handed. Souvenir polished wood from outside sources can be purchased at the concessions.

Part of the Painted Desert falls within Petrified Forest north of Route 66. A looping detour leads to views of bright, eroded mesas extending to the northern horizon. The preserve includes Indian ruins, and a display of petroglyphs crams Newspaper Rock (page 39), near Blue Mesa.

Painted Desert Inn and Rainbow Forest Lodge offer meals, gasoline, and souvenirs. You can picnic but not camp, and the road linking US 66 and 260 is closed at night. Nearest lodgings are at Holbrook, 20 miles west.

# EL MORRO NATIONAL MONUMENT

REARING 200 FEET from the western New Mexico plain, El Morro (the Headland) beckoned generations of travelers. For at the foot of this sandstone crest gleams the desert's priceless treasure—a pool of water. Weary men made camp beside it. Then, painstakingly, they scratched their marks on El Morro's smooth face, scarring it with history in the raw. Indians cut pictures of hunts. Conquistadors carved haughty reports of triumph in the new land. Juan de Oñate, New Mexico's Spanish colonizer, left an engraved calling card dated "the 16th of April of 1605"—the first European inscription in the Southwest.

Today's travelers picnic amid El Morro's wild scenery, 53 miles from Gallup. And many search the rock for names of pioneer ancestors, dusty cavalrymen, and wagon-train drivers who pulled up at the old landmark, quenched their thirst, and gratefully signed the stone register.

**Even the knotholes are petrified!** Its "stone trees" reported in 1851, Petrified Forest became a monument in 1906, one of the Nation's first.

# GREAT SAND DUNES

"This is one national monument where you can write your name all you want—in the sand, that is!" The superintendent of Great Sand Dunes enjoys dropping this remark to visitors whose "Kilroy was here" instincts have been frustrated by "Do not deface" signs in other national park areas.

"Write it in letters a yard high! And put in your home town, if you like. The wind will erase it all by morning anyhow."

Here in southern Colorado, where desert meets mountain, the winds give and the winds take away. From the southwest, from the heat-hazed expanse of San Luis Valley they come, driving the loose sands along. As the airs rise to surmount snow-capped 14,000-foot peaks of the Sangre de Cristo Range, they lose velocity and drop their gritty burden. After untold centuries, these sands of time now smother some 50 square miles, with crests soaring a staggering 800 feet above the valley floor, highest dunes in the inland United States.

The dunes are at their loveliest during the changing light of dusk or at sunrise, when the picture below was made. Visitors are encouraged to tramp and play to their hearts' content. Open all year, the 57-square-mile monument provides picnic and camping facilities, including wood and water. Alamosa, Colorado, 36 miles southwest, is the nearest town with accommodations.

# CAPULIN MOUNTAIN

FROM MAY THROUGH JULY, Capulin Mountain National Monument presents the contradictory spectacle of a once-raging volcano seemingly tamed by wildflowers. The spurting lava is stilled, the choking ash has drifted away, and gay bluebells, daisies, Indian paintbrush, and lupines mask the black slopes.

Seven thousand years ago, northeastern New Mexico reeled with its most recent subterranean churnings. Capulin Mountain, formed then, is a perfect example of a cinder cone, created by welling lava which sputtered and popped like

grease in a pan as trapped gases burst free. Cooling as it fell back, the frothy cinder debris slowly built Capulin's cone.

Today the peak's serene symmetry belies its furious birth. And its lush vegetation continually surprises travelers who reach it across the dry expanses of the High Plains. Deer, porcupines, and squirrels abound, and bird song fills the air. Over the summit, 8,215 feet above sea level, golden eagles soar.

A good all-year road spirals the cone, ziggurat-fashion, passing through moist climate zones supporting juniper, piñon, and ponderosa pine, and higher, squawbush and chokecherry (for which the Spanish gave Capulin its name). The crater rim, 1,000 feet above the surrounding plains, affords a five-state view. Foot trails circle the one-mile lip and descend to the crater bottom 415 feet below.

The monument has a picnic area but no water. Raton, New Mexico, 29 miles west, offers accommodations. The famous Folsom site is nearby. Here finely chipped projectile points have been found with the bones of extinct bison hunted by Stone Age Americans.

**First footprints** of day mark Colorado's Great Sand Dunes, a stormy sea of drifts held restless captive by the towering Sangre de Cristo's giant curve.

269

RALPH GRAY, NATIONAL GEOGRAPHIC STAFF

# THE SOUTHWEST REVEALS
# A PANORAMA OF
# ANCIENT INDIAN CULTURES

A KACHINA stands on a kiva roof, bearing a bough of evergreen, symbol of eternity. Kachinas, incarnations of the gods, come to reward the good, punish the evil, and bless a semiarid region with rain and fertility.

The people we call the Pueblo (Spanish for village) intently follow the ritual, already ancient when gold-hungry Coronado came seeking the Seven Cities of Cíbola. These Pueblo Indians of Arizona and New Mexico—the farmers, cowboys, filling-station attendants, and students who live in 26 dusty, flat-roofed adobe villages of the Hopi, Zuñi, and Rio Grande tribes—are the Southwest's true aristocrats. Their ancestors were Basket Makers who settled amid these mesas and canyons before Christ was born.

They had no metal tool, no wheel, no beast of burden. Yet these peaceful, democratic farmers learned in time to build compact villages of cut stone. Their cities rose in terraces from canyon floors, and clustered high in cliffside caverns. They made and traded fine pottery, cloth, exquisite turquoise jewels. Then these cities fell empty, their ladder poles sticking like fingers from underground kivas that no longer throbbed with ceremonies. Mountain lion and mule deer inherited the silent realm.

When the 19th century world began to hear of vanished "cliff dwellers" and their strange fortresslike homes, fancy ran riot. A highly civilized non-Indian race built them 20,000 or 30,000 years ago, then grew effete, and was vanquished by barbarians, some people said. Or perhaps dwarfs built them, because the windowless chambers (actually granaries) were so small!

Only when archeologists began to bare these ruins, the National Park Service to protect them, and the National Geographic Society to date them by deciphering tree rings locked in their ancient beams did the true prehistory of the Southwest emerge into light.

*The following 40 pages show the ancient cities as they look today, and describe the lives, joys, trials, and migrations of their builders.*

Pueblo Bonito, still a "beautiful village," spreads its ruined grandeur beneath the north rim of

# CHACO CANYON

*By RALPH GRAY, National Geographic Staff*

ET'S BYPASS THE SUBURBS and head straight for the big city."

Edwards Park and I were on a tour of a dozen national parks and monuments containing gloriously preserved dwellings of vanished Southwest Indian villagers. Ahead, near New Mexico's northwest corner, lay Chaco Canyon with its Pueblo Bonito, the largest single ruin in the National Park System, and the mother city of many of the sites we would visit.

Chaco Canyon. Like Greek city-states, Indian towns flourished along the floor 1,000 years ago.

During our years with the National Geographic we had heard a lot about this extraordinary prehistoric apartment house that The Society had excavated in the 1920's. Now we were to see it for ourselves.

Through empty range land northeast of Gallup our car raced a chain of blue-black thunderstorms. Lightning danced around us. Rain cascaded. An unbridged arroyo filled fender high with raging runoff. Afraid to cross it, I stopped. Ted grumbled at the delay.

"Pueblo Bonito has waited a thousand years to greet us," I told him. "Another hour won't matter."

By sunset the wash had drained, and we drove on through gathering twilight to Chaco Canyon National Monument. It was too dark to see Pueblo Bonito as

273

we pitched our tent under a ramada or shelter of boughs, started a campfire, and fixed supper. We saw no one; no one saw us. Yet as we sat in the flickering fire-light, we felt that hundreds of eyes were watching us from behind ghostly walls. Mysterious small noises seemed to speak of muffled footfalls and the shushing of children as families peeked out in dreadful quiet at the strange intruders.

DAWN finally reached through the tent flap and dispelled the fancies of the night. The city was dead, its inhabitants long gone—but what a monument they left! In the glaring horizontal rays of earliest morning the towering walls gleamed yellow against the deep blue sky. Beyond them rose the burnished cliff of Chaco Canyon. Silently, we drank in our first view of the highest example of the golden age of Pueblo architecture.

Pueblo Bonito's city plan forms a huge capital D. The rounded side, rising as high as 40 feet, is backed close under the cliff. An Indian stairway of rocks and wooden poles brought us to the north rim of the canyon where we looked down on the splendid three-acre ruin. Its 800 rooms, clinging together like cells of a honeycomb, huddled beside the outer walls. From the two central plazas, 32 kivas stared up at us with round, empty eyes.

Later, browsing among the ruins, we marveled at scrupulously even masonry —sometimes actually sealing off what had once been doorways and windows. Our guide, in spirit, was Neil M. Judd, the renowned archeologist who excavated the "beautiful village." Having discussed Chaco late and long with him before leaving for the Southwest, I could almost hear him beside me, telling how the Bonitians were forever building new additions and closing off old rooms—perhaps because they got too stuffy to live in. While it was alive, the whole town must have kept stretching and shifting.

We inspected the rounded outer wall. "See that filled-in window?" a ranger began, as if proving Judd's point. "When the city was young, that opened to the outside. But as the town turned more and more into a fortress against raiders, it had to be sealed off. These people learned to live with danger."

We walked from chamber to chamber, sometimes ducking under brush and adobe ceilings, with roof beams as good as new. We passed bins with scattered corn cobs in them, metates where women had ground corn meal, pottery fragments lying everywhere. We found it easy to imagine that the dusky owners were just ahead of us, keeping out of sight, or that they'd merely left for the weekend and would return tomorrow.

Dry Southwest air has helped preserve the look and feel of ten centuries ago. But it was seven National Geographic expeditions (1921-27) that removed 100,000 tons of rubble and transformed a dusty mound into a travel magnet of transcendent grandeur. Most archeological digs produce cross-section trenches of little interest to the average viewer. But in completely unearthing Pueblo

**"Place-of-the-braced-up-cliff"** Navajos called the ruins. Rangers explain that a monstrous slab of cliff, tottering over the village for centuries, was "propped up" with puny sticks and stones by super-confident Bonitians. It crashed in 1941, leaving its fragments (foreground) for sightseers.

275

J. BAYLOR ROBERTS, NATIONAL GEOGRAPHIC PHOTOGRAPHER

Neil Judd, Curator of American Archeology at the U. S. National Museum when he led the National Geographic expeditions, reconstructed Bonitian life from buried fragments. He described the villagers as backyard farmers who raised corn, beans, and squash, and hunted rabbits atop the mesas.

Women ran the home; they made pots and wove baskets, tanned skins, plaited sandals, swept with grass brooms. They were also the master masons. Children fashioned tiny ladles and pitchers—the clay still bears imprints of small fingers.

Bonito, Neil Judd and his helpers laid bare the secrets of pre-Columbian civilization for all to see, understand, and enjoy. Troweling amid crumbling stones, Judd uncovered a genuine—and beautiful—treasure. He glimpsed a flash of color and carefully removed a magnificent turquoise necklace while his Indian workers, lured by some telepathy, gathered silently to watch. With infinite patience, a Bonitian craftsman had polished and drilled the 2,500 stones.

Big as Pueblo Bonito is, it is but one of more than a dozen sizable ruins along an eight-mile strip of Chaco Canyon. Within the monument's 32 square miles rose a little empire of separate villages, supporting some 6,000 people—the largest concentration of population in the prehistoric Southwest. Major sites

### Turquoise treasure emerges from the dust of centuries

Indians of the Southwest prized turquoise as a mystic symbol of water and sky. Judd shared their awe the day his trowel cut away earth to reveal this breath-taking ceremonial necklace. His tiny brush delicately swept away the sand. At last the blue-green stones shone in all their ancient splendor.

What labor went to mine the precious stones, what patient hours to shape the 2,500 beads and four pendants by rubbing on sandstone, to pierce each with sharpened flint! Marauders missed this prize during Pueblo Bonito's decline.

Thousands of visitors to National Geographic headquarters in Washington inspect the necklace yearly.

O. C. HAVENS AND (RIGHT) B. ANTHONY STEWART, NATIONAL GEOGRAPHIC PHOTOGRAPHER

accessible most of the year include Pueblo del Arroyo, Hungo Pavi, Una Vida, huge Chettro Kettle, and Casa Rinconada, where pit houses date from A.D. 700.

Two centuries later, Pueblo Bonito started to rise, reaching its zenith about the time William the Conqueror invaded England. By 1299, Chaco was deserted. Droughts, raids, overworked soil, all had worn down the thriving culture. The people drifted off, probably planning to return. But they settled instead in better-watered regions, and the sands blew into the empty windows of their once-loved home.

Saddened at the thought, Ted Park and I pulled stakes and drifted off, too. We felt that somehow we had made friends with these proud Bonitians—a people white men had never seen.

**This desert citadel** in its heyday sheltered 1,200 in 800 terraced rooms. Four stories tall at outer wall, Pueblo Bonito was America's largest apartment house until 1882.

W. LANGDON KIHN

278

**Tree rings, a link between climate and human history, give archeologists the key to the past.**

As excavations progressed in the '20's under Neil M. Judd's direction, more and more became known about the pre-Columbian civilization at Pueblo Bonito, but one question hung tantalizingly unanswered. How old was this supreme example of Pueblo culture?

Dating by tree rings (dendrochronology) was then in its infancy. This method is based on nature's practice of adding concentric growth rings to the outer edges of tree trunks each year. Specific years and cycles of years can be identified in different trees by thick and thin rings. A good year with lots of rain adds a wide growth ring, a drought year adds little.

The rings can be read long after cutting, sometimes even after charring. Thus the pines Bonitians felled with their Stone Age axes provide the key to dates of their home-building. Comparing these Chaco beams with those in other areas, Mr. Judd found the Chaco beams were cut years earlier. But what would the date be in our calendar?

To anchor Pueblo Bonito's floating tree-

E. F. CARPENTER AND (RIGHT) A. E. DOUGLASS

**With nature's calendar, they trace the wax and wane of Indian cultures in the Southwest.**

ring chronology to the calendar, the National Geographic Society sent out three expeditions led by Dr. A. E. Douglass of the University of Arizona. No living trees could be found locally that had stood in Pueblo Bonito's time, so Dr. Douglass worked back from living trees, dead stumps, and beams from Spanish missions, Hopi pueblos, and ancient Pueblo sites. Painstakingly matching the tell-tale rings, he pieced together an unbroken chronology from the present back to A.D. 700. This told him when the Boni-

tians started to build (919) and when they reached their peak (by 1066).

The final link of present to past appears below. The upper chart is tied to the calendar; the lower, at the end of the undated chronology, records tree rings of a beam from Showlow, Arizona. Drought years (long lines) match perfectly! At left, a core from a beam in Oraibi, Hopi town still inhabited, reveals 24 narrow rings (white arrows) of the Great Drought, 1276-1299, that saw Pueblo Bonito abandoned to the sands.

**Impregnable Balcony House** yields to sightseeing invaders. Its builders, entering their eagle's-nest home, traversed a narrow ledge then threaded the Needle's Eye (opposite page), a small aperture that tests today's king-size explorer. An hour touring well-preserved cliff ruins transports park visitors back to the Stone Age.

# MESA VERDE

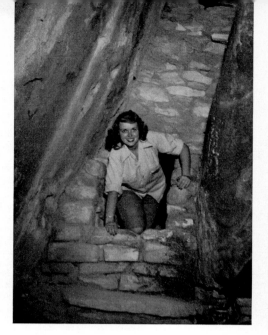

*By DON WATSON, Former Park Archeologist,*
*Mesa Verde National Park*

O N A SNOWY DAY IN DECEMBER, 1888, two cowboys rode across little-known, canyon-sliced Mesa Verde in the southwestern corner of Colorado. Suddenly Richard Wetherill jerked his horse to a stop.

"Charlie, look at that!" He pointed. Charles Mason's eyes went wide. Across the canyon a silent stone city lay sheltered by an enormous cave. Stone houses, piled story upon story, rose to the arched cave roof. It reminded the two men of a cliff palace, and thus they named it. Swirling snowflakes hid some ruins; rubble and bushes concealed others. But in all, ten ruins lay cold and silent within their range of vision.

If the cowboys could have stood in the same spot some two and a half centuries before Columbus, they would have seen humming activity. Some 400 Indians lived in Cliff Palace, protected from enemies and elements. In courts and on terraced housetops women bent over cooking fires. Old men and women toasted their arthritic bones and talked of bygone days when "things were better." In the mealing rooms young women and girls plied grinding stones, reducing brightly colored corn to precious meal. The constant rasping of stones was made bearable only by the melodious notes of the grinding songs. Chanting priests, in underground kivas, added a deep undertone.

At Balcony House, an adobe-paved court spreads beneath another vaulted roof. On three sides stand beautifully built two-story houses. Along the fourth is the sheer cliff. A low wall kept children from falling 700 feet to the canyon floor. In the rear of the cave is a beautiful spring of clear, cold water. Seven or eight centuries ago, this was a simple farming hamlet of perhaps 80 people. During growing season men trotted up toe holds cut in the cliff and cared for crops on the great green mesa above. Crafts took much time. Women shaped pottery by hand; from plants and minerals they concocted paints. When the

**Cliff Palace, Mesa Verde's largest village, crowds beneath a sandstone roof**

Canyons that scar the 15-by-20-mile table mountain hold some 800 cliff dwellings, from huts tucked in crevices to this cave metropolis of 200 family rooms and 23 kivas. Exploring this lost world, the visitor begins at the park museum. Its evocation of 1,300 years of mesa life readies him for Basket Maker pit houses, crude early pueblos, and imposing cut-stone cliff villages he can reach on two loop drives.

**Roof beams** like these record Mesa Verde's past. In their tree rings archeologists read that the cliff dwellings rose here in the 12th and 13th centuries. America had no potter's wheel then to help women shape their bowls. Sun Temple's roofless rooms (right) stand atop the mesa, where hundreds of ruins await excavation.

firing was over only a heap of ashes remained, but from within those ashes came black-on-white pottery of superlative beauty—mugs, pitchers, ladles, canteens, jars, and bowls, gracefully shaped and artistically decorated.

Men produced cotton cloth, weapons, tools, and the all-important ceremonial objects. Each man could make any of these, but he preferred to specialize. Here lived a flint chipper; there a rope maker; across the court a weaver. Exchange of goods was by barter, often by gambling. At any time of day a group of men were betting on some game of chance: arrowheads against sandals; a feather blanket against a necklace. An inch of beads would buy a bow; a foot of beads, almost anything a man needed.

The sun, rising over the opposite canyon rim, awakened Balcony House. After a simple breakfast of corn bread and meat, villagers went to their tasks. Women changed the juniper-bark diapers of babies, bound happy infants to their cradleboards, and hung them on the ends of roof poles to swing in the breeze. Long days on the pillowless cradleboard flattened the back of every Cliff Dweller's skull. The strange deformity lasted through life.

284

Turkeys were driven out of the cave to feed along the slopes. Children and dogs swarmed over the canyon walls, making life miserable for squirrels and chipmunks. When the sun grew too warm, men left their fields and dozed or worked at crafts. Later, hunters returned with deer and mountain sheep.

At the elaborate evening meal some version of corn bread baked on flat stone griddles was inevitable, with a thick stew perhaps, or green corn, or a pot of green beans. Venison roasted over coals was a delicacy. A fat prairie dog or a grouse brought happy exclamations from hungry men. Each family gathered in a tight little circle around its steaming pot. Fingers dipped in recklessly. It was a noisy meal—the better the food the more finger-sucking and lip-smacking. After it was over, a deep, rumbling belch complimented the cook.

Near the end of the 13th century, nature turned against these Indians. Year after year crops failed, springs dwindled, and nomads menaced the famine-weakened farmers. Turning their backs on their homes, families drifted south-ward. Shortly, every pueblo, every cliff dwelling was silent. Only the wail of the coyote and the mournful call of the owl echoed through the empty canyons.

285

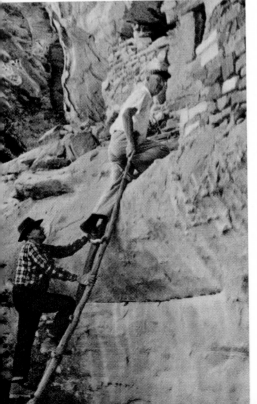

## Wetherill Mesa: National Geographic seeks new light on cliff dwellers

HIGH among majestic cliffs where Indian chant and laughter echoed for 1,300 years then died two centuries before Columbus, the National Park Service and the National Geographic Society have begun a major archeological project to shed new light on the prehistoric builders of this lonely realm. On Wetherill Mesa—a hitherto undeveloped area of Mesa Verde National Park—it will open imposing cliff dwellings to the American people, relieving pressure on the park's other much-visited ruins.

"The Society is proud to take a leading part in this important work," said Dr. Melville Bell Grosvenor, its President and Editor, announcing a $50,000 grant to launch the scientific program.

**Dr. Grosvenor** inspects Mug House. Topping the ladder, he found the canyon floor "several million feet below—when you look back!"

**Long House,** rivaling Cliff Palace in grandeur, sleeps beneath a massive stone canopy at Wetherill Mesa. Dr. Lyman J. Briggs (center), Chairman of The Society's Committee for Research and Exploration, surveys the long-silent, fortresslike dwellings. Waking to National Geographic-National Park Service excavation teams, Long House will soon become a magnet for Mesa Verde visitors, already numbering a quarter of a million a year.

They arrive on US 160 via Cortez or Durango, Colorado, served by Frontier Airlines; buses to park in summer.

The 80-square-mile park and its museums are open all year, but only from early May to late October can you join guided trips through the cliff ruins, hear campfire talks, pitch tents in the free campgrounds, or stay at Spruce Tree Lodge. (By 1966 all accommodations, and greatly expanded facilities, will be concentrated nearer the park entrance.) Trails beckon horseback riders and hikers, but the latter must get a permit before setting out; it's easy to get lost in these labyrinthine canyons.

Mule deer, coyotes, bobcats, and mountain lions roam the piñon and juniper forest that covers lofty, cliff-edged Mesa Verde and inspired its Spanish name, "Green Table." 287

**Scientists study** Wetherill Mesa's ruins. Besides many sites atop the mesa, three sizable cliff dwellings are slated for excavation under the leadership of Dr. Douglas Osborne (foreground). They are Long House, second largest of Mesa Verde's cliff villages; Mug House; and Step House.

Mesa Verde has one of the largest concentrations of prehistoric ruins in the United States. Until its establishment as a national park in 1906, it suffered from amateur "pothunting" and many splendid sites were damaged. Of its hundreds of known ruins, few have been scientifically excavated and opened to the public.

Deep drifts of undisturbed rubble at the Wetherill Mesa sites indicate a wealth of undiscovered treasure.

**Castlelike ruins** lend a medieval look to Hovenweep (Deserted Valley), named by the Utes.

# HOVENWEEP

FRIGHTENED FARMERS once lived here in the gaunt, erosion-gutted Four Corners region where Utah, Colorado, Arizona, and New Mexico meet. Their enemies: thirst and marauders. They built their pueblos on ledges and in open caves, clustered about springs at the heads of box canyons. On the rimrock above rose the symbols of their fear: square watchtowers with loopholes commanding the open mesa. Other forts protected homes, the terraced garden plots, the stored crops—and the precious water bubbling from the springs below.

Six such settlements make up Hovenweep National Monument, four in Colorado, two in Utah. Their distinctive stone towers—square, circular, D-shaped, or oval, conforming to natural foundation rock—have no counterpart in historic pueblo architecture. Each has one small door.

The Square Tower Group in Utah (left) comprises 19 buildings. The largest, Hovenweep Castle, has walls 60 feet long and 20 feet high and is a superb example of pre-Columbian masonry. When did the Hovenweep people abandon these structures? Probably around the end of the 13th century, when famine and raids also drove their cliff-dwelling relatives at nearby Mesa Verde toward the Rio Grande.

The unpaved access to Hovenweep sites gives the average motorist pause. Ask at Cortez, Colorado, or Blanding, Utah, about road conditions. There are picnic grounds at ranger headquarters at the Square Tower Group, but be sure to bring your own water, fuel, and supplies.

# AZTEC RUINS

THESE SPLENDID BUILDINGS have nothing to do with ancient Mexico's "Halls of Montezuma." To white settlers, any Southwest Indian ruin was apt to be "Aztec." These, in New Mexico's northwest corner, perpetuate the misnomer. Pueblo Indians flourished here, beside the cottonwood-shaded Animas River, influenced first by the culture of Chaco Canyon, then of Mesa Verde. Early in the 12th century they built their masterwork: a huge rectangular apartment village enclosing a plaza. It rises three stories at the north wall and contains some 500 rooms. Masonry is straight and even, as at Pueblo Bonito.

One huge circular kiva, built during the Chaco period, was restored to its former glory by Earl H. Morris of the American Museum of Natural History. From the central plaza, today's amateur archeologists descend into this 48-foot-wide room through an antechamber. Four square pillars support the peeled log roof beams. Rectangular masonry vaults in the floor may once have been covered with planks to serve as foot drums, stamped upon during ritual dances, while watchers lined the bench along the wall. Another raised rectangle was the fire box. Curiously, no one has found the sipapu, that small, mystical hole through which earth spirits emerged to commune with Indian celebrants.

The easily reached 27-acre monument, open every day of the year, is 14 miles east of Farmington, which has travel facilities and accommodations. Thousands of motorists take a breather at Aztec Ruins and make a short tour that reveals more of the Southwest's vanished civilization than they might garner in days of scrambling among the scattered ruins of larger park areas.

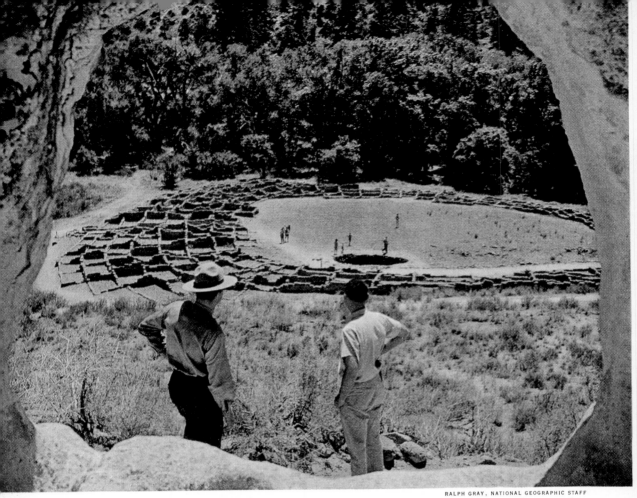

**Prehistoric picture window** looks out on ruined Tyuonyi, once a fortress city.

# BANDELIER NATIONAL MONUMENT

BANDELIER, in the upper Rio Grande Valley of New Mexico, is a beginning and an end. Here, along little Frijoles Canyon, that slices the wooded Pajarito Plateau, Southwestern archeology began. But here also the golden age of a gentle, master-building people came to an end. We find evidence of their once-great skill in the deserted ruins of site after site through the Southwest—monuments that strike awe and wonder in us today.

Here stands Tyuonyi, a 400-room fortified town, built in the form of a circle by Pueblo refugees from Chaco Canyon, Mesa Verde, and other drought-ridden and beleaguered areas. These farmers, builders of permanent homes, weavers of fine cloth, potters, and traders moved into already-settled Frijoles Canyon around the start of the 14th century. Soon its cliffs echoed the voices of masons, the crack of stone against stone as slabs were hand-split to fit Tyuonyi's even walls. Mud and pebbles served as mortar. Trees, felled with stone axes, supported flat roofs. With an eye to bands of marauders, Tyuonyi's builders put entrances in the roofs. Ladders took the place of doorsteps. Almost all ground-floor rooms were windowless; few connected with each other.

These Pueblos emerged on their ladders to greet the bright morning, shouldered their digging sticks, and made for the gardens watered by Rito de los Frijoles (Bean Creek). Wives swept out the dwellings that were their undisputed domain. Perhaps they replastered a wall, then settled down to plait sandals and baskets. Children romped with such toys as a feather on a string. Boys, trembling with excitement, were initiated into secret all-male lodges that met in circular underground kivas. The community elected its leaders. Pueblos did not tolerate strong men or hereditary chiefs.

Tyuonyi's dwellings piled up two and three stories high, with sheer, blank outer walls to keep attackers at bay. Nevertheless, raids and famine eventually drove the villagers away. By 1580 the fragrant smoke of their cooking fires no longer wreathed the canyon. But when the Swiss-American scholar Adolph Bandelier came upon the site in the late 19th century, the flavor of early life in Frijoles Canyon re-emerged in his notable novel *The Delight Makers*.

Pre-Columbian ruins in the southwestern United States were carelessly called "Aztec" or "Moqui" or dismissed as merely "Indian" until Bandelier lavished years of scientific study on them and added a fascinating chapter to American ethnology. He in turn is remembered here in the silent and empty ruins that so inspired him—for a national monument that preserves them bears his name.

**Some Bandelier homebuilders hacked dwellings from cliffs of tuff, a cemented volcanic ash**

Like cliff swallows, many Indians nested high above the central pueblo; others burrowed into the base of the cliff and built masonry additions in front—so-called talus houses. These cubicles, measuring about six by nine feet, may have housed arrivals who found Tyuonyi's 400 rooms already taken and established a suburb in the tuff.

The creek that slaked thirsts and watered crops still sparkles nearby. Monument guests can camp near it, or (May through September) bed and dine at Frijoles Canyon Lodge adjoining the visitor center and museum. Guided pack trips probe the 33 square miles of wilderness south of the main ruins. A nine-square-mile detached section contains unexcavated sites. Motorists pass through it on the 46-mile drive from Santa Fe.

JUSTIN LOCKE

**Keet Seel,** Arizona's largest cliff dwelling, sprawls in a lonely cleft streaked by minerals

# NAVAJO
## NATIONAL MONUMENT

and blackened by cooking fires that burned two centuries before Columbus discovered America.

ILENT, EMPTY, tucked away in northeastern Arizona's maze of wild and solitary canyons lie three magnificent cliff ruins, Keet Seel, Betatakin, and Inscription House. Their sightless windows brood over sun-washed canyon floors as if waiting for their owners to return after 700 years and pick up the fabric of their daily lives. Among Keet Seel's mellow walls, the visitor feels the centuries slip away. He stands removed in a desert wilderness,

11 miles by horse trail from the campground and ranger station, dozens of miles from the nearest village.

Betatakin, reached by a steep trail described as "one mile down and 15 miles back," sleeps in a soaring alcove 400 feet high. In so vast a setting the town seems puny, until close examination reveals its true size. And at the foot of its steps the spring which once filled ancient jars still flows. Thirty-three miles away, Inscription House, named for the mysterious date, 1661, scratched on a wall, nestles high in another cave.

It takes a little muscle to see Navajo's ruins, but they yield awesome reward for the determined and the hardy. They rest within the Navajo Reservation, yet the Navajos are newcomers compared to the Anasazi or "Ancient Ones." Fearing lingering spirits, local Indians shun the old sites, where dried corn cobs lie deep in the stone silos, where wooden beams look sound as ever.

294  **Betatakin** (Hillside House) clings to sloping rock high in its stagelike setting. Villagers stored vegetables in windowless, rodent-proof chambers and strolled across patios to visit neighbors. Drought and soil erosion drove the last dwellers southward about A.D. 1300. The ruin was discovered in 1909.

RALPH GRAY AND (RIGHT) EDWARDS PARK, NATIONAL GEOGRAPHIC STAFF

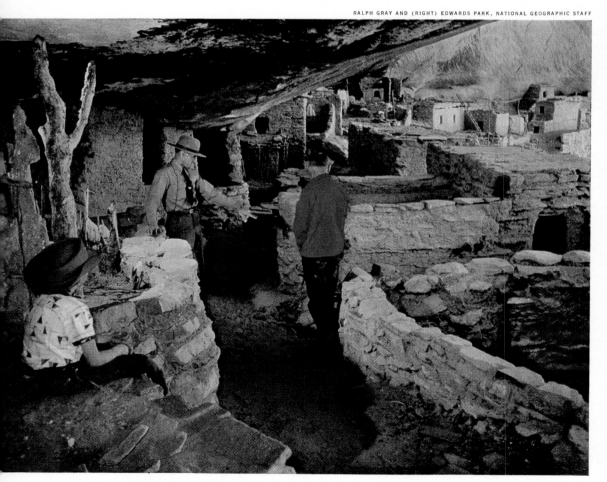

**Main street** of Keet Seel, sleeping city of the wilderness, threads among its 160 rooms.

# CANYON DE CHELLY

*By RALPH GRAY, National Geographic Staff*

I HEARD CANYON DE CHELLY before I saw it. Lying in my sleeping bag on the rim, I listened to the faint falsetto song of a Navajo herdsman greeting the sunrise from the canyon floor. I had camped during the night. Now I went over to the cliff's edge and saw for the first time this breathtaking, red-walled slash in the northeastern Arizona plateau. The ground dropped away before me a sheer 500 feet to a sandy rift a quarter of a mile wide. A cottonwood grove lent shade to the hogan and corral of my singing Indian. From a cave in the opposite wall the ghostly twin towers of White House Ruin peered up at me.

Hundreds of other cliff dwellings cling to crevices and alcoves along the jagged, 25-mile length of Canyon de Chelly (pronounced shay) and its branch canyons, del Muerto (Canyon of Death) and Monument. And here amid the gaunt reminders of a vanished civilization, Indians live today, tend their sheep and goats, plant their corn and peaches, build their hogans and corrals. Here, deep within their huge reservation, they have the right to remain forever.

For this is sacred ground to the Navajos. They believe their ancestors emerged from these mysterious gorges. Here they returned in time of peril—when Spanish soldiers and later the U. S. Army hunted down Navajo raiders. Then, in 1864, frontiersman Kit Carson and his cavalrymen trapped The People—some 8,000 of them—in their sanctuary, rounded them up, and moved the entire tribe to the hated Bosque Redondo reserve in New Mexico. The proud plateau dwellers languished and died from heat, humiliation, and homesickness.

JOHN EDWIN HOGG

Finally, in an act of humanity, the United States returned the remaining Navajos to their beloved canyon country where they have now become the largest Indian tribe in the land.

But long before the Navajos made Canyon de Chelly their own, it was home for other Indians. Mummy Cave Ruin (right), one of the best examples anywhere of the Great Pueblo Period (12th and 13th centuries), was itself a rank newcomer, being built on top of Basket Maker pit houses 2,000 years old. Early excavators of this 80-room village found lovely turquoise and shell jewelry, beaded cloth, as well as mummified remains.

Twenty centuries, however, is but a wink in the staggering scale of time that created Canyon de Chelly's stratified walls, and carved such monoliths as 800-foot-high Spider Rock. Here erosion has made one of the world's most

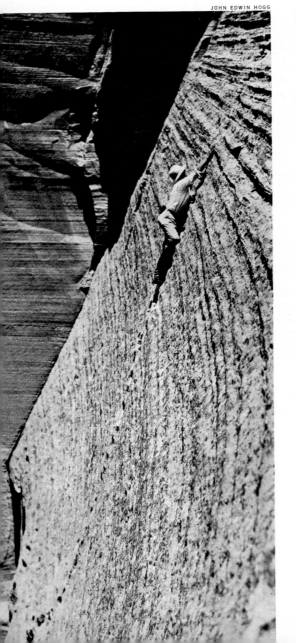

**Going home the hard way.** Some Indians climbed to their cliff dwellings by finger and toe holds. Most used ladders. With these pulled up at night, thresholds were secure from nomad raids. A three-story, cut-stone tower (right) guards Mummy Cave Ruin.

EDWARDS PARK, NATIONAL GEOGRAPHIC STAFF

298

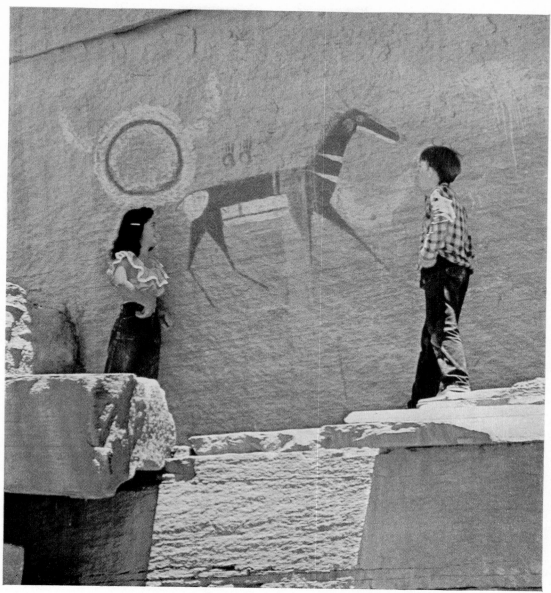

**This Navajo antelope** has coursed the sandstone walls of Canyon del Muerto for 150 years. Other designs in the region are pre-Columbian.

stupendous treats for the eye. People journey to this remote, 131-square-mile national monument mostly to marvel at nature's handiwork. But they soon find that exploring the ruins of an ancient culture adds an archeological dividend. And the casual presence of the Navajos gives flavor to the entire scene.

Best routes are northerly from Gallup, New Mexico, or Holbrook, Arizona, (both on US 66) or east from US 89 and Tuba City via the Hopi villages. Roads recently have been paved. You can camp on the south rim, or stay (May 15—Oct. 15) at Thunderbird Ranch, Chinle, Arizona, near the superintendent's office at the canyon mouth. The ranch conducts canyon tours in a special vehicle.

**Ashen towers** of White House huddle beneath a beetling, iron-stained cliff. This 150-person pueblo was begun in the 1060's, at the time the Normans conquered England.

301

RALPH GRAY AND (ABOVE) EDWARDS PARK, NATIONAL GEOGRAPHIC STAFF

# SUNSET CRATER

By EDWARDS PARK
*National Geographic Staff*

**Like toothpaste** from a tube, viscous lava squeezed up from volcanic fissures. It may still look soft, but clambering over Bonito Lava Flow can cut shoes to shreds.

THE young park ranger pushed back his hat. "To get an idea why Sunset Crater is a national monument you've got to put yourself in the year 1064. You're an Arizona Indian, living in a pit house, trying to farm these highlands east of the San Francisco peaks.

"You're worried by tremors and rumblings underfoot. So you pack up your family and take off. Soon your farm blows sky-high. The earth flames. Rocks soar skyward followed by a rain of cinders. Reddish lava oozes from cracks in your cornfield. When things cool off, you come back for a look. This is what you see—a newborn mountain, jet black."

I stared with new interest at Sunset Crater, a 1,000-foot cinder cone, its cratered crest stained red and orange as though tinted by the setting sun. Around its base stretch acres of somber earth, softened only by stubborn pines that have fought through the cinder blanket.

"Sunset Crater smothered many cornfields," the ranger continued. "But it also kicked off a land rush. Its ash, settling for miles beyond the lava, trapped rainfall. Returning Indians found new grass growing through cinders."

Eager to stake a claim in the black bonanza, Indians headed for Sunset Crater from all corners of the Southwest. Languages and customs mingled, dwellings

**Youngest** of nearly 400 volcanoes around Flagstaff, Arizona, Sunset Crater spewed ash and cinders over some 800 square miles. Near the foot of this once-fiery cone a lava cave contains ice all year. Snow sometimes blocks road to the five-square-mile monument in winter.

and great pueblos rose—like those preserved at Walnut Canyon and Wupatki nearby. But eventually winds stripped away the fertile, moisture-retaining blanket of ash. Crop failures drove families from the again-barren land.

Sunset Crater remains, hulking above its lava field amid fumeroles and small splash craters. Bonito Lava Flow curves from its base like an inky glacier. Wind-blown cinders form contoured dunes. Knife-edged squeeze-ups show where cooling lava was forced out of cracks, then froze upright.

"We don't have any camping or picnicking facilities in the monument," the ranger told me, "but we're only a half-hour drive from Flagstaff, a favorite stop-over for travelers. It's my job to keep kids from breaking their necks tumbling down the cone and generally to talk their dads out of climbing it. For every step you make you slip back two."

I soon saw what he meant. Cinders gave way under me in rustling cascades as, short of breath because of the 8,000-foot elevation, I mounted the slope. But the crest was worth it. I circled the lip of the black, 400-foot-deep crater and examined yellow sulphurous rock and crimson-hued ash that explain the sunset coloring. To the west towered the San Franciscos, Arizona's highest peaks. Northeastward stretched the Painted Desert with its Navajo hogans and Hopi villages. The Hopis still look on Sunset Crater as the home of their Kana-a kachinas, friendly spirits who see to it that Indian storerooms are crammed with corn. In this other-world setting I found the legend easy to believe.

WILLIAM BELKNAP, JR.

**Horned toads,** living for centuries amid Sunset's cinders, have developed camouflage.

**Rangers say** it's quite possible to walk, not fly, down Sunset Crater's steep flank. But youth prefers soaring leaps over the rattling cinders.

# WALNUT CANYON

PRESENT A MAN with a ready-made roof, floor, and rear wall, and he'll build a house. Walnut Canyon, a 400-foot gorge, proves the point. Stone Age Arizonans settled along the canyon's gray walls in deep-cut recesses between shelflike limestone ledges. They built front walls of masonry and partitioned off each one-room house from its neighbors. When newcomers flocked into the area after Sunset Crater's eruption, the cliffside town grew to more than 300 attached dwellings, as orderly as row houses.

Establishment of Walnut Canyon as a national monument stopped careless "pot-hunting" that had destroyed many dwellings. Now travelers stopping at nearby Flagstaff can drive in any day of the year and take a 50-minute hike around the village's "Main Street," 185 feet below the canyon rim. Along this path, 900 years ago, strode the homecoming hunter or farmer, sniffing the cooking odors and greeting children as they played outside their T-shaped doors. Far below on the canyon floor walnut trees shaded the creek.

# WUPATKI NATIONAL MONUMENT

NESTLING BELOW A LAVA MESA, red-walled Wupatki marks the culmination of Arizona's 11th century land boom. Here Sunset Crater's soil-enriching cinders had their kindest effect. As settlers moved into the basin between the San Francisco Peaks and the Little Colorado River, Wupatki (Tall House) mushroomed to a three-story,

100-room pueblo beside its precious spring. Cultures from north, east, and west mingled with that of migrants from the south who built a masonry ball court on which to play their regional game.

A 40-mile drive from either Flagstaff or Cameron, where accommodations are available, brings visitors to Wupatki's sandstone walls. More than 800 other ruins dot the 56-square-mile monument, open all year. Two fortresses, the Citadel and Wukoki, command views of the Painted Desert. Navajos herd sheep outside silent Wupatki, abandoned by drought-stricken farmers 700 years ago.

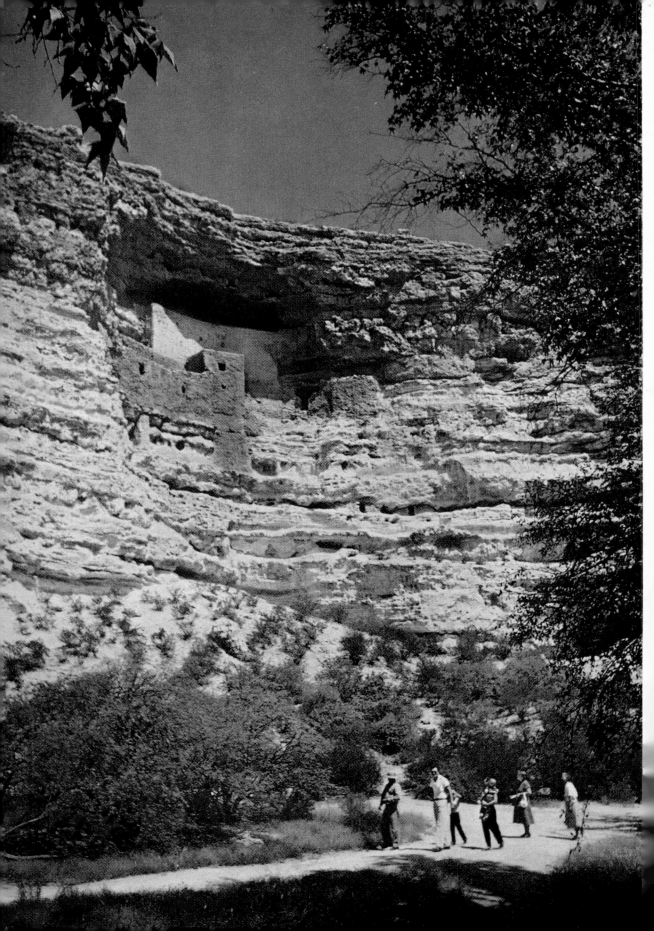

# MONTEZUMA CASTLE

To REFUGEES from the parched plateau country to the north, the green irrigated fields along central Arizona's Verde River were salvation. And here amid the vestiges of a southern pit-dweller culture they built their high-perched masonry apartment houses. Montezuma Castle, standing high and dry in a limestone cave during some 550 years of neglect, remains 90 percent intact. Ceiling timbers in the five-story, 20-room pueblo are as sound as ever. The original earth mortar still seals the walls. Plaster on the inside retains the handprints of the 13th century Indians who patted it smooth.

Montezuma, the Aztec emperor, had nothing to do with this structure. But it is well-named a castle. Its inhabitants, who farmed along Beaver Creek, scaled ladders to reach the only entrance. Protected passageways lead to other floors. The topmost level suggests a penthouse. Its walled terrace, commanding a view of distant peaks, must have served as a battlement for ancient warriors.

The national monument, some 60 miles from Flagstaff or Prescott, includes a detached area, Montezuma Well, where cliff dwellings flank a deep pool that watered irrigation ditches. Picnickers and passing motorists find cotton textiles and other well-preserved relics in the two museums, open all year.

# TUZIGOOT NATIONAL MONUMENT

It STANDS AGAINST THE SKY, an oblong citadel capping a limestone ridge in the Verde River Valley. Around it sprawls a maze of weathered walls. Apache nomads named it Tuzigoot, "Crooked Water," for a nearby lake. Who knows what the great village was called by its people seven centuries ago!

Like their neighbors at Montezuma Castle, 27 miles away, Tuzigoot's builders sought a defensible site. Since no cliff offered shelter, they chose the highest point they could find. As dry farmers moved into the irrigated valley, the hilltop pueblo grew 500 feet long with 110 rooms. Each family lived in a chamber averaging 12 by 18 feet. Returning from the fields, the father swung down a ladder from a hatchway in the roof. His wife had food ready in red pottery she had made. She wore deer-bone hairpins and perhaps a bracelet of sea shells traded from the Gulf of California. While he repaired his farming tools, the youngsters played with carved toys and figurines.

These items lie on display all year in Tuzigoot's museum, one of the Southwest's largest. A mining company owning the ruin safeguarded it from "pothunters" until excavation in 1933-34. To see its treasures and recapture the life that throbbed on the hilltop until overpopulation, famine, disease, and inter-pueblo strife ended the valley's heyday, travelers need only swing off US 89A.

**A pocket-size edition** of Mesa Verde's Cliff Palace, Montezuma Castle rates as one of the Nation's best preserved cliff dwellings. Inaccessible to visitors, it shares the pockmarked cliff with other prehistoric homes.

309

J. BAYLOR ROBERTS, NATIONAL GEOGRAPHIC PHOTOGRAPHER

**White man's steel canopy** protects adobe Casa Grande tower, "America's first skyscraper."

# CASA GRANDE

THIS 40-FOOT RUIN juts like a burned-out beacon from the desert floor of Arizona's Gila River Valley, dominating the cactus and mesquite as it once did villages clustered about it. Crumbling walls are all that remain of houses in the national monument. Only traces of a widespread irrigation system are etched on the sunburned flats. But the four-story watchtower that kept vigil over prehistoric farms now attracts thousands each year. Visitors drive from Phoenix or Tucson to the site two miles north of Coolidge and hear rangers explain the 600-year-old landmark and the two cultures it represents.

Settling here in the first century A.D., the Hohokam (Ancient Ones) built houses of brush and mud, made red-on-buff pottery, cremated their dead, and turned parched lands green with watered crops. In the 13th and 14th centuries Indians from the north settled among them. These Salado or Salt River people built Pueblo-style homes of adobe, painted their pottery black, white, and red, and buried their dead. They adopted the Hohokam's amazing irrigation works—some canals, 25 feet wide and 15 deep, extended 15 miles—and erected the Casa Grande, fashioning its four-foot-thick walls from wet caliche, a limy clay.

When Father Kino, a Spanish missionary, named the tower in 1694, he noted its smooth walls. Later pioneers, cowboys, and settlers scratched names and dates; one puzzler is an ancient Cretan design, cut with a metal tool. Two "calendar holes" pierce opposite walls. On each March 7 and October 7, the rising sun shot a beam of light through both holes, signaling the start of planting and harvesting.

# TONTO NATIONAL MONUMENT

THE SUN, rising above Arizona's Salt River Valley, shines into two caves in a serene side canyon, warming the walls of the Tonto Cliff dwellings. Six centuries ago, it signaled Salado Indians to tend crops or hunt deer among the junipers on the canyon rim while women gathered mesquite beans and saguaro fruit on the talus slopes. Now the two-story pueblos where ancient potters, cotton weavers, and yucca sandalmakers plied their skills slumber while visitors snap pictures and picnic.

A trail climbs to Lower Ruin where some 20 families lived behind a protective wall. Upper Ruin, half a mile away and 300 feet higher, is twice its neighbor's size. It commands a view of Roosevelt Dam's huge reservoir, which drowns the plots irrigated by Tonto's builders. The two-square-mile monument, 65 miles east of Phoenix, is open all year.

# GILA CLIFF DWELLINGS

DEEP in southwestern New Mexico's Mogollon Mountains stands a yellow volcanic cliff with five caves, three of them linked by natural archways. Well-preserved dwellings crowd these cavities, high above a trickling stream on the canyon floor. But venturesome persons who ride 50 jolting miles in a truck to this remote national monument find more than ruins to reward them. Stark wilderness beauty awaits—and the haunting mystery of a people who lived here, then vanished, leaving their fingermarks in the adobe walls. Gila Hot Springs Ranch offers accommodations and transportation from Silver City.

311

40

Reno

Sacramento River

101

99w

1

Lake Tahoe

Carson City

50

Sacramento

395

6

8a

Muir Woods
NATIONAL MONUMENT

Yosemite
NATIONAL PARK

San Francisco

50

Stockton

120

Mono Lake

6

San Joaquin River

140

Devils Postpile
NATIONAL MONUMENT

95

Hollister

152

Merced

41

Bishop

Kings Canyon
NATIONAL PARK

Monterey

Fresno

180

Beatty

Pinnacles
NATIONAL MONUMENT

King City

198

Lone Pine

Death Valley
NATIONAL MONUMENT

95

101

99

Sequoia
NATIONAL PARK

Paso Robles

41

Shoshone

NEVADA
CALIFORNIA

6

Bakersfield

395

127

466

Baker

Mojave

Santa Barbara

Barstow

66

91

66

Los Angeles

Twentynine Palms

Joshua Tree
NATIONAL MONUMENT

Pacific Ocean

Salton Sea

San Diego

99

PART FOUR

# THE GOLDEN WEST

WAGON MASTERS filed their trains through South Pass, tossed a final gibe at wisecracking Fort Hall trappers, and headed down the California Emigrant Trail. If you asked the dust-chewing drivers where they were bound, like as not they'd answer, "To see the elephant!"

The elephant meant anything that stretched belief. It meant gold for the taking . . . or going bust. It meant free land, new grandeur . . . or only disillusion.

These pioneers crossed the Great Basin, a saline, sagebrush desert. They cursed through towering ranges of snow-scarfed peaks. They threaded awesome forests and meadows of hip-deep grass. They skirted lakes and streams filled with eager fish, and whole mountainsides of wildflowers.

They saw the elephant, all right! Some even found gold. And they fell in love with California, where nature not only sustained the body, but nourished the spirit.

Today the phrase is dead, but the urge to go west still lives. With ease and pleasure, travelers explore Death Valley, the Sequoia groves, the clear vistas of the Sierras. And they see things most forty-niners never saw: the waterfalls, the granite walls, the luxuriant floor of Yosemite, the Incomparable Valley.

313

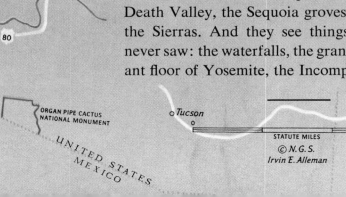

STATUTE MILES
0                    150
© N. G. S.
Irvin E. Alleman

**Jacob's ladder** aims for the sun as it scales Half Dome's granite scalp nearly a mile above the valley. California's Yosemite National Park, vacation paradise for more than a million each year, lies on the Sierra's western slopes about 150 miles from San Francisco.

# YOSEMITE

*By PAUL JENSEN*

*National Geographic Staff*

THE LAST 600-foot stretch was the hardest. Half Dome's shoulder humped before me, rock rising starkly to the summit of Yosemite's celebrated landmark. I had hiked eight miles from the valley floor. Here at 8,350 feet I felt the muscle rust of months in the office.

I gripped the hand cables that point the way up the sharpest pitch. Fifteen feet, then rest and blow. . . . Fifteen feet . . . I hauled myself straight into the eye of the two o'clock August sun. Fifteen feet. . . . At last the grade eased off and I walked out on an 11-acre stone desert hanging in the sky.

Curved slabs of granite shingled the summit like cabbage leaves. These slabs jut into space to form a visor over Half Dome's fractured face, so I crawled the last few feet on hands and knees. I took a firm hold on the outermost rock, swallowed, and peered down.

The cliff cut back 80 feet under me, then dropped sheer as a skyscraper wall for 2,200 feet, twice the height of the Empire State Building. From there, bare rock plunged at an angle some 2,500 feet more. I was perched above one of the world's most awesome drops and I plead guilty to vertigo. But the immensity of the sight that spread before me soon drove away my qualms.

**Yosemite Falls leap** in spring flood, shaking the earth with the force of their combined 2,425-foot plunge—North America's highest. August drought reduces the falls to a gossamer spray, fades red snow plants atop Glacier Point.

316     **Dark Wawona Tunnel leads to this dazzling vista: cliffbound Yosemite Valley**

Stern El Capitan (left), rising 3,600 feet above the pine- and fir-clad floor, contains enough granite for three Gibraltars. Bridalveil Fall's

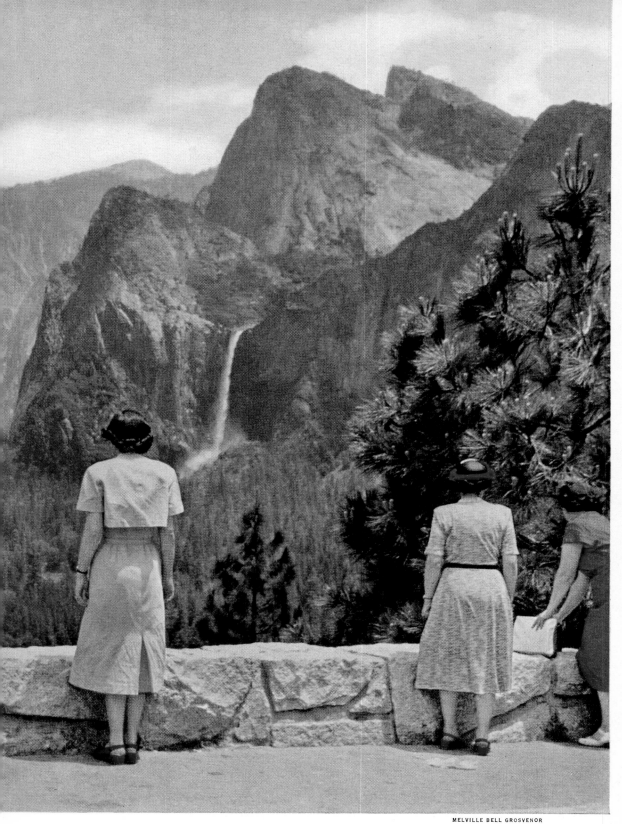

plume of mist seems to drop out of a lost world. The 620-foot cataract, strongest during May's thaws, wears a triple crown: Cathedral Rocks. Its sparkling waters feed the Merced River, which flows through the seven-mile valley. Half Dome projects on the distant skyline.

317

**Yosemite's living tunnel, Wawona Tree in Mariposa Grove, was cut in 1881 for stagecoach traffic.**

Yosemite's Big Trees were discovered by Joseph R. Walker's expedition to California in 1833. Coast redwoods were found by Spaniards in 1769.

In 1852 an English botanist named the Sierra tree *Wellingtonia* in honor of the British general. But patriots, eager for an American name, were delighted when scientists decided the Big Tree belonged to the coast redwood's genus, named *Sequoia* for the Cherokee who gave his tribe an alphabet.

*Sequoia gigantea's* fissured bark (above right) grows up to 24 inches thick. Asbestos-like, it resists fire. The tree's heart is dead. Only inner bark and outer rings, or sapwood, live to carry water and food.

Three groves escaped the glaciers that wrapped Yosemite during the Ice Age.

318

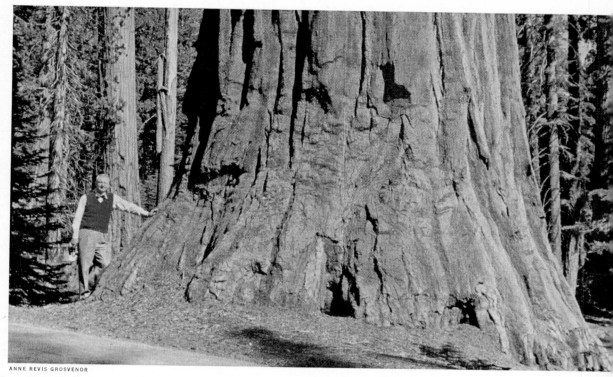

**"Too old to die," giant sequoias are the champion heavyweights of the plant world.**

Flashing with fish, Yosemite's 200-odd lakes offer fine sport, sometimes catches as hefty as this trout. Packing their fishing rods, many vacationers take off for Tuolumne Meadows to camp and cast in wild solitude. Here marmot and ground squirrel scold yellow-haired porcupine. Mule deer browse this high country in summer with their fawns (left). Winter drives them down into Yosemite Valley or Grand Canyon of the Tuolumne.

Taking its name from *Uzumati,* Indian for grizzly bear, Yosemite has none left. But black bear are common, begging beside roads as they do in other parks. Early guardians of Yosemite, when it was still a state park, had a problem with poachers. The national park was established in 1890.

319

1 **Ten million years ago,** Yosemite Valley was a lush lowland flanked by gentle hills. Half Dome's ancestor (center) rose only 1,500 feet above the sluggish, winding Merced River. Rains drenched the subtropical vegetation.

How
Yosemite
Valley
was
formed

2 **Gradual uplift of the entire region,** several million years later, caused the Merced to cut a V-shaped valley. Cooler climate fostered hardwoods and evergreens like the first sequoias. Yosemite's landmarks began to take shape.

320     *Paintings by EUGENE KINGMAN*

Mirror Lake glittered like quicksilver nearly a mile straight below, and to the left Yosemite Valley spread its evergreen carpet. At least 20,000 people must have been in the valley, nucleus of the great national park. But the only signs of life were cars—tiny beads strung along threadlike roads.

I raised my eyes to a sea of domes, ridges, forests, and snow-patched peaks that filled the eastern horizon: the Sierras rising in magnificent tiers. Closer to my right, Mount Watkins hulked above Tenaya Canyon. Behind me, past 18 miles of pines and firs, I could picture Mariposa Grove's immense sequoias. Fifteen miles ahead I could make out peaks flanking the Grand Canyon of the Tuolumne. Between the valley and that great granite gash sprawled the wild high country of Tuolumne Meadows (page 36) where the Tioga Road cuts across the park. Sierra Club members, particularly, seek out this wilderness tract. And here I would soon go—to see the canyon, another Yosemite Valley in its own right; to roam the lofty meadows with their canvas cabins spaced a day's hike apart; to examine the glacial polish that so entranced naturalist John Muir, granite expanses that still glisten from the buffing of ancient ice. Besides, I had appointments with impatient trout in half a dozen lakes and streams.

All this was Yosemite. What an array of riches! I gazed at Glacier Point (page 22), still imposing even though it was now 1,600 feet below me. How it had towered above when I arrived in the valley the evening before! Driving in from the South Entrance, I emerged from Wawona Tunnel and pulled up as

**3**     **A final shrug of earth's shoulders** hoisted the Sierra Nevada to snow-capped eminence, while the rushing Merced chiseled out its bed in the rising rocks. El Capitan (left) faces Cathedral Rocks. Evergreens cloak the slopes.

**4** **A frozen sea smothered the valley** as glaciers pushed in from the east. Rock-shod ice carried away one side of Half Dome, obliterated the Merced River's sharp bends, widened the valley floor, and created hanging glens.

everyone does at the sight of the immense natural portal that frames Yosemite Valley's forested floor—El Capitan's overwhelming brow glowering at the leaning spires of Cathedral Rocks, where earlier in the summer Bridalveil Fall wavers in the valley breeze. Farther up the valley, Upper and Lower Yosemite Falls make the ground shake then with their combined drop of some half mile, one of the world's greatest. At times, half a dozen waterfalls lace the seven-mile valley.

That evening, gloom had pervaded the valley. A boy, trying a short cut from Glacier Point, had gotten trapped on a shelf inches wide, 1,500 feet up the cliff. Darkness fell and prevented rescue, so rangers talked to him all night with a loudspeaker to keep him awake. Moral: stay on the trails!

SITTING serenely now on Half Dome's noble crest, I felt proud and elated at my climbing feat. A chipmunk scurried out from under a slab, came flirting over, and started eating my crackers as tame as you please. Suddenly I felt foolish. Why, people came up here every day—this was one of the best-fed chipmunks in the park!

Coasting back down the trail, I passed through thickly forested slopes to Little Yosemite Valley. This hanging glen ends abruptly where the Merced River, swinging past Liberty Cap, spills from the spout of a giant's pitcher. After a pulsing, thunderous 594-foot drop at Nevada Fall, the river charges to a final

**5** **Glaciers returned twice more,** deepening the U-shaped valley and polishing the granite monoliths ice had sculptured. The last advance, extending just past El Capitan, left it, Half Dome, and Cathedral Rocks much like today.

**6** **Lake Yosemite,** impounded by glacial debris, reflected the grandeur of its walls for several centuries. Its shallow basin gradually silted up, and today evergreen forest clothes the bottomland, center of park activities.

**Forest patches cling like cockleburs
atop Yosemite's glacial sculptures**

Half Dome (left) rears its bald head to survey
its wilderness domain. Lost while hunting bear
in 1849, William Penn Abrams blundered into

"a valley enclosed by stupendous cliffs" where a round-topped peak seemed "sliced with a knife." But first to explore and name Yosemite were members of California's Mariposa Battalion who entered the valley in 1851 to subdue Chief Tenaya. Lower right: Tenaya Canyon.

325

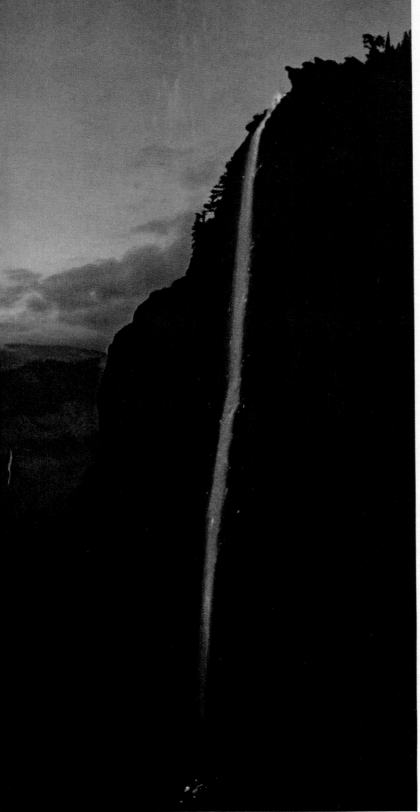

## The firefall cascades from Glacier Point every summer evening

In the 1870's a settler pushed hot coals off the cliff, starting a tradition. Others tried flaming gunny sacks, fireworks, even bombs to heighten the spectacle. Today's fire-builder uses fir bark, burned down to embers.

In the darkness, a call floats up from Camp Curry, "Let the fire fall!" A long-handled rake does the rest. Most coals burn out by the end of their 900-foot fall.

By day, Glacier Point, 3,250 feet above valley, offers a spectacle of Yosemite Falls (below).

MELVILLE BELL GROSVENOR

J. BAYLOR ROBERTS, NATIONAL GEOGRAPHIC PHOTOGRAPHER

317-foot plunge down Vernal Fall, then boils along its gorge past Happy Isles.

When I reached the valley floor, it felt good to soak my feet in the tingling, ice-melt water of the Merced as it swept past the hotel, lodge, and campgrounds of the Yosemite Valley community. Crowded? Yes. But Yosemite, like our other splendid parks, brings out the best in people. Utter strangers, relaxing together after dinner, share experiences like old friends.

That evening this magic bond among thousands of tanned, tired visitors strengthened spectacularly. Tents, cabins, and hotel emptied just before nine o'clock. We gathered outside, eyes trained at the dark overhang of Glacier Point. Suddenly there was a stir—a soft whispered exclamation—as far above a leisurely finger of glowing coals pointed down, seemed to hesitate, then fused into a shimmering, incandescent stream: the firefall. It made my day complete.

Oh yes, the boy on the ledge. Certainly the park rangers got him down—with 500 feet of rope and that brand of skill and courage that has become routine.

**YOSEMITE NATIONAL PARK** *Central California. 1,189 sq. mi.*

**Features:** Glacier-sculptured Sierra wilderness. Leaping waterfalls, sheer-walled Yosemite Valley, Grand Canyon of the Tuolumne. Three groves of giant sequoias; 200 bird, 78 animal species.

**Activities:** Visitor center, Yosemite Village; Happy Isles nature center (page 27). 216 mi. of scenic roads; 751 mi. of trails. High Sierra pack and hiking trips. Horses at valley, Wawona, Tuolumne Meadows. Boating, fishing (Calif. license). Nature walks, campfire programs, junior rangers (ages 7-13), firefall in summer. Skiing winter.

**Weather:** Summer days pleasant, nights cool. (Valley elev. 4,000 ft.)

**How to get there:** From west, Calif. 140. South, Calif. 41. East, Calif. 120 (over Tioga Pass, 9,941 ft.; trailers at night only, closed winter). See map at back of book. Southern Pacific, Santa Fe Ry., United Airlines to Fresno or Merced, Calif.; TWA to Fresno; bus to park.

**Accommodations:** Hotels and lodges (three open all year), cabins, tents. Write Yosemite Park and Curry Co., at park. Camp and trailer grounds crowded mid-June—Sept.; first come, first served.

*For further information write Supt., Yosemite National Park, Calif.*

**Skiers throng Badger Pass as winter cloaks Yosemite in its old white magic**

Beginners and experts can test their skills at this ski development on the road to Glacier Point. Tows, trails, a ski school with special classes for children, even a baby-sitter service for skiing parents await the thousands who come mid-December to mid-April.

The chaletlike ski house serves meals on a terrace facing one slope. It furnishes warmth and comfort for the day's end, when skis are waxed, muscles relaxed.

Skiers lodge at Wawona or Yosemite Valley. Some find ample thrill in the valley, where heavy snow sends avalanches rumbling down cliffs, and the spray of Upper Yosemite Falls clings like crystal to the rocks.

# MUIR WOODS

COME TO THE WOODS, for here is rest," said John Muir, and what better place than this lovely little haven at the foot of Mount Tamalpais just north of the Golden Gate. Superlatives are not for Muir Woods; its 510 acres preclude camping or long hikes; its trees are not as tall as some. But they grow almost in the shadow of bustling San Francisco—a virgin stand of coast redwoods, *Sequoia sempervirens.*

Like *Sequoia gigantea,* the Big Tree of the Sierras, the coastal species has rosy wood and may live more than 3,000 years. But its bark is chocolate, not cinnamon; it usually sprouts from burls at the base of living trees, not from seeds. The craggy giant of Yosemite and Sequoia bulks like a lighthouse—the world's most massive tree. The slimmer coast redwood towers like a mast to a world-record 364 feet.

John Muir loved them both, as he did all wild things. Landing in San Francisco in 1868, the young Scot turned his back on the city and set out afoot to explore the wilderness. His stature was slight, but his stamina prodigious. He'd simply put some bread and tea in a bag and "jump over the back fence," sleeping in hollow logs or on pine needles. Caught by a blizzard, he'd burrow in the snow and wait it out. During a Yosemite windstorm, he climbed a great pine to exult in its wild thrashing. He never shaved, never carried a gun, was never attacked by an animal. He never got sick except for a spell in the city when his stomach rebelled from eating "properly" in restaurants.

His beloved sequoias? Muir could not bear to see man wipe out in a day what nature took millenniums to produce. "No doubt these trees would make good lumber after passing through a sawmill," he said, at his soft-spoken, sarcastic best, "as George Washington after passing through the hands of a French cook would have made good food."

His writings crystallized public sentiment in favor of saving our natural heritage. In Theodore Roosevelt he had a strong ally, and today's national parks and forests reflect the vision of these two.

Vigorous to the end, Muir died at 76. To recall him there is the 226-mile John Muir Trail in the Sierras—and Muir Glacier in Alaska. But the small forest just across the bay from San Francisco is perhaps his most fitting memorial. Here people come as to a cathedral, half a million a year, to walk quietly among the great trees, listen to the birds, watch salmon spawn in Redwood Creek, and to remember that our parkland riches did not come easy—they are the legacy of men who fought hard for an ideal. Men like John Muir.

B. ANTHONY STEWART, NATIONAL GEOGRAPHIC PHOTOGRAPHER

# DEVILS POSTPILE

GOLD-HUNTING PROSPECTORS and restless pioneers were first to take note of this 900-foot-long colonnade of basalt rising 200 feet out of the eastern California forest. To them, the sight was other-worldly; they called it Devils Postpile. Naturalist John Muir wondered at its origin, and so do visitors today, as they arrive via US 395.

Geologists say that a Sierra volcano spewed lava here perhaps 150,000 years ago. The deep river of liquid rock cooled too quickly; like a hot dish set on ice it cracked. Later a great glacier laid bare the edge of this freak formation and polished the upper ends of the packed posts. Sightseers mounting the easy trail remark that the top looks like a huge mosaic or tile inlay.

Once part of Yosemite and still under that park's superintendent, this national monument, 7,600 feet above the sea, offers surprising variety in its 798 acres. Here in summer you can picnic, fish and swim in Middle Fork of the San Joaquin River, hire horses nearby, and hike to Rainbow Fall, where the river takes one sheer leap to a green pool 140 feet below. The monument even has hot and cold running springs. The Soda Springs bubble with naturally charged water, the makings for free sodapop. Reds Meadows Lodge and store are close by.

# PINNACLES NATIONAL MONUMENT

BURIED TREASURE awaits its finder among the weird peaks of Pinnacles National Monument—or so say hopeful romantics in the Coast Ranges of central California. The notorious bandit Tiburicio Vasquez supposedly hid stagecoach loot in a gulch hereabouts. Many a visitor has searched for Vasquez' cache, but each has settled for the scenic treasure that enriches all who explore these extraordinary formations.

In summer, a park naturalist tells the story of the Pinnacles' creation: how slow-flowing lava welled up through a fissure and formed a dome-shaped mountain. Violent eruptions piled the dome high with rubble. Then—during 30 million years—erosion chewed this volcanic mass into grotesque crags and 1,000-foot spires where golden eagles, turkey vultures, and many other birds now nest. Green even in winter (high point is 3,305 feet), the preserve is open all year. Hiking and riding trails thread its 23 square miles; two pass through canyons so narrow that falling rocks have wedged, forming cave roofs. Prudent campers provision at nearby Hollister or King City and bring their own fuel to the free tent or trailer sites; the mantle of brush produces no wood to spare.

**Climbing a stairway to the sky,** a hiker surveys the rugged Sierra scene in Devils Postpile National Monument. The splinters of basalt, about two feet thick and 40 to 60 feet high, cluster like great organ pipes.

FRED G. HINES

# SEQUOIA AND KINGS CANYON

*By JOHN M. KAUFFMANN*
*National Park Service*

THE HIGHWAY writhed up the Sierra Nevada ramparts. Behind, drenched in June sunshine, lay California's San Joaquin Valley; ahead beckoned the hazy ridges of Sequoia National Park.

Up this canyon, a century before, Indians led a rancher along dim trails to see an incredible wonder—the giant sequoia trees, largest of living things. Now, thanks to highway engineering, more than a million visitors each year drive these heights.

I rounded a bend and caught my breath. Before me stood the Guardsmen: four sequoias like pillars of a city gate. Cinnamon-red trunks rose massively amid the green. I parked and walked over to a group of trees. An auto paused, its driver grinned: "You look like a midget!"

He was right. In the Giant Forest we are all Gullivers in a Brobdingnagian world. I found the Sentinel Tree watching over hundreds of other Gullivers eagerly buying film and camping supplies. "Relax, youngsters," the old trees seemed to say. "Your lives are short enough. Enjoy them!"

**A wary doe** takes to the High Sierra Trail in this giant twin-park wilderness of silent forests, savage canyons, and granite peaks, an easy day's drive from Los Angeles or San Francisco.

B. ANTHONY STEWART, NATIONAL GEOGRAPHIC PHOTOGRAPHER

I raised my tent between two sequoias where the long light of sunset would filter through the boughs to make the trunks glow. I unpacked my gear. Then the welcoming committee arrived: inquisitive robin, bumptious chipmunk, and truculent jay, panhandlers all. The jay hopped onto my table, scolding for food.

At suppertime the forest filled with fragrant wood smoke, children's laughter, faint notes of a guitar. Families gathered, each united in primeval comfort around its evening fire. Birds began to sing, flute answering tiny flute in trilling antiphony—elfin music sung to giants.

*Crash!* I recognized what rangers call the "Trash Can Symphony." Bears were busy tipping over receptacles in search of tidbits. A mother bear and her cub shuffled by. I knew they would not harm me if I did not molest or feed them, so I settled back against a tree to read by lantern light.

A coyote chorus was my dawn alarm clock, and a delegation of deer trotted by to see I was making the most of the morning. I joined the stream of human ants circling the base of the General Sherman, most massive and one of the oldest of living things. I wondered how many tons of tree towered here, high as the Capitol dome in Washington, D. C. Some say 2,000, with enough wood to build 40 five-room houses. The 272-foot trunk is nearly 37 feet in diameter.

"I feel so . . . infinitesimal," murmured a young woman as she gazed upward.

"I feel like a youngster," replied a white-haired grandmother with a twinkle.

Egypt was conquering an empire when the Sherman sprouted. The tree was a thriving adult when Greece flowered into its Golden Age. And on a winter's night when a great star blazed over Bethlehem, this tree stood straight and tall, already more than 1,500 years old.

Next to the Giant Forest, Grant Grove is the best known and most accessible of the parks' 24 groves of *Sequoia gigantea*. The General Grant Tree, which is second in size to the General Sherman and thought by many to be even more impressive, is widely known as the Nation's Christmas Tree. In addition, Congress designated it a national shrine honoring America's war dead.

CLIMB the mountains and get their good tidings!" Alta Peak, rising northeast of the Giant Forest 11,211 feet above sea level, seemed to echo John Muir's exhortation. A friend and I shouldered knapsacks one morning and plunged into red-fir forest. Above timberline we panted onto Alta's snow-splotched summit to gaze upon an endless world of mountains. From north to south the Great Western Divide sawed the sky. One summit far beyond must be 14,495-foot Mount Whitney, high point of the Sierra Nevada—the Snowy Range.

Since most of the snow melts away in summer, Muir, I thought, had a better name: The Range of Light. Dawn turns its peaks into pinnacles of pearl. The midday sun shimmers across the pale rocks with blinding intensity. The light mellows as afternoon wanes, and at sunset the cliffs blaze with alpenglow.

**Sequoias of Giant Forest** tower over pygmy campers. The two parks protect thousands of these ancient Big Trees, native to a 4,000—8,000-foot zone in western Sierras. Trunk tapers little, hence tree's enormous mass.

B. ANTHONY STEWART, NATIONAL GEOGRAPHIC PHOTOGRAPHER

THE TRACT OF LAND ON WHICH THIS TABLET HAS BEEN ERECTED, TOGETHER WITH FOUR OTHER TRACTS OF LAND, ALL WITHIN THE HEART OF THE GIANT FOREST, WAS PURCHASED FROM PRIVATE OWNERS WITH FUNDS SUBSCRIBED BY THE

NATIONAL GEOGRAPHIC SOCIETY
TOGETHER WITH AN APPROPRIATION BY THE
CONGRESS OF THE UNITED STATES

THESE AREAS WERE DEEDED TO THE UNITED STATES ON DECEMBER 30, 1916, FOR THE BENEFIT OF AND TO SERVE THE PEOPLE OF THE NATION.

**A grove says thanks** to those who saved it. The Society's contributions helped stay the saw (p. 31).

**Earth's biggest living thing: the General Sherman Tree**

High as a 25-story building, this 3,500-year-old conifer sprang from a winged seed no larger than a rolled-oats flake—a tiny package for such a mighty life.

Sequoia roots are shallow; should erosion unbalance it, a great tree could topple while still in its prime.

Sequoia and Kings Canyon National Parks are so large that one can hike or ride for days. I explored the High Sierra Trail, high road to Hamilton Lakes, Kaweah Gap, and down the Big Arroyo toward the mile-deep canyon of the Kern. The more I ventured, the more I longed to push deeper into the Sierra fastness. For "there is a love of wild nature in everybody," John Muir wrote, "an ancient mother love ever showing itself whether recognized or no, and however covered by cares and duties." Nearly 40,000 people each summer pack into this back country.

I encountered scores of outdoorsmen and women—even campers so young they were carried papoose-fashion. One pigtailed six-year-old strode proudly down the trail carrying her own hefty little knapsack. There were Scouts, too, and rock climbers and fishermen. At Wanda Lake an angler showed me a fine catch of golden trout, the most sublime

**Campers' moving day:** fun for the family, work for the burros.

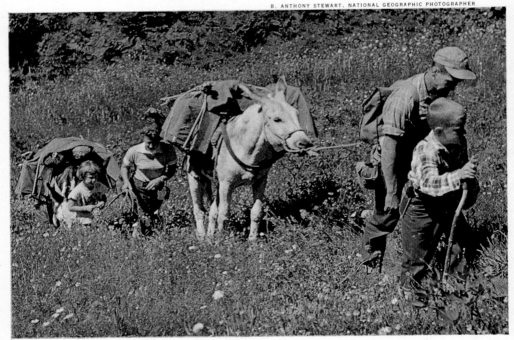

**FOLD OUT, DO NOT TEAR**

344     **In a world of golden eagle** and fighting trout, nature entertains Boy Scouts at glacier-carved Hamilton Lakes, two days' hike from the road. Angel's Wings jut above.

**Dancing flames** warm campers at Bearpaw Meadow tent camp, a mile and a half high. Alpenglow and full moon bathe California's roof at twilight.

of fish, the Sierra's own native glory. Long ago the waters must have trapped the reflections of a sunset and transformed them into living things.

This is stupendous country, incredible country, where superlatives seem inadequate—Le Conte Canyon, Black Giant, Dusy Basin, Grouse Meadows, Lake of the Fallen Moon, and finally Kings Canyon, plunging more than 8,000 feet from mountaintop to river bed. So measured, it's the deepest in North America.

## SEQUOIA and KINGS CANYON NATIONAL PARKS *Central California. 1,314 sq. mi.*

**Features:** Spectacular High Sierra setting for world's biggest trees, continent's deepest canyon, state's highest mountain.

**Activities:** Visitor center at Giant Forest. Scenic roads into both parks. Hiking, riding trails. Wilderness camping, fishing (Calif. license). Guided tours, nature walks, campfire programs; skiing in winter.

**Season:** Parks open all year. Most activities June—Sept. (nearly rainless days, cool nights). Elevation at Giant Forest 6,400 ft.

**How to get there:** Calif. 180, 65, or 198 from US 99. See map at back of book. So. Pacific, Santa Fe Ry., United Airlines to Fresno or Visalia, Calif., TWA to Fresno; bus to park in summer. Trails to high country from Owens Valley, east of Sierra, on US 6-395.

**Accommodations:** Lodges, cabins among sequoias; tent chalet on High Sierra Trail. Camp Kaweah all year. Write Sequoia and Kings Canyon Nat'l Parks Co. at park or (Oct.—May) Visalia. Camp, trailer sites (p. 32).

**Services:** Coffee shops, supplies, garage, gas, church in summer. Camp, ski gear rental.

*For further information write the parks' Superintendent, Three Rivers, California*

**An awesome inferno unfolds
beneath Dante's View:
waves of salt and sand rub
wounds where earth's crust sank**

Gold-seekers, struggling to break out of this fiery trench, had little eye for the scenic riches more than one-third million visitors enjoy each year.

Eastern California's Death Valley extends 140 miles from north of Ubehebe Crater, where an eruption shook the ground early in the Christian era, to south of Saratoga Springs, one of many water sources desperate forty-niners failed to find. Some 550 square miles lie below sea level. In the salt-rimmed depression at far left is the Western Hemisphere's lowest spot—minus 282 feet. From Dante's View, the visitor can look beyond it at 14,495-foot Mount Whitney (not shown), California's highest peak.

Thunderstorms may rage in the mountains, but most rainfall and runoff evaporates or is absorbed before reaching the valley floor. Despite aridity, more than 600 kinds of plants thrive, among them desert holly, salt-bush, cacti of a dozen kinds, mariposas, lupines, and dahlias. Sunflowers turn to their god. Primroses and poppies splash color in the vast basin.

Visitors (below) are intrigued by Death Valley's "riddle of the sands." What causes large rocks to move and leave tracks on the level clay floor?

JOSEF MUENCH

# DEATH VALLEY

*By EDWARDS PARK, National Geographic Staff*

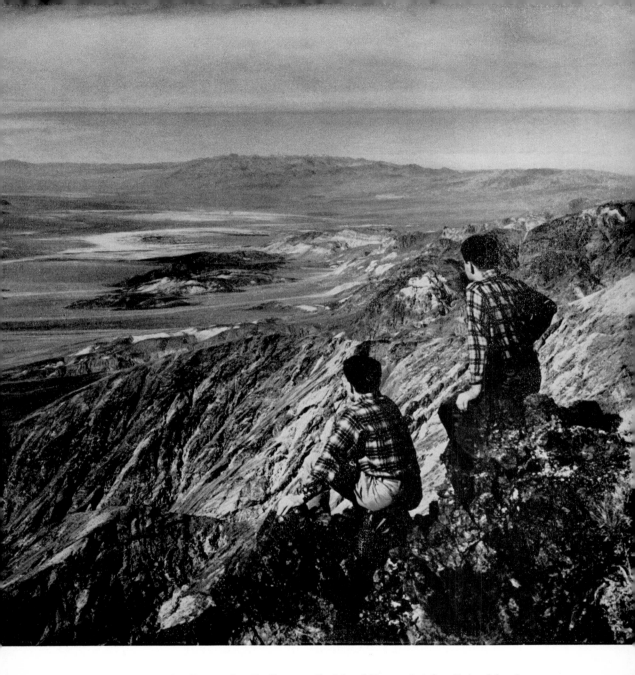

Tomesha, the Panamint Indians called it: "Ground Afire." And in the height of summer there is no better name for this sun-tortured trench between blistered ranges. But when a group of forty-niners blundered into it, they renamed it Death Valley.

Drive in from the east through Daylight Pass to get an inkling of how those emigrants felt. Short-cutting to the gold fields, they had crossed a weary succession of deserts and barren hills. At last they came to this range, seemingly topped by a peak flying a banner of snow. Surely these must be the Sierras! They flung themselves at the bald mountains, wrenched their groaning wagons through the washes and gullies, then stared in numb despair at the trick nature had played.

347

Fringe-toed lizard hugs its sand dune haven. Burrowing with special toes (below), shy *Uma notata* "swims" into loose sand to avoid enemies or blazing sun. Valley folks say when lizards blow on feet to cool them, it's hot!

Spiny lizard, sporting a prickly collar, hunts insects in the shade, hibernates in winter. A 7-inch tail is half his length.

Miles yet from the Sierras, they stood amid the Amargosa Range. Between them and the peak whose snow had lured them—11,049-foot Telescope Peak, high point of the forbidding Panamint Range—spread a desolate sink, four to 16 miles wide, mostly below sea level. Rather than turn back, they decided to cross the salt-crusted, lava-smeared plain.

Thus the trap snapped on them.

In your car today you can drive freely and comfortably along the valley floor

348

Death Valley's 20-mule team pulls again—for TV.

and spend the night at Furnace Creek with its irrigated date palms, its inn and ranch, its tennis courts and swimming pool. Here the Jayhawkers, one of the emigrant parties, scrabbled frantically for water. You may park beside the Devils Golf Course, that strange rubble of crystalline salt pinnacles and gravels that stretches down the valley 40 miles and is 1,000 feet deep. This bed of an Ice Age inland sea blocked the Bennett-Arcane party when they sought escape to the south. Your road skirts close under the brooding Panamints where those slow-dying men and women finally clawed their way out of the valley, then looked back on it and cursed it with a lasting name.

Death Valley—a bitter name, and hardly a just one, for life abounds here. The kit fox, desert coyote, and Bailey bobcat pad across the desert floor at night. Rabbits and ground squirrels scurry through the mesquite. Only sand dunes and salt beds are bare of plants—and the pale green pickleweed, resistant to salt and alkali, braves the very edge of the Devils Golf Course. Water flows sweet in many subsurface veins. Gardens flourish. Except in summer, when temperatures have hoisted to a poleaxing 134°, Death Valley's climate smiles on man by day and treats him to technicolor sunsets as lowering rays play on the eroded, mineral-stained hills. Nights are often cool.

It took the ubiquitous prospector to discover that the place was livable. One of the lost forty-niners, searching for the gunsight he had accidentally knocked from his rifle, found a chunk of rich silver ore. His story brought miners with their burros. Though no one ever located the Lost Gunsight Mine, other strikes were made. Boom towns sprouted along the mountains, howled on Saturday nights, then withered away, leaving slag heaps of broken bottles. In 1880 a destitute couple, trying to scrape a desert living, learned of valuable borax and how its deposits look. Aaron Winters felt he might have seen some of that stuff in the valley. He went and looked, and for years the 20-mule teams hauled 36½-ton loads of borax from the works at Harmony.

Two generations ago mules hauled borax on the grueling 10-day, 165-mile desert trek to Mojave.

**DEATH VALLEY NATIONAL MONUMENT**   *California-Nevada. 2,981 sq. mi.*

**Features:** Desert showplace in "North America's basement"; lowest point in hemisphere.
**Activities:** Visitor center at Furnace Creek; illustrated talks. Roads lead to Dante's View, Panamint overlooks, dunes, borax works, Ubehebe Crater, Scotty's Castle. Trail up Telescope Peak. Horses at Furnace Creek.
**Season:** Most activities Oct. 15—May 1 (weather is pleasant). Roads open all year.
**What to bring:** Jacket for cool evenings.

Sunglasses, binoculars, camera, light meter.
**How to get there:** Highways through monument intersect US 95, 91, 395. By rail or air to Las Vegas, Nev., where cars can be rented. Airstrips in monument for private planes.
**Accommodations:** *Oct.—May.* Furnace Creek Inn, Ranch, Stove Pipe Wells Hotel; write Death Valley, Cal. *All year.* Scotty's Castle (Goldfield, Nev.); cabins at Wild Rose Station (Trona, Cal.). Camp, trailer grounds.

*For further information write Superintendent, Death Valley, California*

**Death Valley Scotty lived in Alhambran splendor in this castle but kept the secret of his easy-going wealth**

A former trick rider in Buffalo Bill's Wild West Show, Walter Scott hit the 1905 headlines when he emerged from Death Valley with padlocked sacks of gold, scattered bills like confetti on Los Angeles streets, and hired a train for a record run to Chicago. For years he fostered the legend that a hidden gold mine kept his pockets jingling. Actually, a millionaire friend set up Scotty just for laughs.

The pair built this $2,000,000 mirage in concrete, with its imported tiles, hand-carved woodwork, and crenelated towers, in the 1920's. It perches 3,000 feet high in Grapevine Canyon at the valley's northern end. The "desert rat's" fabulous home, now a hotel and museum, opens to hourly tours.

**"He went thataway!"** gesture the tufted Joshua trees of Lost Horse Valley.

# JOSHUA TREE NATIONAL MONUMENT

BY MOONLIGHT they raise grotesque arms as if supplicating a pagan goddess. By day these outstretched arms, seeming to point to a promised land, reminded westward-trekking Mormons of Joshua at prayer—hence the name Joshua tree. Ranging up to 40 feet high and 14 feet around, this overgrown member of the lily family lives—who knows?—perhaps 500 years. It produces no telltale rings.

In southern California, where the Colorado and Mojave Deserts meet at the Little San Bernardino Mountains, 872 square miles bear this shaggy plant's name. From monument headquarters at Twentynine Palms the road follows a gently rising plateau. Scarlet-tipped ocotillos and cholla cacti give way to Mojave yuccas; Joshua trees take hold around 3,000 feet. Suddenly at Salton View, 5,185 feet in the sky, the land tumbles away to reveal distant Salton Sea, 235 feet below the ocean, and San Gorgonio Mountain, 11,485 feet above. Beneath lies San Andreas Fault, the great earthquake-making rift. Campgrounds await all year. Bring water, firewood, warm clothes—even summer nights may be nippy.

351

PART FIVE

# THE PACIFIC NORTHWEST

THIS IS THE BIG WILDERNESS—a land of fire and ice gentled by a cloak of green and washed by Pacific swells. Its trees are big, its mountains big, its spirit as big as all outdoors.

Cataclysmic eruptions shook this region in the yesterday of geologic time. Molten lava seared its signature on earth's face; volcanic surges heaved up noble Rainier, Lassen, and long-gone Mazama, in whose flooded basement now lies Crater Lake.

Today the fires are banked and ice grips the Cascade peaks. And in the shadow of Olympic glaciers where summer is a fleeting thing lie ocean beaches and the green growing miracle of the rain forest.

Lewis and Clark staked a claim to the Northwest in 1805, but prairie schooners were slow to follow on the Oregon Trail. Returning today, pioneers would find much of the young land's solitude unchanged. As park visitors do, they could hike for weeks in dense evergreen forests, flowered alpine meadows, an untamed realm of rock and snow. They'd rest by fish-filled streams now roaring, now muted to a trailside chuckle, and top off the day with campfire yarns as leaping flames sent sparks to join the stars.

0                                        150
STATUTE MILES
© N.G.S.
Irvin E. Alleman

*A New York family explores a wilderness of rain forests, glaciers, and flowered alpine meadows in western Washington*

# OLYMPIC
## NATIONAL PARK

*By PAUL A. ZAHL, National Geographic Staff*
*Photographs by the author*

A SNOWBALL whizzed past me, followed by a peal of laughter. "Happy Fourth of July, Daddy!" What a strange Independence Day! That morning my wife and I and our two small children, Eda and Paul, had left our cabin in the Elwha Valley and driven up mile-high Hurricane Ridge—into a sky-touching world of dazzling snow.

Below lay steep, densely forested ravines. Beyond, an arc of snow-capped peaks saw-toothed across the horizon, topped by the crags and glaciers of Mount Olympus, 7,954-foot high point of Washington's Olympic Peninsula. Northward the landscape tumbled abruptly toward Pacific waters fingering through the Strait of Juan de Fuca to produce Puget Sound. There, above a blue haze, we could distinguish Vancouver Island, Canada.

Two weeks earlier we had left our New York apartment and set out in search of a wilderness. Here, in the 1,400 square miles of Olympic National Park, an up-and-down world of wonders, we found it. Spurning the elegance of Lake Crescent Lodge and other hotels, we settled for nearly three months in a one-room log cabin. Living centered around a wood-burning stove, with papa responsible for chopping wood, children for filling the woodbox, and mamma for stoking the fire and preparing meals. Radiating from this base, we could ex-

**In cathedral-like rain forests** of the Olympic lowlands, giant conifers struggle sunward from the matted floor where life and death keep pace. On the snow-chilled heights bloom wildflowers like the bluebell above.

355

**Lookouts** scan for telltale smoke among Olympic's treasured trees. If fire breaks out in remote areas, planes drop equipment to fire fighters.

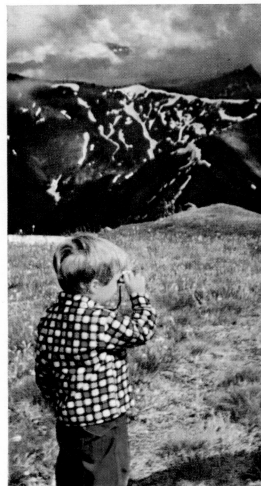

plore hot mineral springs, inky-blue Lake Crescent with its sentinel Storm King mountain, miles of rain forest laced with plunging streams and cascading rivers, and the high country with its peaks, jewel-like lakes, and scouring glaciers. There was Enchanted Valley and the long, narrow strip of park land along the Pacific. There were Roosevelt elk, deer, marmot, mountain beaver, and bear.

We had made this day's ascent to seek wildflower meadows that should by now have set Hurricane Ridge aglow. But the only glow came from snow. Rangers had warned that this was a late spring, "but a few days of warm weather and flowers will pop as if they had springs under them."

Well, we had those few days of warmth. So where were the wildflowers?

**Crowning the park wilderness,** these majestic ranges are visible far at sea. Sighting them in 1788, English navigator John Meares named the highest peak Mount Olympus—home of the gods.

My wife resolved the dilemma. I heard shouts and saw her point down the mountainside to a sprinkling of golden dots around a snow patch. We skidded down into the midst of thousands of glacier lilies nodding yellow heads close to the melt-soaked turf, some pushing boldly through the snow—our first sign of spring in the Olympic high country.

The Olympic Peninsula is as unusual in climate as it is geographically and botanically. Moisture-laden Pacific winds are deflected upward by Olympic peaks. The resulting rainfall on the western slopes reaches 140 inches a year, and around Mount Olympus precipitation is an amazing 250 inches. Yet by the time these winds cross the peninsula they are nearly dry. Thus, while the west side is the wettest region in the continental United States, an area 50 miles to the east, in the Olympic "rain shadow," approaches aridity.

The downfall on the western slopes has produced one of the most luxuriant temperate-zone rain forests in the world. From temporary quarters in the lower Hoh Valley we would drive day after day to the end of the spur road, then

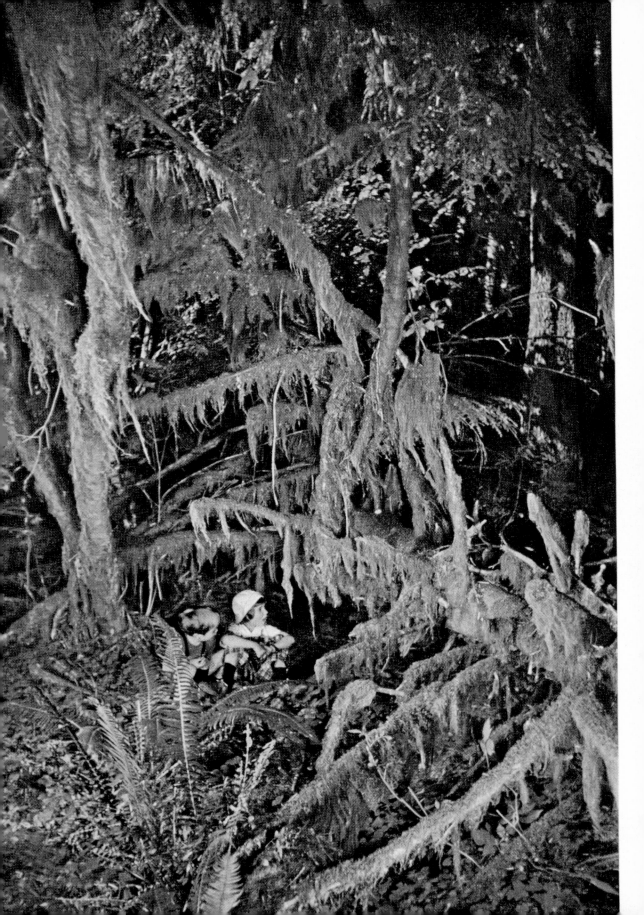

set out on foot up the trail. Papa had to carry junior a good part of the way, and once had to fish Eda out of a stream; but aside from such minor hazards the going was easy. Yet, pressing in on the trail is a forest as wild and primeval as any in the world. Up the Hoh Valley, the world's largest Sitka spruce boasts a circumference at chest height of 51 feet 6 inches. Near the valley mouth, the world's largest western red cedar has a girth of 66 feet 1 inch. In the Queets River Valley is the largest Douglas fir (53 feet 4 inches around), and on the east fork of the Quinault River, the record western hemlock (27 feet 2 inches).

Though many big trees towered 200 feet beside the trail, what dominated the scene was the profusion of smaller species—understories of big-leaf maples, vine maples, ferns, lichens, fungi, Oregon oxalis, and the smaller life of this prodigious tangle. Club mosses hung from nearly every branch, covered nearly every surface in trailing strands and great sweeping tufts like the magnified beards of invisible elves and hobgoblins. We felt we had entered a nether world—mysterious, almost palpably quiet.

Clouds hung low on our first visit to Hoh Valley's rain forest. Then the sun came out and a brilliant yellow-green light replaced the somber shadows. Like pale mist it filtered through the vegetation, reflected by a billion chlorophylled surfaces, bathing us in a soft yet all-pervading glow.

This great rain forest has been standing relatively undisturbed for centuries. With much of it in the climax state (a climax forest is one that has developed to its maximum extent), profuse growth continues, but the overall mass barely changes. Creative and destructive processes have reached equilibrium.

When an old tree crashes, a hundred seedlings, stimulated by the light, leap up to fill the space, though only one or two reach full growth. Meanwhile, lichens, fungi, bacteria, ants, termites, and beetles set upon the fallen giant and convert it into humus. Seeds from living conifers light upon it, and soon a virtual nursery of new evergreens sprouts and grows, often in straight colonnades, from the decayed trunk. Their roots may loop around the side of the fallen log; trees on stilts are not uncommon. Finally the disruption caused by the crash is corrected, and the forest regains its balance.

Animals, too, inhabit this moss-draped world, but the visitor is hardly aware of them. Now and then an invisible bird sings high in the trees, a black beetle scurries across the trail, or a chipmunk performs briefly on a log.

**Not Hänsel and Gretel,** but Paul and Eda Zahl sit in the hushed stillness of a moss-draped fairyland. Only bird notes from atop 200-foot Douglas firs break the eerie silence. Park roads lead to rain forests of the Hoh, Queets, and Quinault Valleys. Trails continue through green-lit worlds where beetles (right) explore their own forests of matchstick lichens.

**Life teems on the rain forest's floor;** a new world opens for Eda.

$\mathbf{D}$URING the summer my family and I made no fewer than two dozen trips to Hurricane Ridge. Packing a substantial lunch and other necessities for keeping two small children tranquil, we would leave the cabin early and spend the day in meadows of wildflowers.

Vegetation on the heights has a dramatically brief life cycle; blossoms must be developed quickly and seeds matured and hurriedly disseminated. We could sense an element of biological urgency in these alpine meadows. The great

360

UPPER LEFT: Bright spore capsules wave atop a moss plant. Winds will scatter reproductive cells as they sift from pods. (Enlarged 3 times.)

LOWER LEFT: *Nidula*, a common fungus, cradles spore masses like a clutch of eggs. The closed pouches have not yet matured. (Enlarged 3 times.)

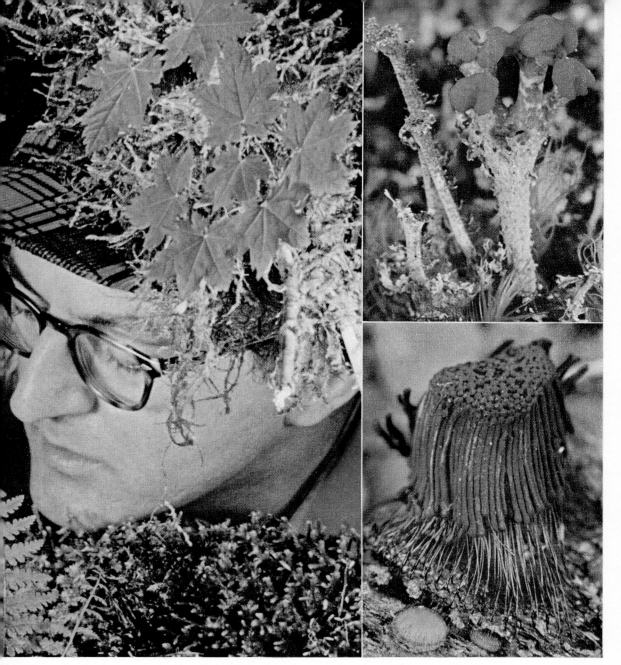

Among these tiny plants live frogs, salamanders, slugs, shrews, and mice—but no venomous snakes.

woolly-coated bumblebees seemed to fly more energetically and hum more purposefully than those in the valley.

We would find space among the flowers to spread our blanket. We would glance toward the crags of Mount Olympus, half hidden in clouds, and down at flowered meadows running steeply into a thick border of evergreens, standing prim and clean. I would wander off looking for a particularly rich field of purple-blue lupine; and then great swirls of mist might roll in, sometimes so

361

UPPER RIGHT: Scarlet-crested *Cladonia,* coral-like lichen, carpets sunlit earth and rocks. Brilliant tips cast spores to the wind. (Enlarged 3 times.)

LOWER RIGHT: *Stemonitis,* a mold on the border between plants and animals, slides its matchlike spore cases over rotting logs. (Enlarged 3 times.)

**Lupine and white buckwheat** mantle Hurricane Ridge,

UPPER LEFT: Petals turn back to form tails of Jeffrey shooting stars, *Dodecatheon jeffreyi*.
LEFT: Grass widow, *Sisyrinchium douglasii,* is not a grass, but a relative of the iris. Blossoms often last only a day. (Enlarged 1½ times.)
LOWER LEFT: *Phacelia sericea* clusters its flowers at tip of a foot-long stem, thrusts antennalike stamens from the blooms. (Enlarged 1½ times.)

a mile above the sea, during the brief alpine summer.

BELOW, CENTER: Indian paintbrush, *Castilleja,* reverses usual flower pattern. Tiny green blooms peek between bright orange-red leaves and bracts. It cloaks many far-western valleys.

BELOW: Delicate *Anemone hudsoniana* wears a coat of silky hairs. A member of the buttercup family, it thrives on high meadows and rocky slopes. (Enlarged 1½ times.)

dense that we would have to return to the car or seek shelter in the modern ski lodge perched high on a scenic clearing.

One day in this mountainous Eden we might find a particular meadow yellow with buttercups; a week later, blue with larkspur, white with phlox, or orange with columbine. Our joyous adventures among these delights were marred only once by anxiety.

We had been photographing columbine near where the clearing dropped perilously into a 200-foot ravine. My wife suddenly looked up, her voice shaky. "Where's Eda?"

Little Paul was sitting in a nearby patch of wallflowers, engrossed with a nectar-seeking bee. My eyes swept the area, including the precipice rim. I shouted, "Eda! Eda!" No reply.

I ran to the edge, but the sight I feared was not to be seen, and I thanked God. In enlarging circles I searched wherever flowers were high enough to conceal a child.

Then I heard a whisper: "Daddy, *please* stop making all that noise. Do you want to scare the marmot?"

Too relieved to be angry, I saw Eda behind a rock, intent on a large, woodchuck-like rodent. Just then it let out a blasting whistle and scrambled into its hole. I listened silently to a lecture from Eda on disturbing animals in a national park. When it was my turn, Eda got a return lecture on hazards of mountain travel for unaccompanied first-graders.

Once when the fog came up thickly during our picnic lunch, we saw a figure materialize. "Hello," I shouted. No answer. What we had thought human was a handsome doe. To the children's delight, she went straight to my leather camera case,

**Elk stroll a slope** deep in Enchanted Valley. The park protects the largest remaining

sniffed, then began chewing with alarming vigor. Before I could point out that it is against park regulations to feed animals, Eda presented the deer with a peanut-butter sandwich. The animal accepted gratefully, turned, and fled into the mist.

At the park superintendent's suggestion I joined three of his staff for a trip into Enchanted Valley, a part of the Olympics that few people have seen. A day's drive from park headquarters at Port Angeles took us to the park's south side. After another long day on horseback we forded the east fork of the Quinault River and entered the valley itself.

Down an unbelievably high escarpment poured a series of waterfalls, some leaping from ledge to ledge 500 feet at a time, some sweeping down in great bridal veils, others zigzagging like fragments of frayed thread. In the rosy light

364

herds of Roosevelt or Olympic elk.

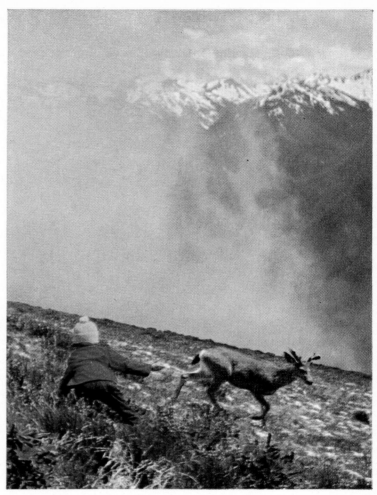

**Blacktail buck** on Hurricane Ridge spurns Eda's friendship. More than 50 different mammals, including bear and cougar, inhabit the park. "Whistler," the marmot (below), digs his den between rocks.

of evening the valley's northeast wall seemed to be bleeding in a hundred places. Each waterfall disappeared into a glistening, echoing ice cavern.

That night around the fire in a log chalet Coleman Newman, the park's elk specialist, mentioned that the park's four or five thousand famed Roosevelt or Olympic elk are shy and thinly spread in summer. But he agreed to scout the upper valley with me. Early in the morning we moved into a clearing near the river. Newman ducked. I followed his example as a group of elk moved cautiously out of the woods. Against the snow we counted some 90 great elk—cows and calves, but no antlered bulls—carefully making their way across the sloping side of a huge cone of snow.

Weeks later on a trip to Bogachiel Peak, on High Divide, Newman and I spied more elk through our binoculars, this time magnificently antlered bulls. We watched 1,000-pound behemoths streamline their antlers back against their shoulders and batter through what seemed impenetrable forest growth.

I wanted my wife to join me on a trip to the glaciers of Mount Olympus, but with the children, that was out. So I chopped a week's firewood and left the cabin to my family, by now used to the deer, squirrels, chipmunks, and even bear that were their neighbors.

From the Hoh Valley, ranger Hugh Bozarth and I headed up the rain-forest trail on saddled mounts. Climbing and camping, we finally reached the glassy surface of Blue Glacier, close beside the cloud-mantled pinnacles of Mount Olympus. We rigged crampons and ropes and hiked over the ice to peer into yawning blue crevasses and explore vertical knife edges at the glacier's melting front. Between the craggy summits of Olympus a domed field of ice cracks off under the weight of new snow to feed six great glaciers. One icefall stood a quarter of a mile away, a crumbling cliff 500 feet high, with fallen blocks below. The 50 or so Olympic glaciers are only remnants of what they were. Blue Glacier, where we stood, shortened by more than 800 feet in only 15 years.

O N THE Olympic Peninsula, rain or overcast in one valley or on one peak does not necessarily mean that the same prevails elsewhere. "What's for today?" Eda would ask as our cabin stirred to life in the morning. I would glance at the ridge. "Looks clear as a bell. It's Hurricane Ridge for us." Or maybe: "Ceiling too low. How about the Soleduck forest, or Lake Crescent, or Blue Mountain, or the Ocean Strip?"

The national park's mile-wide Ocean Strip runs for about 50 miles along the peninsula's western coast and includes three Indian reservations. You reach it on US Highway 101, the road that circles the park's main mountain mass with spur roads poking inland through valley openings.

One day we headed for the strip—first, to view a whale that had washed ashore a few miles south of Ruby Beach; second, to visit the coastal village of Lapush and show the children some real American Indians. You have to see this Olympic coastline, added to the park in 1953, to believe it: great needles of bare, occasionally tree-studded rock rising straight out of the surf; sculptured caverns and rock bridges; sheer shore cliffs; heaps of white drift logs; glistening beaches; tidepools teeming with life; and sea birds everywhere.

The whale, of course, had no business being there. Its carcass might have fascinated tourists a month earlier; by now nature had taken its inevitable course. One whiff from more than 50 feet away and we turned and ran. Climbing

**Tracking a fugitive flower** to its rocky lair, the Zahls discover Piper bellflower (page 34), one of 10 flowering plants that grow only in the Olympics. Beyond tower the 7,000-foot Needles.

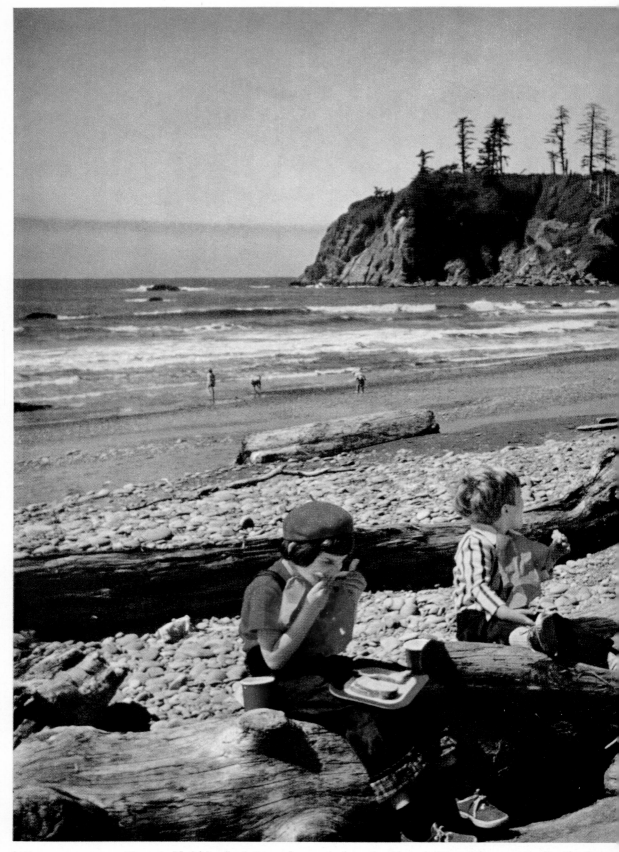

**Tree-studded isles flank the rocky coast** where the Olympic Mountains meet the Pacific. Sea

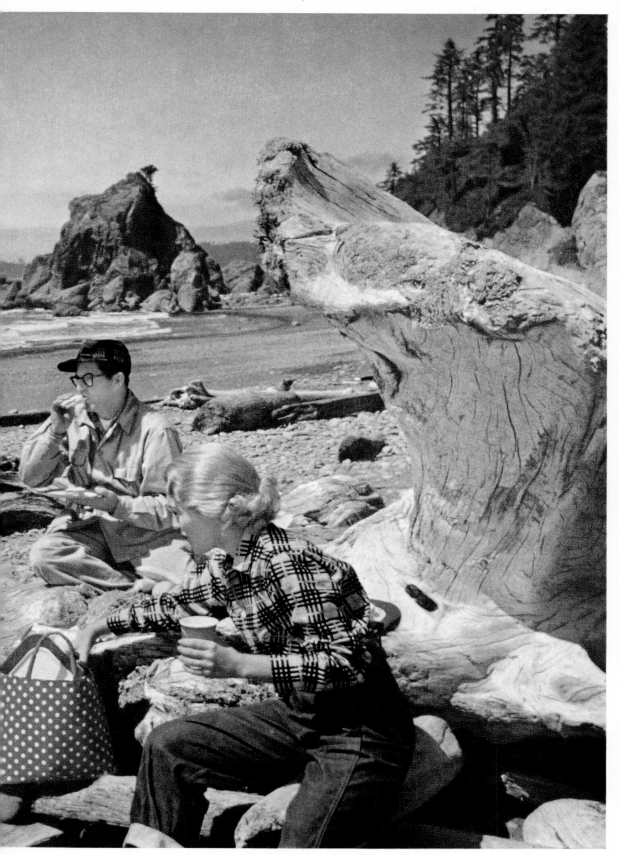

birds skim creamy surf; seals bask on warm ledges; deer and bears share beaches with families like the Zahls.

back up the sea-cliff trail, we headed northward toward Lapush.

In this picturesque fishing village, Eda found her Indians, some in outboard-propelled dugouts, smelt-fishing in the bay. She noted that neither their garments nor speech differed from our own.

One September morning, lumber jackets and heavy underwear gave way to city clothes as we prepared for the homeward trip. I knew that bull elk, coats sleek and antlers sharp, were clearing throats for autumn's mating calls; that bears were fattening on late-season berries, getting ready for the big sleep; that wildflowers were withering and winds gathering force.

Soon winter would whiten this mountain land, turning it from a paradise for summer naturalists, campers, and hikers into one for skiers. But the summoning of school bells back East saved us from the temptation of staying longer.

**Salmon fleet** idles at Lapush, Indian village at the mouth of the Quillayute River on the park's Ocean Strip. Below: Nets dip silver smelt that ride high spring tides to spawn in the sand.

**Coastal Indians** once harpooned whales from huge dugouts. Adept carvers, they recorded their legends in wood. This Makah wears the symbolic headdress of the Wolf clan.

371

**OLYMPIC NATIONAL PARK** *Area 1,400 sq. mi.*

**Features:** Only park embracing snow-capped peaks and ocean beaches, rain forests and alpine flowers. Olympic elk.
**Activities:** Visitor center at Port Angeles. US 101 nearly circles park; spur roads to key areas. 600 mi. of trails. Horses, guides at Sol Duc Hot Springs, Elwha River. Hiking. Trout, salmon fishing. Nature walks, campfire programs. Skiing at Hurricane Ridge weekends Dec.—Mar.
**Season:** Park open all year. Best weather summer and early fall. Deep snow at high elevations Nov.—June or July.
**What to bring:** Rough-it clothing, warm jacket, rain gear.
**How to get there:** US 101. See map at back of book. Also ferry across Puget Sound and Hood Canal. To Port Angeles by air or bus from Seattle, by ferry from Victoria, B. C.
**Accommodations:** Lodges, inns, cabins; write Olympic Peninsula Hotel and Resort Assn., Box 156, Port Angeles. Campgrounds high and low, some accessible to trailers.
**Regulations:** Don't disturb nature. Fires outside campgrounds by permit. Wash. fishing license in certain areas.

*Write Supt., Olympic National Park, Port Angeles, Wash.*

# MOUNT RAINIER

By MERLE SEVERY, National Geographic Staff

THE GREAT MOUNTAIN played coy with us as we approached it over Chinook Pass from Yakima on the east. We caught only tantalizing glimpses through clouds clambering over its shoulders of rock and ice. We wound through somber forests of fir and hemlock, past glacial moraines and waterfalls. Fallen timber streaked the slopes where avalanches

374　**Midsummer sun meets winter snow** above Paradise Valley. Some 300 miles of trails probe the park wilderness; 90-mile Wonderland Trail circles Rainier. Mount St. Helen's cone rises beyond Tatoosh Range.

B. ANTHONY STEWART, NATIONAL GEOGRAPHIC PHOTOGRAPHER

**Wind and water hollowed** this fairyland grotto in Paradise Glacier. Filtered sunlight tints the walls a luminous blue. Mount Rainier's flanks support more glaciers than any other U. S. peak outside Alaska.

RAY ATKESON

had thundered down. Arriving amid the swirling mists at Sunrise, 6,400 feet high on a northeastern spur, we found families of little firs huddling together, like jagged islands in a foggy sea.

"Guess we won't see Rainier today," said my wife Pat as she spread lunch. Squirrels and chipmunks came to greet us. Birds flew in to share our picnic.

Then the surging fog parted and Rainier filled the sudden blue sky. Blinding sun danced on fresh snow. Enormous glaciers seemed poised over our heads.

Again the mists billowed in, and behind the swirls loomed a mystic mountain in a surrealist painting. An eerie chill enveloped us and we hastened on.

NEXT MORNING, outside our window at Longmire the 14,410-foot white giant stood majestically alone in a cloudless sky. We drove up to Paradise Valley, 5,500 feet high on Rainier's south shoulder, and there roamed parklands ablaze with autumn reds and mounted slopes dotted with dark green spires.

We surveyed blue-green crevasses and seracs on Nisqually Glacier and heard the rumble of ice crashing into the milky stream that snakes below its debris-littered snout. In the crisp distance snow-crowned Mount Adams and Mount St. Helens poked above the sawtoothed Tatoosh Range. Loping up mountain trails through sun-splashed alpine meadows, we felt a million miles from anyone, in a lofty, timeless realm. "Reminds me of *Heidi*," Pat said.

Later, stopping along Stevens Canyon road, carved out of Rainier's broad southern flank, we hiked over granite ledges polished in gentle swells and troughs by ancient glaciers, and peered into a breath-taking chasm at glacial melt frothing over rocks 180 feet below. At afternoon's end the wind died; no ripple blemished Rainier's mirror image in Reflection Lake. The sun's failing rays climbed the icy summit as we returned to Paradise, and the Nisqually valley flamed from wall to wall. The evening star had risen above the silhouetted Tatoosh peaks when we rode down off the mountain.

"Want to see how Paradise looks in winter?" Superintendent Preston Macy and his wife asked us that evening in their Longmire home. "The snow was 30 feet deep, with drifts of 40 and 50 feet." A color slide flashed on the basement screen. Just the chimneys of Paradise Inn showed above the curving dunes of snow. "Altogether we measured 992 inches of snowfall there last year!"

We heard the back screen door slam, then again impatiently. "Raccoons," smiled the soft-spoken Macy. "They say they're hungry. Wild animals seem instinctively to know they are protected in our national parks."

Mount Rainier National Park has something for everybody. Each summer, a million or more visitors, lured by the Cascades landmark so convenient to Seattle and Tacoma, delight in the alpine flowers that garland it to glacier's edge.

Pat and I found autumn peace on the quiet slopes, before winter's breath turned them into a skier's delight. But perhaps Rainier's special appeal is to the wilderness camper and climber, whose adventures the next pages record.

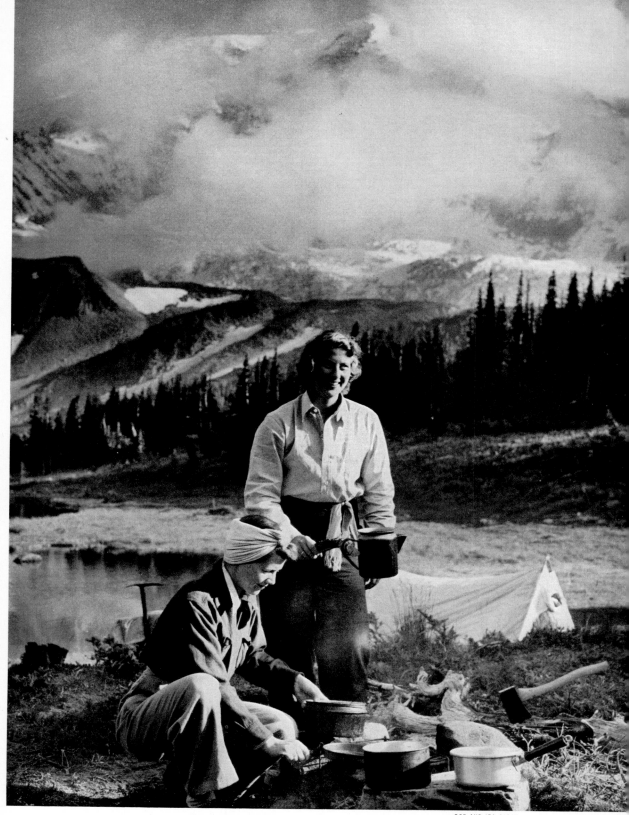

**Campers prepare a trailside supper** below cloud-swept Carbon Glacier. Nine campgrounds and many trail shelters serve outdoors enthusiasts in the 378-square-mile park. For hotels and transportation write Rainier National Park Co., Box 1136, Tacoma 1, Wash.

380 **Only a narrow slice** of packed snow stands between the climber and an 80-foot plunge. Horizontal lines mark Nisqually Glacier's yearly accumulation of ice. Rainier is mountaineer's favorite among Pacific Northwest peaks.

**Alpinist safeguards** a teammate's crossings by snubbing his climbing rope around anchored ice ax used to chop frosty footholds on steep slopes. He secures the rope's other end around waist and shoulder with a bowline on a bight (right). Later he may loop it into a sliding sling to rappel down cliffs (page 17). Spike-studded crampons (below), strapped to climbing boots, give firm footing.

381

## High-altitude adventurers thread a maze of chasms

Climbing season, June to Labor Day, brings hundreds of enthusiasts to Mount Rainier. From lofty campsites climbers look down on lakes, rivers, and roads spread out as on a huge relief map. At night they watch the twinkling lights of distant cities.

Parties trying for the summit must register with a ranger and show they are physically fit, properly equipped, and experienced. Teams check every inch of nylon rope, cram lightweight foods in waterproof containers into compact packs. Most start from Paradise Valley after lunch, reach Camp Muir at 10,-000 feet, and lay over until midnight. They try to get to the top and back below Gibraltar by 10 A.M. before intense sun brings icefall dangers. They lunch at Muir, return in afternoon.

Crossing a glacier, two to four rope together. Their rhythmic "rest step" is geared to thin air. Between steps they pause three seconds, time for a full breath. Reflected sunrays can cause bad burns in half an hour. Climbers quench thirst with oranges, canned juice, and candy drops dissolved in melted snow.

Twenty-six glaciers cling to Mount Rainier; ages ago some may have reached Puget Sound. As brittle flows hump over rocks, huge cracks open. Some could swallow a hotel. Crevasse floors provide fair shelter in extreme cold because glacier interiors stay around 32°. On the summit, caverns melted out by volcanic steam offer refuge.

These men cross a snow bridge on Winthrop Glacier, one of six ice rivers originating at Rainier's summit. They head for distant Steamboat Prow.

BOB AND IRA SPRING

# CRATER LAKE

*By MERLE SEVERY, National Geographic Staff*

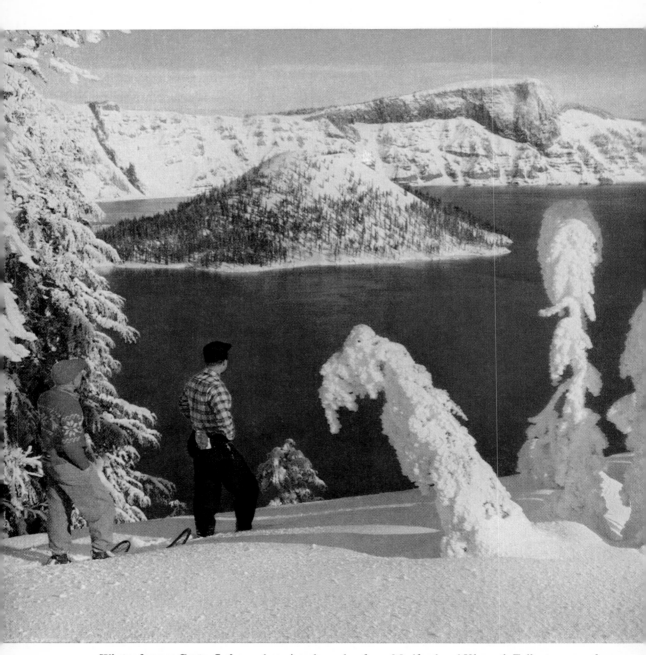

**Winter frames Crater Lake,** and ermine-draped conifers bow to its regal blue. The lodge and cabins at Rim Village are closed and the campgrounds buried under snow, but Oregon roads from Medford and Klamath Falls stay open for winter sports enthusiasts, who find the national park's skiing superb. Peak tourist season is late June to mid-September, when park buses con-

Y OU REALLY HAVE TO SEE IT to believe it. I had stared at plenty of blue water, but nothing to match Oregon's inland wonder. Telling my wife Pat about this lake and how blue it was, I found words just wouldn't do. I'd have to take her there and show her. Even so I wasn't the first to fumble the descriptive ball. In 1853 the great inkwell's discoverers tried "Deep Blue Lake." Next group in named it "Blue Lake." Others gave "Lake Majesty" a whirl, and finally everyone gave up and settled for "Crater Lake." But Pat, never at a loss for words, would surely come up with exactly the right phrase.

We drove into the park, high on a saddle of the Cascade Range, and pulled up along Rim Drive. There, as we stood on the lip of the gigantic rock bowl and gazed out on that circle of impossible blue, the Nation's deepest lake looked like 20 square miles of western sky that had slipped out of place and lay at our feet.

Transfixed by the crater's strange stillness, as though all the sounds of modern life had been swallowed in this clean, azure world, I sniffed fragrant evergreens, felt the crisp mountain air, and braced myself for the flood of adjectives, the torrent of apt superlatives that inevitably must burst from Pat's open mouth.

"Gol—*ly!*" she said, and all was stillness again.

We skittered down a path that zigzags to water's edge. No beaches whiten the crater's rock and cinder wall, plunging so steeply that 100 yards from shore in one place the lake is already 1,200 feet deep. We hired a boat and rowed out on the lake—I rowed, Pat hummed "From the Land of the Sky-Blue Water."

"Look," she said, cupping water in her hands, "it's not blue at all."

"No different from the water in your tap," I told her. "Only purer."

"It's the sky's reflection," she said hopefully. Passing clouds took care of that. The water was blue, blue sky or not.

nect with trains and planes, and naturalists tell the blazing story of the crater's origin. Visitors tour the rim, take a 2½-hour launch trip round the lake, hike, fish, and boat to Wizard Island (left).

## How Crater Lake was formed  *Paintings by EUGENE KINGMAN*

1 **A mighty volcano** once seethed with fire where Crater Lake glistens today. Many thousands of years ago molten rock deep in the earth welled up through a fissure in the earth's crust to build Mount Mazama in southern Oregon. Like other Cascades peaks, this lusty mountain enlarged itself with lava flows.

"Then what is it?" she persisted. "Don't tell me it's all done with mirrors."

"Almost," I said, glad I had done my homework. I explained how sunlight, scattering in such clear, deep water, so free of suspended living and mineral matter, has all its colors absorbed except blue. The blue rays rebound upward.

"Living matter. . . . Aren't there any fish in the lake?" she asked.

"Rainbow trout and sockeye," I told her, "but not until man put them here. Fish had nothing to feed on, so they planted shrimp for them to eat."

I was resting on my laurels when she came back: "What do the shrimp eat?"

She had me there. ("Diatoms, microscopic single-celled plants," a friendly ranger told us later without the slightest trace of strain.)

Pat continued to stare mesmerized into the translucent depths. "What a place to drown in," she mused. Six inches in a bathtub would do the trick, I'd always thought, and I couldn't see how the extra 1,995½ feet would make a bit of difference. But I pulled a little quicker on the oars, and Wizard Island's cinders grating on the boat bottom came as a welcome sound.

Hiking up the uncanny 760-foot cone I told Pat this was really Llao's head. "Llao who?"

"Llao, the Klamath Indian god who ruled from a throne beside the lake." And I went on to tell how his arch enemy Skell captured Llao, took him to the

386

2   **Glaciers formed** on Mazama's lofty flanks even as the volcano wakefully puffed. Geologists have found ice-scratched rocks sandwiched between thick layers of lava, showing that new eruptions smothered white-cloaked slopes. Fallout of pumice and ash buried the surrounding land in a blanket of fertility.

3   **Fire-breathing Mazama** grew to magnificent stature, building gradually to nearly 12,000 feet, and gave birth to a secondary cone on its western shoulder. Whenever the giant slept, glaciers cooled its head, and forests mantled its ashy slopes. Then fresh waves of lava would seethe down valleys, wiping out growth.

**4** **The last advance of ice** wrapped the Cascades in a chill, white cover. Mazama spawned frozen rivers that moved in resistless majesty down slopes and valleys. Yet far underground the volcano's furnace still smoldered. As the ice retreated, some 20,000 years ago, the stage was set for Mazama's final act.

**5** **The stub of a mountain** is all that remains of majestic Mazama. Probably for weeks the earth trembled, the skies were black with dust, and white-hot magma avalanched down the slopes. Finally, with a rending crash the summit fell, leaving a giant caldera or volcanic pit six miles across and 4,000 feet deep.

highest cliff, and there tore him to bits and cast them into the lake. Giant crayfish, subjects of Llao, ate the pieces, thinking them parts of Skell's body. Then the head was thrown in and the crayfish saw their mistake. Their tears raised the level of the lake. Llao's head became Wizard Island.

"Don't believe a word of it," puffed Pat as we reached the top and peeked into the crater within a crater. "Now tell me how it really happened."

The big show, of course, was Mount Mazama's volcanic spree 7,600 years ago, quoth I, leaning heavily on everything rangers and guidebooks had told me. The grumbling volcano blew its heart out in an explosion that blackened noonday skies and spread pumice far into Canada. How apt that Indians later shied away from this place as a battleground of the gods! Mazama spewed six and a half cubic miles of ash and rock over the land and emptied even more lava through fractures in its base. It didn't truly "blow its top"—the hollowed-out summit simply collapsed into the void. Where a peak rivaling Lassen and Rainier had stood there was only a 4,000-foot hole—a catch basin for centuries of rain and snow. Wizard Island was a volcanic afterthought.

The lake's other island—Phantom Ship with its mastlike pinnacles—we saw from the 36-mile Rim Drive. We skirted 8,938-foot Mount Scott, highest peak in the 250-square-mile park. We stopped at overlook after overlook, each with its special vista, and wound past Hillman Peak (Hillman was the prospector who nearly stumbled into the lake at Discovery Point).

"Now that you've seen this phenomenon, what would you name it?" I asked.

"How about 'Crater Lake,' " Pat suggested.

6 **Mazama's last gasp built Wizard Island,** a cone that erupted from the rubble-choked crater floor. Rains and snows filled the Nation's deepest lake; it has neither inlet nor outlet. Today's annual precipitation of 69 inches keeps lake level fairly constant. Walls rise nearly 2,000 feet above the water in places.

# OREGON CAVES

A LUCKY MAN was Elijah Davidson. With his old muzzle-loading rifle he wounded a bear and chased it down a hole. The story does not go on to say whether he retrieved his bear, but lighting a pitch torch, he found himself in a weird underworld of winding passages and decorated chambers. And if Elijah was fortunate in discovery that August day in 1874, so have been the many thousands who have followed his trail into Oregon Caves.

One of these was Joaquin Miller, the Poet of the Sierra, who often sang the praises of "The Marble Halls of Oregon." Chandeliers, columns, miniature waterfalls, even bric-a-brac, all rendered by the relentless seepage of water bearing dissolved limestone, embellish these cool, silent rooms. Coveralls and rubber shoes, available near the entrance, are a good idea when taking the mile-and-a-quarter guided trip, for the electrically lighted caves are damp.

Near the California line, Oregon Caves National Monument opens its mountain chateau and cabins in summer. You can picnic within these 480 acres, but Greyback Campground is eight miles away. A nursery tends children while parents explore; you must be over six to enter these lovely, fragile chambers.

# LAVA BEDS NATIONAL MONUMENT

VIOLENCE KEYNOTES this northern California scene. Here volcanoes flamed in centuries long past. Lava spewed from 17 cones, cooling into porous chunks. Rivers of fire flowed from fractures and crept into gullies. There, hardening on the outside while the molten interior drained off, they formed lava tubes and caves; when roofs collapsed these became trenches and chasms, sometimes 100 feet deep. Fumaroles belched and hissed gas, then left dead chimney shafts probing far underground.

Into this black labyrinth in 1872 came a band of Modoc Indians who had broken free of the reservation they unwillingly shared with the Klamaths, their traditional foes. Defeating a cavalry force, the ill-armed Modocs, encumbered by women and children, took to the lava and fought the United States Army to a standstill five months. Their leader, "Captain Jack," deployed his warriors, never more than 71, through the serpentlike trenches. He stood off odds of 15 to one, dodged artillery fire, rearmed his braves with captured rifles. In one pitched battle he wiped out two-thirds of the attacking bluecoats, killing four out of five top officers.

Rock forts and foxholes still stand. Bleached bones of slain horses lie underfoot, and you almost expect to hear the crack of an Indian rifle. But campers and picnickers can explore in safety the lava bridges and statuary, the Indian inscriptions, and the caves with "lavacicles"—stalactites of once-molten rock.

**A riot of green** in Fern Cave contrasts with Lava Beds' dry landscape overhead.

On the ice floor of Skull Cave, Indians refrigerated bighorn and pronghorn meat. The bighorn are gone, but mule deer winter in the monument's 72 square miles. In spring, wildflowers burst into bloom among the lava flows—a new and less violent eruption, ever pleasing to the eye.

# LASSEN VOLCANIC NATIONAL PARK

WAGON TRAINS heading for the Sacramento gold fields found Lassen Peak a welcome landmark. An old volcano, probably as extinct as most of its sister peaks in the Cascades, northern California settlers judged it. Only a few saw signs of life. In 1865 a backwoods hunter named Bumpass reported steam vents hissing and mud pots bubbling and spitting beside the mountain.

They say Bumpass led a newspaper feller to the display, cautioned him to watch his step, then himself broke through the crust and dunked a leg in boiling mud. He was so mad he clean forgot to cuss. As if to make up for that lapse, the thermal basin is today called Bumpass Hell.

In May, 1914, Lassen awoke. For a year it belched ash and cinders in more than 150 explosions. Then red tongues of lava lapped from the crater and seared the mountain's flank. Deep snow melted in a rush, sending a torrent of

392     **Lassen's lava shoulders** wear patches of summer snow; skiers sometimes find August sport. From this road (8,512 feet) it's a 2½-mile hike to summit. Lakes invite boating, fishing, skating. A bus links Redding and park in summer.

**Electric quiz board teaches youngsters to identify birds. Light shines when name and picture match.**

mud and giant boulders plunging into the valleys. A mighty, low-angle blast mowed down trees on Raker Peak, three miles away, neatly peeled the bark, and drove sand an inch into them.

Lassen's eruptions died away in 1917, and out of the devastation emerged a wild and beautiful national park. Cones, crags, lava beds, the seething Bumpass Hell and Sulphur Works all recall the violent past. But forests and lakes make this a hiker's and camper's park, with eight campgrounds and 100 miles of trails. Motorists can follow a self-guiding road tour leading to lava flows and wild-flower meadows alike.

Still a landmark, the 10,466-foot peak reminds westbound air passengers that San Francisco is near. A nice old volcano, people think. Extinct, of course.

More likely, Lassen is merely dozing.

**Lichens spread gold** on the bark of firs. Nature programs are given at Manzanita Lake, summer hub of the 166-square-mile park. Superintendent's address is Mineral, Calif.

CHARLES E. MOHR

## PART SIX

# THE EAST

IN THE WEST, nature shouts; in the East, she whispers. No bottomless canyons yawn beneath your feet; no awesome peaks thrust two miles into the sky. Tucked away in corners of a softer landscape, Eastern parks are a city dweller's ideal retreat.

More than three centuries of civilization have almost erased the silent forest that greeted the first settlers. But along Maine's rockbound coast and in Appalachian highlands, on the windswept dunes of Hatteras and in Florida's jungled Everglades, you will find a miracle: Hemmed in by farms and cities, nature is not overcome. And around these wilderness shrines lingers the spirit of pioneers who sought a new land's liberty.

Beside Acadia National Park, sturdy New Englanders set out to sea, as their fathers did, in "thick o' fog," even if the sky is "armin' up fer a blow." And in cabined coves in the Smokies, lean mountain men whose speech bears Shakespeare's lilt "stick to their fancy" and "hain't afeared of nary a man nor b'ar they is."

Clinging sternly to old freedoms, these people personify the unconquerable spirit of the parks—where nature still weaves her spell on those who seek her out.

395

0        200        400
STATUTE MILES
© N.G.S.
*Irvin E. Alleman*

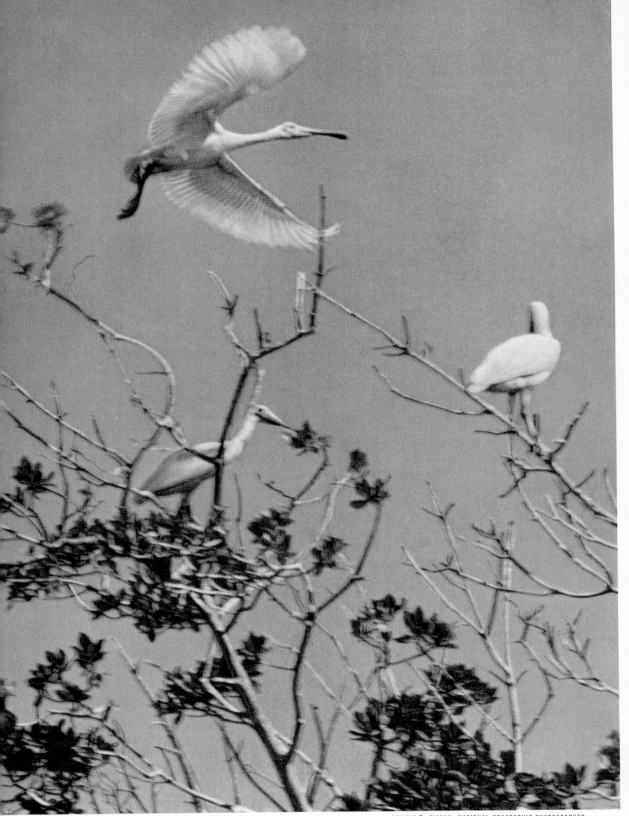

396     **Roseate spoonbills,** almost exterminated, staged a comeback when protected from ruthless hunters seeking their plumes. Here in Everglades National Park, a zoo without cages on Miami's doorstep, rare tropical birds, strange mammals, and the Nation's only crocodiles find sanctuary.

Airborne ballerina: the wood ibis

# EVERGLADES

*By DANIEL B. BEARD*
*Former Superintendent, Everglades National Park*

THE DENSE CANOPY of red mangrove trees bordering Squawk Creek gave way to the open vastness of the Everglades. All morning, National Geographic artist and naturalist Walter A. Weber and I had worked our way through uncharted waters from our camp at Little Banana Patch, Florida, historic campsite of the Seminole Indians and perhaps the ancient Calusas before them. Walt, armed with cameras, binoculars, sketch pads, and other tools of the wildlife artist in the field, was anxious to record firsthand some of the spectacular birds and animals that make subtropical Everglades unique among our national parks.

Every bend of the stream looked the same—monotonous thickets of spraddle-rooted mangroves growing along the swampy shore. As our outboard motor churned up the sepia waters and weeds, a never-ending procession of yellow-

**Flying carpet** of southern Florida is a water sled driven by an airplane propeller. In such boats, patrolling rangers skim over vast wilderness marshes beyond reach of roads and trails enjoyed by park visitors.

WILLARD R. CULVER AND (ABOVE) ALLAN D. CRUICKSHANK, NATIONAL AUDUBON SOCIETY crowned and black-crowned herons pumped their way out of the trees and flew ahead of us. Their disturbed squawks give the stream its name. The stream shoaled and we began to pole our skiff. A flock of white ibis lazily circling in the distance was the only sign of life on this hot, midwinter afternoon. Hammocks, the tree islands of the Everglades, dotted the landscape.

We ran against a fallen cabbage palm log and could go no farther by boat. A nearby hammock, dominated by a large mahogany tree, beckoned. As we struggled toward it, knee-deep marl sucked at our feet, sawgrass tore into our clothing. Breaking through cocoplum bushes into the hammock, we paused to catch our breath and grow used to the dim light. It was like stepping from a sunlit street into a movie theater. Oaks, reddish-limbed gumbo limbo trees, wild tamarinds with their lacy leaflets, wild coffee bushes, and vines almost blotted out the sun. The sing of attacking mosquitoes was the only sound.

Our trip through waterways in this vast Everglades sanctuary gave us a close look at many of its wonders. Here since time immemorial, ibis, egrets, herons, and other birds have gathered each year to nest and rear their young. Squalling, fighting, pushing, chattering birds by the thousands—here is more excitement, more doing, than at Coney Island on the Fourth of July. Flights of adult birds are continually coming in with food or to give nest relief to their mates. Other flights are going out, while high overhead the swing shift, perhaps, is taking its recreation in lazy, soaring circles.

First birds come to Everglades in December. They are the wood ibis, commonly called "flintheads." In reality, they are storks. These huge birds are a wonderful sight, the pure white of their plumage in the bright sun contrasting with the jet black of their wing tips. Then come American egrets to choose nesting places close by, followed by snowy egrets, Louisiana herons, and others. Last to arrive are white ibis. By the end of February the rookeries are filled with birds; by late June they are about empty.

We once took a visiting scientist to East River Rookery. Not only the number and variety of birds amazed him. "Have you any idea," he exclaimed, "what an enormous amount of food it takes to feed just one bird? Here are hundreds of thousands, and they all must eat." The birds feed on fresh-water crayfish, minnows, snails, frogs, and maybe even a baby alligator now and then. They choose their nesting site by instinct, or intelligence if you will—near their food supply yet protected from raccoons, bobcats, and other enemies.

On that trip we passed a manatee and its calf in a shallow bay. The manatee, or sea cow, is a mammal that has adapted to a marine environment. Surprisingly large and usually sedentary, manatees "graze" on grasses of bay bottoms. Little is known about them because they are still rare, and hard to observe except when they poke their noses up for air. We got between the cow manatee and her calf.

**"There's one!" An alligator basks amid water lettuce**

Corkscrew Swamp rivals nearby Everglades as a wildlife sanctuary. Thousand-year-old bald cypress trees spread knobby roots in the ooze. Birds scream overhead; water moccasins glide in quiet pools. As at Everglades' popular Anhinga Trail, a boardwalk leads into the swamp.

The National Audubon Society helped preserve both Corkscrew and Everglades. Audubon president John Baker (above) points out a young four-foot gator to Mrs. Melville Grosvenor. The photographer, National Geographic's president, stretched full length on the walk to catch its portrait.

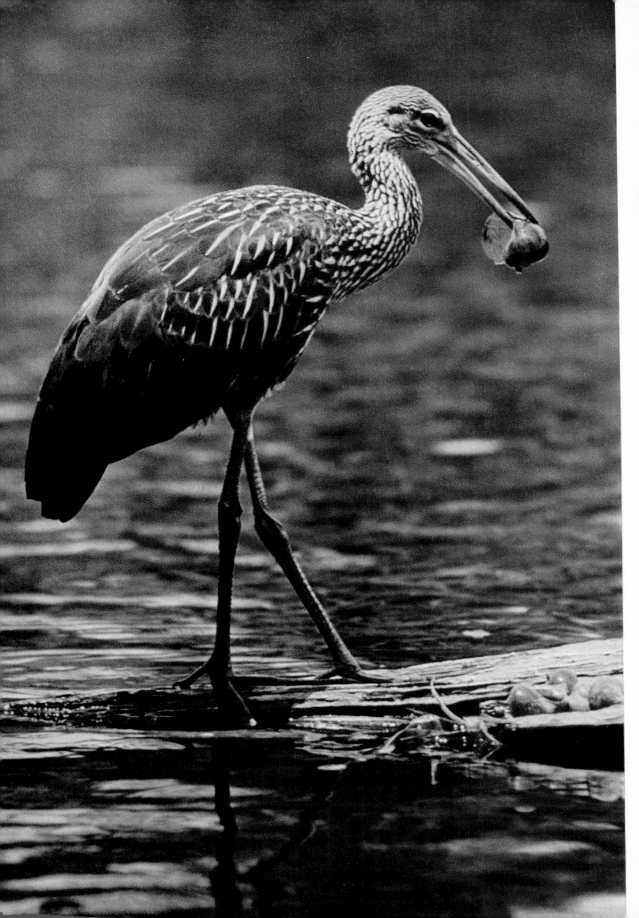

Frantic, she hurled her ungainly bulk clear of the water—not in the graceful curve of a porpoise, but in a tremendous "bellywhopper" that made the scientist ask nervously, "Do they ever jump into the boat?"

"Sure, lots of times," fibbed our boatman, swinging the wheel hard aport. "We take 'em home and milk 'em."

The long, swinging arm of the Florida Keys protects the shoal expanse of Florida Bay. In many ways the bay resembles the Bahamas, with its sprinkling of mangrove keys and crisscross of propeller tracks made in the shallow bottom by fishing boats.

In summer, it is a shimmering mirror reflecting the statuesque cumulus clouds parading over the distant Everglades. Sometimes it is lashed by the merciless fury of a hurricane still unabated by crossing any land mass. In winter, when a "norther" strikes, the surface is churned into a milky froth as waves wash the marl bottom.

Some of the rarest and most beautiful birds in the United States live here. It is startling to see a flock of roseate spoonbills—big pink birds with crimson splashes—coming into Bottle Key in Florida Bay. Rare reddish egrets, known locally as red-necked herons, can be quickly identified by their unheronlike habit of chasing down their killifish prey. Another famous Florida Bay creature is the pugnacious great white heron, with seven-foot wingspread. No other large bird in North America lives in such a restricted range—30 by 50 miles. Audubon discovered the big white birds and captured several.

Crocodiles also inhabit the bay and the mainland's south shore. Years of persecution by man have made the saucy croc timid; but there's still something sinister—and majestic—about these last of U.S. crocodiles.

How to tell one from an alligator? "Don't worry," I often reply. "If you see a croc, you'll know it." Actually, the crocodile has a long, slender snout; the alligator's is shorter and blunter. Crocs stick to salt water, gators to fresh water.

## EVERGLADES NATIONAL PARK

**Features:** Largest (2,188 sq. mi.) subtropical wilderness in U.S., teeming with wildlife, at Florida's southern tip. Marshy prairies, mangrove, cypress swamps fringed with tidal rivers, lakes, bays, and beaches.

**Activities:** Visitor centers at Flamingo, Royal Palm Station. Nature talks, guided walks, boat tours. Tarpon, marlin fishing offshore.

**Season:** Park open all year. Most birds nest in winter; temp. usually 60°–80°. Summers hot, humid.

**What to bring:** Cottons, visor cap, light jacket. Insect repellent, sunglasses, binoculars, telephoto lens.

**How to get there:** US 1, 41, Fla. 27. Air, rail to Miami (40 mi.); bus to park. By cruiser on inland waterways.

**Accommodations:** Motel in park; write Everglades Park Co., Flamingo, Fla. Campgrounds at Flamingo and Lone Pine Key. Motels in Miami, Homestead, Everglades, Key Largo.

**Services:** Restaurant, stores, gas, marina, charter boats at Flamingo. Hospital, churches in Homestead.

**Regulations:** Back-country camping by permit. No teasing alligators. Fla. fishing license in fresh water.

*For information write Superintendent, Box 275, Homestead, Florida*

**Florida's elusive limpkin,** named for its halting gait, is a wading gourmet that probes for snails. Folklore says its echoing nighttime shrieks sound like a little boy lost forever in the swamp.

FREDERICK KENT TRUSLOW

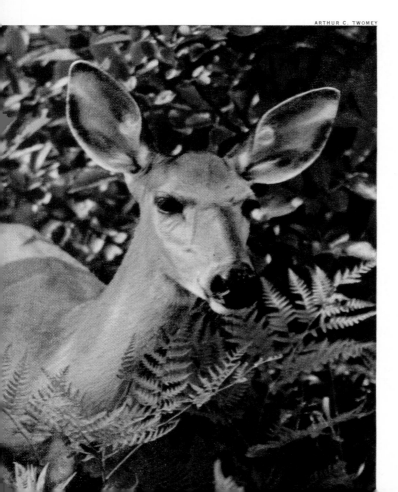

**Cuthbert Lake Rookery,** where wood ibis by the hundreds crowd their mangrove-island home, is one of Everglades' largest nesting grounds.

The park encloses only part of the vast sea of tall grasses and sedges, spotted by tree islands and laced by waterways, that rolls north to Lake Okeechobee. Called "a continent in the making" because these amazingly flat lands emerged from the ocean in geologically recent times, the Everglades at highest rise barely 12 feet above the sea.

Unreclaimed swamp a generation or so ago, much Everglades land today yields lumber, crops, and cattle. But conservationists fear further efforts to drain and fill lands near the park could change water levels, destroying nature's delicate balance that assures ample food for wildlife.

**Whitetail doe** peeks round a green curtain, reminding that the park is not just an aviary. Bobcat, raccoon, opossum, otter, gray fox, marsh rabbit, and skunk dwell here, as do burly black bears and chattering squirrels.

Along this Gulf of Mexico coast lie the sparkling wilderness beaches of Cape Sable, where giant loggerhead turtles come out to nest each summer. Back of the coconut palms stretch a mangrove swamp, a lake, a series of salt marshes and ponds where white pelicans, roseate spoonbills, rare flamingos, and many other birds rest and feed.

Farther up the coast is Ponce de Leon Bay, the mouth of Shark River and boatway to Whitewater Bay. Mangrove trees—red, white, and black—grow tall here, perhaps taller than anywhere else in the Western Hemisphere. Eastern brown pelicans raise spray as they dive into a school of fish; frigate birds soar effortlessly above, swooping occasionally to pick up a fish while on the wing.

Gradually the shore line breaks into mangrove keys, the Ten Thousand Islands. Here thousands of white ibis roost in summer. Huge flights circling high are a wonderful sight—the bright flash of red feet and red bill against snow-white body.

Beyond, the winding Barron River leads to the picturesque little town of Everglades, where President Truman dedicated Everglades National Park in 1947. For decades, conservationists watched helplessly while ruthless hunters decimated the area's unique wildlife. Now America's families can see these splendid creatures thrive unmolested in a great wilderness preserve.

NATURE'S CHILDREN spring to life on the canvas of National Geographic artist-naturalist Walter A. Weber. Before he set up his easel, he spent weeks boating and hiking the great Everglades preserve, studying his subjects in their habitat. His skilled brush drew inspiration from on-the-spot sketches, notes, color motion pictures and slides. He checked the fidelity of engraver's proofs.

The result: not mere likenesses, but unbelievably accurate re-creations in action of the exotic birds, mammals, and reptiles that make Everglades National Park unique.

B. ANTHONY STEWART, NATIONAL GEOGRAPHIC PHOTOGRAPHER

*A portfolio of Everglades wildlife paintings by Walter A. Weber* ▶

403

## Snowy Egret

To put "a bird on Nellie's hat," shooters destroyed whole rookeries, almost wiped out these dainty egrets by 1910. Today they safely parade their courtship plumage in Everglades National Park.

WALTER A. WEBER

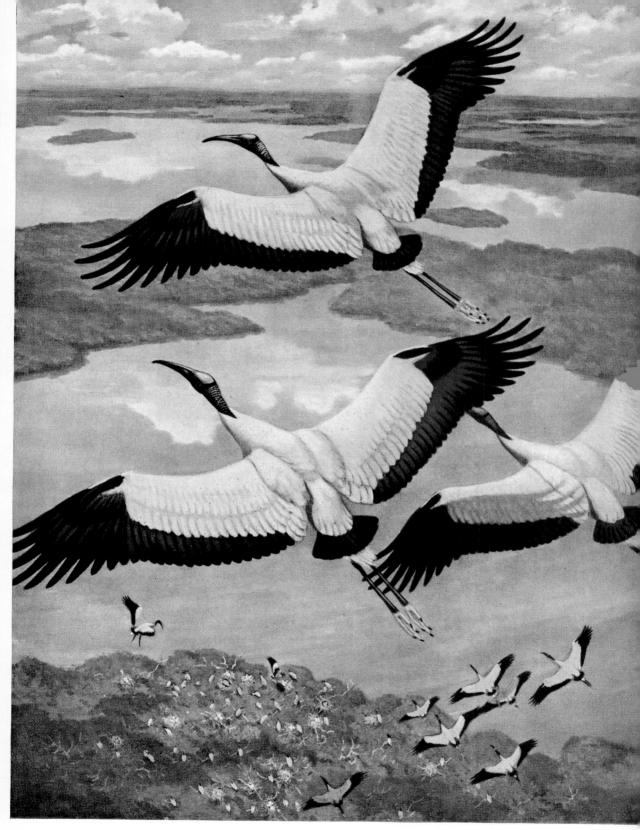

*Wood Ibis*   North America's only stork, the "flinthead" soars above
East River Rookery, where thousands winter amid a
labyrinth of islands. The wary flocks post sentinels when feeding.   405

## White Ibis

Evening sees black-tipped squadrons
winging from Everglades marshes
to roosts on nearby keys.
Audubon watched a crafty white ibis
drop mud into a crayfish hole,
then gobble the little crustacean as
it came up to remove the plug.
Impatient mothers often lay eggs
in unfinished nests.

*Black Skimmer*    Wearing formal dress, this bird skims low over the sea,
scooping up fish and shrimp in its flat lower mandible,
day or night. Its petulant cry sounds like a puppy's bark.

***Black-necked Stilt***   This shrill comedian's antics lead searchers away from
its nest. If rising waters threaten, it pushes twigs
under its eggs, jacking them up as high as eight inches.

WALTER A. WEBER

**White Pelican**

After a slow take-off, these heavy northerners wintering at Cape Sable spiral out of sight. Horny growth on bills forecasts breeding season. If disturbed, white pelicans may desert nest and young.

**Eastern Brown Pelican**

Neck forward, wings back, this ungainly bird plunges into the water after its prey. Unlike its white cousin, it is sociable and does not fear man. Forked tail identifies a frigate bird.

Squawk Creek is named for these raucous dwellers along its
red-mangrove banks. Yellow-crowned (perching) and
black-crowned (flying) night herons fish off their doorsteps.

*Night Heron*

*Reddish Egret* When excited, reddish egrets ruffle their long plumage and change their look. Some, belying their name, are chalk white. These members of the heron tribe hunt killifish in the shallows.

WALTER A. WEBER

In spring, gobblers are often too busy strutting before their hens
to eat; fat reserves sustain them. They seldom fly except
to roosts, but can run like a streak through grass and scrub.

*Florida Wild Turkey*

WALTER A. WEBER

*Water Turkey*   Swimming, the anhinga submerges all but its serpentine neck, whence the name snakebird (page 55). Young birds hiss and leap into the water if alarmed. The neighbors are wood ibis.

413

## Great White Heron

It has the wings of an angel, but sometimes devours young birds. When fishing, it stands like a statue, waiting for prey to swim to it. Hunters used to salt down great whites as food.

WALTER A. WEBER

### American Egret

In breeding season, this majestic white bird trails filmy aigrettes up to 21 inches long. Here it joins the little blue and Louisiana herons in flight.

### Pileated Woodpecker

A jaunty red plume distinguishes this crow-size woodpecker, which dwells in Everglades trees. Strong neck muscles power its triphammer beak.

415

*Crocodile*    Ruddy turnstones scatter before a crocodile, who asks no favors and grants none. Now protected, this long-victimized denizen of salt water grows to 14 feet. Color and pointed snout tell croc from gator.

Limpkins (left) and gallinules ignore an alligator daydreaming in a
cypress pool. Seminoles eat his tail flesh. Hide hunters, firing at torch-reflecting
eyes, almost exterminated him. Teeth alone brought $5 a pound.

*Alligator*

*Manatee*

Everglades lagoons pasture underwater livestock, Florida's air-breathing,
grass-eating manatee. Seemingly put together from nature's spare parts—seal head,
whale flippers, cow flesh—this sluggish mermaid suckles her young.

*Raccoon*

Three masked henchmen join mamma on a stream-border raid. Their plunder: mussels, crayfish, frogs, turtles, birds, eggs. Mainly nocturnal, coons dwell in trees. They often wash food before eating. Marsh rabbit is the innocent bystander.

419

*Puma*    Everglades National Park shelters some of the last pumas east of the Mississippi. On silent pads, the big cat stalks its prey remorselessly, then springs and hurls it to the ground. Its mating call in the night is a wild, unearthly shriek.

WALTER A WEBER

## Otter

An otter pounces; his sharp teeth dispatch a watersnake. Artist Weber reconstructed this Everglades drama from signs of the battle. To the sleek, web-footed otter, the snake was an appetizer. Fish is his favorite fare.

# GREAT SMOKY MOUNTAINS

*By VAL HART*

A BOUT THAT GROUNDHOG you saw yesterday," Sam said. "Tell you how we cook them. First you get yourself a nice fat young groundhog, dress it, and boil it." Sam paused to throw a log on the fire. "Now, if you're out in the woods, you get sassafras or spicewood for season; then you take the meat out of the water and bake it." He smacked his lips. "Wonderful flavor. Couldn't tell the difference if it was coon or bear."

This introduction to mountain cooking made my kitchen and the gray routine of housekeeping in Washington, D. C., seem far away. We were on a pack trip

through Great Smoky Mountains National Park. I glanced at the friendly faces lit by the fire and thought how odd it was that only a few days before we had been strangers: Ruby Bere, Wisconsin bacteriologist; Genevieve Bass, Florida housewife; Elizabeth Yates, a writer from New Hampshire; Bob Sisson, National Geographic photographer; and I. We had met at Tom Alexander's Cataloochee Ranch near Waynesville, North Carolina. Tom was our outfitter and guide. In his very quietness at that moment he seemed a part of the mood of the hills. So did Glenn Messer, Tom's helper, and Sam Woody, our camp cook.

"COME ON, you cowpunchers, let's get going!" Tom yelled early the first day as he led out from the ranch toward Hemphill Bald, the first steep climb. Ruby and I glanced at each other. Both inexperienced riders, we were pleased that our horses took their place in line and moved at all.

Entering the park, we headed northeast along the crest of Cataloochee Divide. We watched clouds in the long distance drifting low, merging with the deep blue haze which gives the Great Smokies their name. This highest section of the Appalachian Mountains straddles the border of North Carolina and Tennessee. Sixteen peaks top 6,000 feet.

Our trail narrowed through a jungle of rhododendron intertwined with dense masses of dog hobble, covering the forest floor. Occasional patches of sunshine lit bright-red partridgeberries. The Smoky Mountains, we soon discovered, conceal surprises for those who venture off the park roads. From quiet jungle darkness we emerged into a sun-drenched meadow where butterflies flitted among the goldenrod, sunflowers, and purple and white asters.

Leaving the crest of Cataloochee Divide, we turned northwest into McGee Branch Trail for the sharpest descent of the 10-day trip—2,000 feet in one hour. The lead horses seemed terrifyingly far below, and the treetops lower still. I wondered if Ruby, like myself, was hanging on grimly and praying that her horse wouldn't go over the side.

In the quiet valley of Caldwell Fork we passed abandoned cabins. Mountain people had lived here years before the Government acquired the land for a park; now the only sign of life was the clawed-off bark of apple trees whose fruit had tempted bears. Off somewhere a ruffed grouse drummed in the loneliness.

Our first night's encampment was on Rough Fork of Cataloochee Creek, in an old homestead clearing. We watched Sam start his fire and caught the tempting odors that rose from it. In no time he produced broiled lamb chops, mashed potatoes, peas, and buttered hot biscuits. Food never tasted better.

Bob Sisson, an experienced camper, gave us good tips: Put on top of your duffel bag the things you'll need in the morning; use your jacket for a pillow; above all, pick a good spot for your sleeping bag, clear away the rocks and twigs, and blow up your air mattress before dark. This sound advice we all ignored. Liz and Ruby, bird and flower books in hand, disappeared around the bend of

424                                                 *Photographs by ROBERT F. SISSON,*

**Laurel brightens a trail** through lush forest that never feels an axe's bite. Nearly as many tree varieties as in all Europe mantle America's most-visited park, where North Carolina meets Tennessee.

an inviting path, while the rest of us lazed about. Later, warmed by a roaring fire, we sang ballads and told stories. Then, by flashlight, Genevieve and I struggled to blow up our air mattresses, find our sleeping bags, and rummage through duffel bags for soap and toothbrushes. Gen couldn't find her blanket. "Here's one Florida cracker who'll sleep cold tonight," she said. We pulled close to the fire and tried to sleep.

But sleep outdoors does not come easily to one used to four walls and a ceiling. We watched a gypsying mist envelop a moonlit trail and listened to night sounds—the splash of a stream, whinnying of our horses, crackles of the dying campfire. "About bears," Gen whispered. No one had mentioned bears. "Banging tin plates scares them off and wakes everybody to help." Fine idea, I agreed, and we tiptoed to the "kitchen." With tin plates by our sides, we finally dropped off to sleep.

Hundreds of black bears range the Smokies sanctuary. Next morning Tom showed us their tracks, and from Trail Ridge he pointed out patches of color—laurel thickets—on Spruce Mountain. Bears like to live in these dense growths, known to mountain people as "woolly heads," "yellow patches," or "slicks." The vastness was overwhelming. The park embraces half a million acres of forest. In a few hours' climb riders pass through sweet gums, umbrella magnolias, and shortleaf pines common in the South; maples, oaks, and hemlocks of the North; and finally into red spruce, fir, and mountain ash atop the highest peaks.

Riding along the crest of Balsam Mountain, in the shadow of magnificent oaks, beech, and basswood, we kept our jackets on. But we quickly took them off when we came out into the hot sun on Ledge Bald. Why are so many Smokies bald? Some scientists say excessive evaporation, caused by winds and altitude, killed the trees. The Cherokees believed their ancestors cleared the tops as lookouts for a monster that was carrying away their children; the Great Spirit sent thunder and lightning against the marauder, and forever after the mountains remained bald. But Tom is convinced that white men or Indians cut them to pasture cattle and the balds will eventually grow back into forest.

It was raining when we halted, but Liz predicted the rain would stop—the jay she had heard meant clearing weather. She and the jay were right. The moon came out and we went to sleep. During the night a mouselike shrew ran across my face and I never knew whether it got into my sleeping bag, because right then I established some kind of Smoky Mountain record for noise and speed busting out of that tightly zipped pouch.

**The camper's hour** comes when aching muscles relax and tongues loosen before the crackling fire. A bear may venture near; this cub begged for bacon.

The park naturalist joined the riders encamped at Walnut Bottom. "A Niagara of mist often wreathes the Smokies, greatest mountain mass east of the Rockies," he said. "Some spots catch 100 inches of rain. Nurtured by deep humus and high humidity, hardwoods here attain amazing size: rhododendrons 25 feet tall, a mountain laurel clump 82 inches through. Climbing 5,000 feet you enter three life zones—it's like traveling from Georgia to Canada."

426

"Ain't never heard nothin' like it," Sam remarked later. "Shrews, you say? Now, was they boomers I'd know what to do."

"What's boomers?" we asked, and Glenn answered for him. "A boomer is the fastest little varmint in the mountains, kind of a red squirrel. Hit goes so fast that if lightnin' strikes the top of a tree whar a boomer is, the boomer can beat it down to the ground, look back up, and say, 'Hit's split!' "

He was right about their speed. Boomers were all over—Tom, Glenn, and Sam saw them often. I only saw where they'd been. But I did see red crossbills. At Round Bottom a flock flew in to take over our camp before the pack horses were loaded. Sam told us they used to swarm around salt licks for the cattle, so the mountain people call them "salt birds."

During the morning's ride we passed through a low gap to Raven Fork of the Oconaluftee. "Over to your right," Tom said, as we forded Raven Fork stream, "is the most beautiful part of the Smokies—the real wilderness area of the park.

Trails that used to lead in there have been closed off for years and no horses are allowed. People can go in, of course, if they can get in."

"Nobody asked my opinion," Glenn said, "but was somebody to ask me, I'd say hit's a place for roughnecks, not city slickers. Especially women city slickers."

Our next overnight stop was to be at Pecks Corner. Tom had spoken of its "nice little country store." Pecks Corner, 5,700 feet high on the Appalachian Trail, proved to be miles from any roads or stores. The joke was on us women, because we had cleaned up especially for a momentary brush with civilization. Instead, a bear came to our camp that night—a friendly black cub, begging food. Later our flashlights picked out two grown bears coming from the spring.

From Pecks Corner our trail led into a spruce and balsam forest called Paul Bunyan's Toothpicks. Under the quiet spell of these high, dark forests with their soft, mossy floors the ancient Cherokee belief in *Yunwi Tsunsdi*—Little People —seems credible. These kindly dwarfs, with hair falling below their knees, lived near the highest mountaintops. They passed the time dancing and beating tiny drums, sometimes worked at night for good people, and always led lost Indian children home.

We had been warned about the Sawteeth, where sharp mountain crests drop off thousands of feet on both sides. No one talked much on this stretch. We were busy holding reins and watching our horses' footing—up almost perpendicular sides, winding among the rocky teeth.

Later Tom told us we were approaching the Boulevard and advised us to stay

428

well off the road because the horses were unused to fast-moving traffic. Of course the Boulevard sign turned out to be a bear-clawed marker pointing up a steep, narrow trail to Mount Le Conte, nearly five miles away. We rode in silence through dense fog, scarcely able to see the switching tail of the horse ahead. The winding trail became a narrow ledge jutting from the side of Myrtle Point, Le Conte's eastern overlook.

"Camp" for the night was Jack Huff's Lodge, its cabins inviting with comfortable beds and roaring fires, its manicured lawns warm in unexpected sunshine. With sudden enthusiasm to watch the sunset, we climbed to Cliff Top, Le Conte's other vantage point. A white churning sea of clouds hid the valley below, and in the distance sunset flamed on the clouds above 6,642-foot Clingmans Dome, second highest mountain in the eastern United States.

Leaving the Appalachian Trail next day, we camped two nights at Walnut Bottom before the final day's ride through virgin forest. We were welcomed back to Tom's ranch with an old-fashioned square dance. People came from miles around for the "hoot-e-nanny gathering." Between vigorous sets, Cal Messer, mountain fiddler, sang for us "Whoa, Ebenezer, Whoa" and "I Got One Old Hat."

Then there were wilderness hikes and the ranch to enjoy—and the annual fair

**Fording Raven Fork, hikers strike out for the park's wildest region**

Not even a horse trail enters the 19,000 acres set aside as eternal wilderness. "Hit's not a place for city slickers," the author was told. But she disagreed and joined a party (opposite) that invaded this "forest primeval."

Packing camp gear on their backs, they pushed up well-named Breakneck Ridge, fought their way through mazes of rhododendrons and matted underbrush, saw torn-up turf where bears had fought. But when they camped beside a serene pool and bathed burning feet in cool mountain water, they realized their reward—a taste of untouched nature amid the densely settled eastern United States.

More than 3,000,000 visit the Smokies each year. "But 99 percent of the people who come here see only five percent of the park," was one guide's rueful estimate.

**County fair with an Indian accent** draws crowds to the Cherokee Reservation abutting the park in North Carolina. These schoolboys perform the eagle dance. Indian drama "Unto These Hills" is staged here summer nights.

on the Cherokee Indian Reservation adjoining the park. Besides the midway exhibits, I was fascinated by the singing contests: singers' faces and lips were strangely motionless, for in the Cherokee language the lips never close. We watched dances, archery, and a violent game of Indian ball.

Mainly a farmer, the modern Cherokee has found another "cash crop": posing in feathers and war paint in front of roadside souvenir shops. "We lost one of our best Sunday School superintendents all last summer because he started 'chiefing,' " one official told us. "Sunday is the busy tourist day."

If only more of these Sunday tourists would leave the park's paved roads and get out into this beautiful American wilderness! It was an experience this city slicker will never forget. And as Tom said, there's something about the water in the Great Smoky Mountains that brings you back.

**A Cherokee** demonstrates the blowgun skill of his ancestors, who fled into the Smokies to escape removal to the West in 1838-39. Eastern Cherokees number 3,000.

**"Leather britches,"** beans strung and dried by Cherokee wives, are traditional winter fare.

**GREAT SMOKY MOUNTAINS NATIONAL PARK** *Tenn.-No. Carolina. 798 sq. mi.*

**Features:** Roof of eastern America, cloaked in virgin forest. Some 1,300 varieties of trees, shrubs, herbs; 50 fur bearers; 200 birds.

**Activities:** Pioneer Museum. Log houses, grist mill at Cades Cove. 109 mi. of roads; Clingmans Dome Highway rises to 6,311 ft. 653 mi. of horse and foot trails (70 mi. of Maine-to-Georgia Appalachian Trail in park). Trout fishing in 600 mi. of streams. Nature hikes, illustrated talks May—Oct.

**Season:** Park open all year. Lowlands warm in summer, mild in winter; summits always cooler. Autumn has least fog and rain.

**What to bring:** Hiking shoes, rough-it clothing, rainproof jacket, camera, light meter.

**How to get there:** See map at back of book. US 441 from Knoxville, Tenn., to Asheville, N.C., crosses park. Air, rail, bus via the two cities; Smoky Mountain Tours in summer.

**Accommodations:** 6 free camp and trailer grounds. Le Conte Lodge (6,400 ft.) by foot or horseback; write Jack Huff, Gatlinburg, Tenn. Hotels, motels, in nearby towns.

**Park regulations:** No feeding bears. Camping, fires outside campgrounds by permit only. Fishing license. Keep pets on leash.

*For further information write the park's Superintendent, Gatlinburg, Tennessee*

**Creaking water wheel** of Virginia's Mabry Mill and century-old North Carolina hand loom conjure up vanishing mountain ways. Rhododendrons (right) adorn the long, long trail.

M. WOODBRIDGE WILLIAMS AND (OPPOSITE) W. E. GARRETT, NATIONAL GEOGRAPHIC STAFF

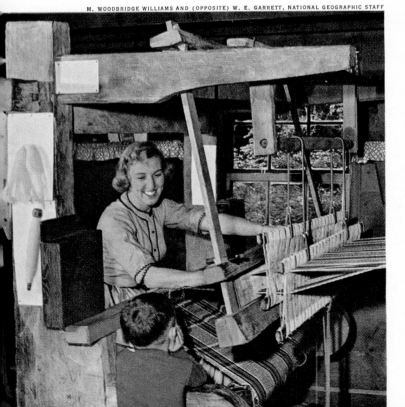

# BLUE RIDGE PARKWAY

THEY should put up a sign: "Slow, next 469 miles. Look out for gentle curves, heart-stopping views, and sudden plunges into the 19th century." This asphalt trail, riding the Appalachian crests between Shenandoah and Great Smoky Mountains National Parks, threads a cool, quiet other-world of grist mill and log cabin, forest and flower.

"Hiking is great—Detroit style," says a relaxed motorist, sampling scenery served cafeteria fashion in this "elongated park."

**Giant gardens flaming in the sky greet the Blue Ridge traveler in June**

"Ride awhile, stop awhile." The parkway's main purpose is not to take you somewhere— once in the highland fastness, you are there. No neon and billboard jungles assault your senses; no stoplights, no goading horns. If it suits your fancy, you can side-trip to 6,684-foot Mount

Mitchell, high point east of the Mississippi, or rhododendron-covered Roan Mountain in North Carolina (above). Spring's bloom of dogwood, azalea, and rhododendron gives way to autumn's reds and golds as Mother Nature, unable to decide on a color pattern, empties her paint pots playfully over the mountainsides.

Museums, trails, camp and trailer sites, sandwich shops, service stations, a lodge at Doughton Park, North Carolina, and summer cabins at Rocky Knob, Virginia, wait discreetly along the way. Much of the parkway is open all year.

# SHENANDOAH

By *ROBERT T. COCHRAN, JR.*

*National Geographic Staff*

436    **Where Indians once tracked deer,** today's car-borne vacationist stops at Baldface Mountain

A DAY'S DRIVE from New York or Pittsburgh, two hours from Washington, Shenandoah spreads its gentle slopes and cool, shady coves like a wrinkled picnic blanket. This slender national park in Virginia's Blue Ridge Mountains provides a handy oasis for Eastern city dwellers when the urge comes to get away from it all. After Great Smoky, it's the most visited of U.S. national parks. Thousands come in spring, when new leaves

Overlook to view forested ranges repeating to infinity. Constant haze gave Blue Ridge its name.

hang like green mist over the forested mountains, and in fall, when the leaves take a riotous, color-splashed curtain call. But seasons do not limit Shenandoah's charm. Skyline Drive winds south from Front Royal 105 miles through the park to Rockfish Gap, where it joins Blue Ridge Parkway. Overlooks, 75 in all, flare outward from the crest-hugging drive. To the east, Virginia's rolling Piedmont flattens as it becomes the distant Tidewater. To the west, Shenandoah Valley's trim farms and apple orchards stretch like a hazy checkerboard around Massanutten Mountain to the Allegheny Mountains beyond.

Many visitors see Shenandoah on a longish Sunday drive. Others camp, or sample the 207 miles of woodland trails. Alpinists might smile at the easy grades, but weekend hikers enjoy puffing to Hawksbill's 4,049-foot summit, highest in the park. Some rent horses at Skyland or Big Meadows and ride to hidden hollows and trout streams where a deer flicks its white flag and bounds away, a gray squirrel scuttles up a tree, and a wood thrush sings.

Quickly forgetting the nearness of great cities, you half expect to meet a painted Indian, a silent buckskinned hunter with his long rifle, or even John Lederer who was first to explore here in 1669. But don't expect the noisy Knights of the Golden Horseshoe, who, booted and plumed, accompanied Virginia's Governor Alexander Spotswood to Swift Run Gap in 1716. This gay band "drank the King's Health in Champagne, and fired a volley; and the Princess's in Burgundy, and fired a volley; and all the rest of the Royal Family in Claret, and fired a volley." Things are calmer now in this 330-square-mile preserve where the wild and quiet beauty of America's first frontier endures.

438

**A cabin and a corn patch** spell freedom to hardy mountaineers. "Corn squeezin' " stills outlawed, they make cottons, pottery, ironwork for sale in nearby park.

### Soft mist swirls through autumn's gold in Shenandoah

Motorists sometimes drive above the clouds on Skyline Drive, rising to 3,680 feet. Except when fog, ice, or snow briefly closes the road, park is open all year.

April through October finds restaurants, service stations, gift shops open. Fishermen break out tackle, and hikers bunk in shelters along the Appalachian Trail. Summer fills camp and picnic grounds, throngs the nature programs. To reserve lodgings at Skyland, Big Meadows, or Lewis Mountain, write Virginia Sky-Line Co., Luray, Va.

A bus traverses park in summer; trains serve nearby Front Royal, Luray, Elkton, and Waynesboro (see map in back).

# CAPE HATTERAS

Hurl TOWERING WAVES, whipped to a boil by Atlantic gales, against a slender barrier of wind-swept sand; add pirates and shipwrecks. From these ingredients, nature brews a magic tonic: Cape Hatteras. Words may describe but cannot explain the lure of the sea at North Carolina's Outer Banks. Just dig your toes in the clean beach sand and face the endless, crashing surf and you'll know why people come back to Cape Hatteras National Seashore Recreational Area.

Winds and the mighty Gulf Stream's colliding with cold Atlantic currents shape this 80-mile stretch of America's stormiest coast, from Nags Head south to Ocracoke Inlet. Dune grass, wildflowers, loblolly pine, and weathered oak pin down the golden grains in places, but there is little permanence in this shifting world of sand and sky, wind and wave.

Hatteras remembers a host of turbulent yesterdays. A summer pageant, "The Lost Colony," portrays England's first colony in North America, which vanished with scarcely a trace from Roanoke Island in the 1580's. Swashbuckling pirate

**Uncrowded beaches** and the white roar of boisterous seas lure an increasing number of vacationists to the Outer Banks. Cape Hatteras Light, highest in United States, warns ships of dread Diamond Shoals.

441

B. ANTHONY STEWART AND (ABOVE) J. BAYLOR ROBERTS, NATIONAL GEOGRAPHIC PHOTOGRAPHERS

442    **Hatteras Island's belt of sand, ribboned with asphalt, guards Pamlico Sound (right) from**

**the churning Atlantic.** Tourists find lodgings, stores, restaurants in villages like Hatteras (in distance), served by bus from Norfolk, Va., via Manteo, N. C. Open all year, the National Seashore offers visitor centers, a maritime museum, campgrounds, beach shelters.

**"Graveyard of the Atlantic,"** the Cape Hatteras region has claimed some 2,200 ships. U.S. Coast Guard men rescued this freighter's crew by breeches buoy. Ship and cargo were salvaged.

Bring sunglasses, light meter for camera; don't underestimate glare of sand and sea.

Edward Teach (Blackbeard) fell before the slashing cutlass of a young Royal Navy lieutenant off Ocracoke Island in 1718. Wilbur and Orville Wright soared into immortality in 1903 at Kitty Hawk when their flimsy airplane skimmed the dunes in man's first power-driven flight.

Today's visitors enjoy the sun and warm waters (page 48), bird-watch at Pea Island Refuge, fish, hunt seashells—even hunt waterfowl in certain areas.

For beachcombers, Hatteras is paradise. The sea casts up driftwood and wreckage—small change from the price paid by those who gambled with it and lost.

**Channel bass** give hefty sport to surfcasters and charter-boat fishermen from Oregon Inlet. Bluefish, sea trout, pompano, amberjack, dolphin, marlin, sailfish run Hatteras waters too. 445

J. BAYLOR ROBERTS, NATIONAL GEOGRAPHIC PHOTOGRAPHER

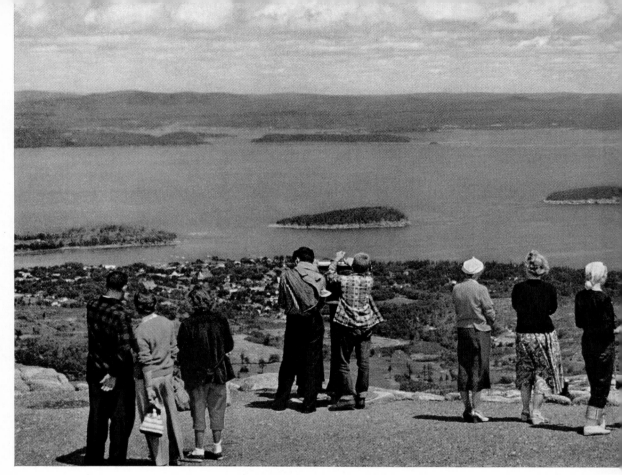

**Frenchman Bay** spreads below Cadillac Mountain, roof of Acadia. The Porcupine

# ACADIA NATIONAL PARK

*By EDWARDS PARK, National Geographic Staff*

A T DAWN an outbound lobster boat pants through a muffling fog, "so thick ye cud stick yer knife in it to mark the passage back." Gray waves boom and suck on kelp-slick rocks. A breeze clears the air and morning's sun warms up the smells of fish scales, tar, pine needles, and 3,000 miles of ocean. Gulls scream above the lobstermen as they chug homeward in midafternoon to sell the catch to summer folk. Finally the lowering sun turns pointed spruces black against the crisp sky.

This is the coast of Maine.

And this is the essence of Acadia, mostly on Mount Desert Island, where mountains tumble to the Atlantic to end in battered cliffs, where breakers claw into twining coves and inlets, where a man can fish with one hand and strip a wind-stunted blueberry bush with the other.

Superlatives adorn this national park, oldest east of the Mississippi and first

446

B. ANTHONY STEWART, NATIONAL GEOGRAPHIC PHOTOGRAPHER

Islands bristle with trees. Famous resort town of Bar Harbor, park headquarters, hugs shore at left.

to be donated to the Government. Nowhere else along the east coast of the United States does such high land overlook the ocean. The pink granite summit of Cadillac Mountain, 1,530 feet above the waves, is the first point on the Nation's coast to catch the sunrise. The road up it many engineers consider the best mountain road in the world, never exceeding a seven percent grade. Somes Sound, cutting the island nearly in two, is the only true fiord on the U. S. Atlantic coast. Mount Desert Island itself has been called the "world's most beautiful" so often that its State of Maine residents, by nature embarrassed by extravagant compliment, are afraid they may start believing it.

Like most Maine coast regions, Mount Desert bounced between French and English hands. Jesuits established a mission on it in 1613. Virginia colonists raided the island; pilgrims from Plymouth, paying off the *Mayflower* expenses with Maine furs, used it as a base. Louis XIV gave the island as a fief to Sieur de la Mothe Cadillac, the French explorer who founded Detroit.

In 1820, when Maine became a state, Mount Desert Island was still remote and obscure. It was not until 1844 that a visiting artist "discovered" the island's secluded beauty and began to talk it up so enthusiastically that a growing stream of summer people turned the little fishing village of Bar Harbor into one of the

447

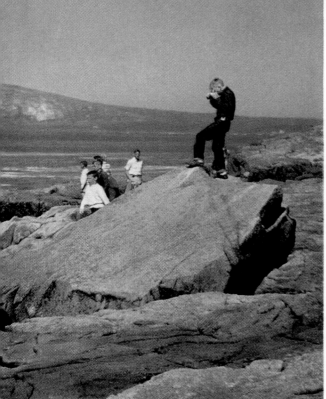

**Surf explodes on Schoodic Point, a salvo in Maine's eternal war between wave and granite**

The tang of brine and seaweed mingles with the perfume of evergreen and bayberry in Acadia. Here on the park's small mainland segment and on Mount Desert Island, rising across Frenchman Bay, motorists find ever-new vistas of the thunderous North Atlantic. Some 100 miles of forest trails wind inland past fish-filled ponds and streams and ascend steep hills. On guided walks, naturalists explain how ancient ice rounded the island's contours.

Acadia is accessible all year by highway; by rail or air via Bangor, Maine; campgrounds, park activities, air service to Bar Harbor in summer only. Fog-wreathed Bar Harbor (below) welcomes yachtsmen and flounder-fishing vacationists alike.

world's most fashionable resorts. By the turn of the century, huge mansions, each staffed by at least seven indoor servants yet invariably known as "cottages," looked down on gleaming yachts that crowded the anchorage. Everyone who was anyone arrived by water. One sporting pair of gentlemen made a practice of sculling all the way from the Union Boat Club at the foot of Boston's Beacon Hill—which must have taken a good bit of the summer.

Through the generosity of such "cottagers" Acadia National Park was born. A square rod of land, donated "for public use" in 1903, started it. Huge slices of private property followed. In 1916 these gifts were turned over to the Federal Government and became a national monument. The park, formed in 1919, now includes about 48 square miles, partly on Schoodic Point on the mainland, and on Isle au Haut. Though ravaged by a forest fire in 1947, Mount Desert has thick woods marching down to the sea cliffs. Far from a desert (explorer Champlain's name meant "wild, uninhabited"), it abounds in lakes, ponds, and brooks. Beavers splash in hidden backwaters. Deer trot along the maze of paths that cut from one viewpoint to another. Bird song is everywhere.

Thronging people seem to vanish from sight along Acadia's roads and trails. Yet the human types that frequent the Maine coast are all here—carloads of exclaiming sightseers in bright shirts, old-time summer residents tending their neat lawns; artists, tennis champions, yachtsmen, tanned children with sun-bleached hair. And among them all are the down-Easters who fill gas tanks

449

**Water turns to wine** in Anemone Cave as tide ebbs, baring rock crusted with tiny red algae. Acadia, combining rich ocean life with plants and animals of woodland, lake, and mountain, is a naturalist's delight.

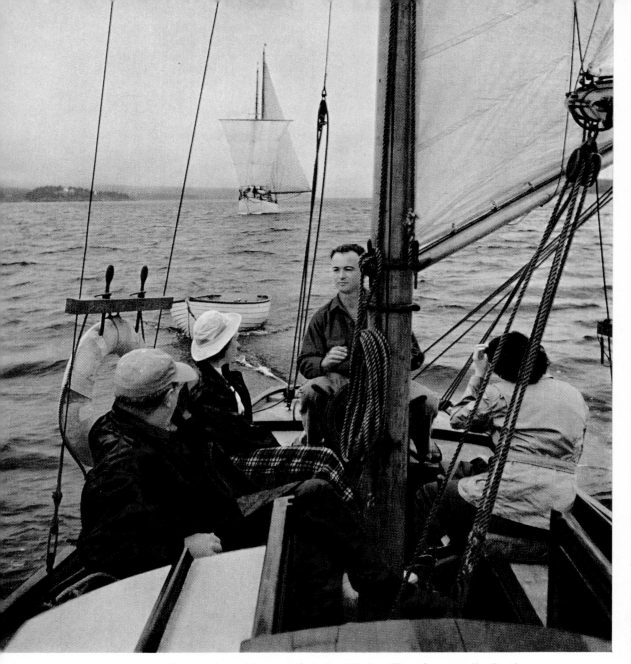

**Summer's yachts** sweep into Bar Harbor like migrant gulls. On these cold, deep waters children learn to race, navies come to call, and park visitors motorboat to the historic museum on Little Cranberry Island.

and grocery orders, answer questions and give directions with sober courtesy (". . . daown the ro-ud past the Haskell bahn, then bear right . . ."). With a sense of relief these year-rounders say goodbye to the "summer complaints" in September—yet with furtive pleasure welcome them again next June. For the summer folk are part of Maine, part of Mount Desert, and certainly part of the park that they conceived and brought to life.

# MAMMOTH CAVE

*By PAUL JENSEN*
*National Geographic Staff*

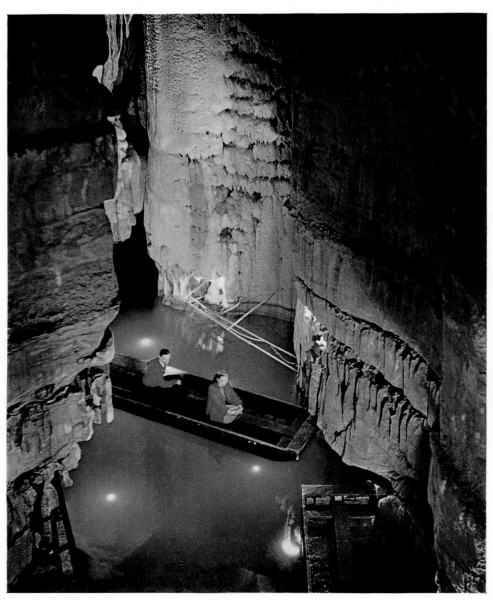

452   **"Through caverns** measureless to man, down to a sunless sea." Coleridge's lines strike a responsive chord in boaters on Mammoth's Crystal Lake, an emerald wrapped in rocky folds 270 feet below the central Kentucky woods. Higher water tables in times past scored the horizontal grooves; dripping water cut the fluting.

THE TOUR LEADER smiled wryly. "Somebody asked The Question again today. In twenty years I bet I've heard it 500 times: How many miles of *un*explored passages are there in the cave!"

We sat on the lawn in front of Mammoth Cave Hotel. Buses from the Frozen Niagara entrance were delivering tour groups nearby.

"Actually," he went on, "the answer is probably thousands of miles. Central Kentucky is honeycombed with caves. Maybe you noticed, driving in this country you hardly ever cross a creek, but you see lots of sinkholes. Rainwater seeps into the ground, dissolves the limestone layers underneath, and the surface caves in. These sinkholes catch more water, and it eats out large chambers and long corridors. Mammoth Cave is mostly ancient stream bed.

"Now you take its 150-odd miles of explored passages and multiply that by the size of this whole flat-bed area and you've got a right smart amount of cave."

I had just returned from the 7½-mile All Day trip and that seemed like a right smart amount of cave to me. Four other tours explore shorter routes.

Tour Supervisor Ritter took me in the Historic Entrance, which a pioneer named Houchin is said to have stumbled on while chasing a bear in 1799. But long before, Indians penetrated its gloom with reed torches to gather gypsum, probably for use as a cathartic. One brave pinned under a six-ton rock was found in 1935. You can see Mummy John in a glass case near the entrance.

Ritter pointed to wooden pipes. "Slaves bored these out of logs," he said. "During the War of 1812 our supplies of nitrates for making gunpowder were cut off. Fortunately for the United States, Mammoth Cave dirt contained saltpeter. The 'peter dirt' was put in wooden vats to leach out the nitrate, the solution was pumped to the surface, the water boiled off, and the all-important salts shipped to the powder works in Philadelphia."

Soon people came to see the now-famous cave. No American could say he knew his country who had not seen Niagara Falls and Mammoth Cave, "the greatest cave there ever was." Tourists came first by stagecoach, then by steamer up the Green River, or by rail to Cave City. Dom Pedro, Emperor of Brazil, arrived, and Grand Duke Alexis of Russia. In 1851, the silent corridors awoke to the golden voice of Jenny Lind, and 25 years later Edwin Booth

**Blind fish feel their way through pools of blackness**

Thousands of generations of Echo River's minnow-size fish had no use for eyes. Darkness also robbed them of pigment; backlighting will reveal the skeleton. Eyeless crayfish scuttle through the Stygian waters, and cave crickets creep on the walls.

*Photographs by W. RAY SCOTT*

intoned Hamlet's soliloquy in a room now known as Booth's Amphitheater.

"Right up there he stood," said Parker Ritter. "Go on, give it a try."

I mounted the rock. My imagination peopled the great chamber below with men in silk hats and lovely ladies in rustling crinoline, carrying parasols. "To be, or not to be," I piped, "that is the question. . . ." The imagined crowd vanished. Ritter alone grinned up at me. Blushing, I descended and followed him meekly to see the Giant's Coffin and the huts where a colony of consumptives had vainly sought cure in the dry and even cave atmosphere. We skirted the Bottomless Pit and Minerva's Dome, threaded the narrow, serpentine channel of Fat Man's Misery, and descended to the River Styx.

Beyond, the cave was not lighted for a mile and a half. Padding along in silence through the puddles of light from our hand lanterns, I felt I really was in a cave. With darting shafts of light we fought back the pressing darkness. At the Snowball Room cafeteria we joined a party taking the Scenic Trip. Suddenly I was engulfed in the chatter of a holiday group. A family from Philadelphia joked with another from Des Moines. One teen-age girl hobbled along with a taped ankle. The doctor had told her to exercise it and by golly she was going to. "Okay," the tour leader grinned at her, "but I'd take the service elevator here—'cause if you get in too much pain we may have to shoot you!"

Off we trooped, taped ankle and all, through the now brightly lit cave. At Mammoth Gypsum Wall we examined the riot of flowers, needles, fluffy masses

**Wooden pipes** carried water for nitrate-leaching vats during the War of 1812. America's sudden need for gunpowder materials skyrocketed Mammoth Cave's price from $116.67 to $3,000 in a single day. A month later, part interest sold for $10,000. Dry, 54° air keeps the 150-year-old pipes from rotting.

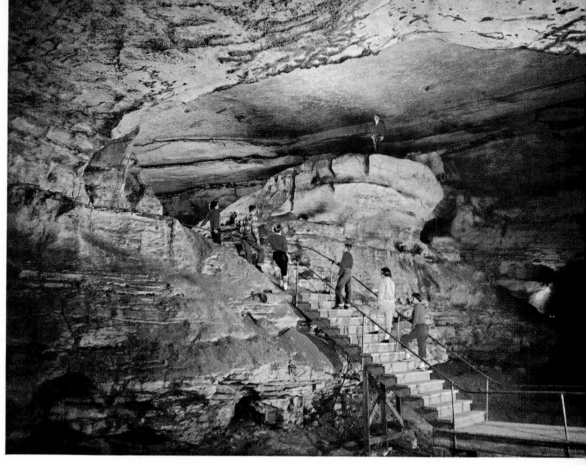

**Booth's Amphitheater:** from this rock the famed actor delivered Hamlet's soliloquy in 1876.

like cotton candy at a fair—all composed of fragile gypsum crystals. At Grand Central Station we met another group. "Who are they?" a woman wanted to know. The tour leader told her they were taking the Frozen Niagara trip.

"Oh," she said abstractedly. "I thought they were left over from yesterday."

Frozen Niagara, most spectacular of Mammoth's onyx formations, is aptly named—a mass of fluted stalactites spilling from a lofty ledge, its motion frozen forever by nature's magic.

On the surface, the sun seemed brighter, the trees and grass greener, the rustling leaves had a crisper sound than before. I became freshly aware of the beauty of these rolling Kentucky lands. In the park's 80 square miles, a bit of American heartland is returning to wilderness. Oak and hickory, poplar, elm, and ash grow strong. And 170 species of birds try to outshout each other.

Half a million visitors come each year to see the cave, 100 miles from Louisville or Nashville, and many linger to camp, hike, fish (you don't need a license), and boat along the Green River. The park and hotel are open all year. One early visitor had different plans. At dusk he held up one of the Cave City-Mammoth stagecoaches, relieving its passengers of $831 and jewelry. Shot soon after, the bandit still had some of the loot. His name: Jesse James.

*Excavating man's oldest known home in
the Southeast reveals a continuous record of
more than 9,000 years of Stone Age life*

# RUSSELL CAVE

BROOKS HONEYCUTT
**Cave men** sharpened bone awls on stone.

By *CARL F. MILLER*
*Leader, National Geographic-Smithsonian Russell Cave Expeditions*

H
E WAS SHORT, naked, and desperately afraid. He ran, bending over to make himself smaller, for an enemy was close behind. Suddenly, a stone-tipped shaft plunged, with stabbing pain, into his back.

The warrior stumbled on, somehow dragged himself back to his dark cave home on an Alabama mountainside, and there he died. No grave was dug. His body, with the spear point still in his back, was simply laid on the cave floor and covered with earth. This Stone Age American lived and died about 1000 B.C., yet he was a comparative latecomer to the great limestone cavern. For at least 6,000 years before his lifetime it had sheltered primitive man.

The remarkable story of Russell Cave unfolded during three seasons of excavation, 1956-58, under auspices of the National Geographic Society and the Smithsonian Institution. To preserve the cave for scientific study, The Society purchased it and the surrounding 262-acre farm near Bridgeport, made liberal research grants to further the work, then presented the site to the people of the United States for preservation as a national archeological monument.

A few inches below the present cave floor we found relics of Indians who lived here during early colonial times. These people, of the so-called Mississippian culture, date from about A.D. 1500 to 1650. Through the next 4½ to 5 feet we read the floor-by-floor record of the preceding Woodland peoples. Bone needles and fishhooks, arrowheads, shell ornaments, all told their mute story.

Imagine with me for a moment Russell Cave as it was then.

Each morning the sun pours into the yawning mouth of the great cavern, 107 feet wide and 26 high, facing east. Just below flows Dry Creek, which turns and

**Life in Russell Cave:** a suitor of the Woodland era offers a finely wrought ax as price of a bride. Eavesdropping, the girl brings clay for her mother's pottery making. Hide canopy diverts dripping water.

PETER V. BIANCHI, NATIONAL GEOGRAPHIC STAFF ARTIST

disappears into the mountain through an even larger cavern next door. The men soon depart into the endless forest. With bows and arrows, stone-headed spears and axes, they hunt deer, bear, wild turkey, and smaller game. Or they scour the woods for berries and nuts. Farming, if known, is primitive. Why farm, when the forest holds food for the taking?

The women squat at work under hide canopies which keep off dripping water. They roll moist clay into ropes, then coil and shape these into wide-mouthed jars, some holding five gallons. They add decoration by pressing carved paddles or coarse mesh into the smooth surface, scratching a design, or painting it with a slurry of hematite. Then they place the pottery on glowing coals to harden. Other women weave sleeping mats from rushes, scrape bear hides with stone knives, or sew deerskin bags. They thread bone needles with animal sinew or

458

**An ancient hunter took to his grave the missile that killed him**

Like a detective sifting debris for clues, the author brushes earth from a skeleton buried about 3,000 years ago; he determines that the cause of death was the white-quartz spearhead near the spine. A later cave man dug into the grave and tossed away the skull and other bones. Spear and arrow points on notebook were found nearby.

Interestingly, a small dog found at a lower level had been given a far more careful burial than the man.

Russell Cave dwellers were abominable housekeepers. Instead of sweeping out their trash, they buried it under fresh dirt. In these layers archeologists read the story of the passing generations.

**Russell Cave** yawns above Dry Creek. Here primitive man found life was good—ready-made shelter, mild climate, clear water, a forest full of game. Members of the Tennessee Archeological Society first probed the site in 1953.

BROOKS HONEYCUTT

BROOKS HONEYCUTT

**Floor levels** in this cross section span 4,000 years. Dips mark fire pits. Ladder of time (left) keys layers to history. Charcoal from about 7060 B.C. was found 10 feet below lowest sign.

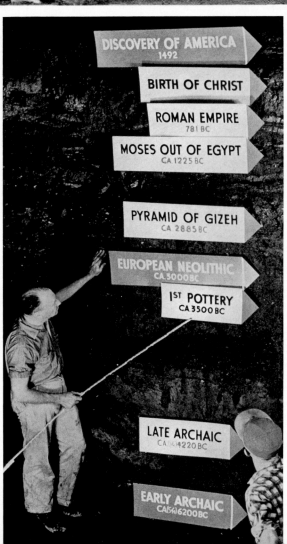

DISCOVERY OF AMERICA
1492

BIRTH OF CHRIST

ROMAN EMPIRE
781 BC

MOSES OUT OF EGYPT
CA 1225 BC

PYRAMID OF GIZEH
CA 2885 BC

EUROPEAN NEOLITHIC
CA.5000 BC

1ST POTTERY
CA 3500 BC

LATE ARCHAIC
CA (5/4) 4220 BC

EARLY ARCHAIC
CA (5/4) 6200 BC

gut. Naked children dash about. As sunset nears, the men return. If the hunt was good, no one will go hungry.

Each family gathers around its fire to eat, laugh, and boast. The hubbub dies; only the glow of embers testifies that humans are here, asleep.

Generations pass. Whenever the stench of gnawed bones and rubbish grows too great for even these untidy people, women bring in baskets of earth and spread a new floor—thus preserving for archeologists a record of their way of life.

My wife Ruth, who works with me, found a stone axhead unlike any seen before at the cave—grooved to fit a notched handle and painstakingly sharpened to a

**Giant's staircase** into the past reached bedrock at 43 feet. Radiocarbon tests dated a hearth at 23 feet as 9,020 years old, plus or minus 350. Scattered artifacts still lower suggest earlier occupancy. At 35 feet the author found a hearth that warmed men possibly 12,000 years ago.

WILLIAM W. CAMPBELL, III, AND
(LEFT) BATES LITTLEHALES, NATIONAL GEOGRAPHIC PHOTOGRAPHERS

**Local students, turned archeologists, sift the dirt of a hundred centuries for stone points and knives,**

**Deer antler** chips flint to a deadly edge. Primitive men split flakes from large pieces of flint with hammerstones, then pressure-flaked the edges with bone tools. This Russell Cave spearhead, though later, shows less skill than the fluted points Folsom man left nearby 10,000 years ago.

Coal miners, who could have quickly emptied the entire cave, were stunned when asked to trowel out six inches at a time in five-foot squares.

Painstakingly they peeled off the layers, examined each trowelful, and passed the dirt along for screening. They squeezed each ounce of wet clay through their fingers and, with precision, dynamited limestone slabs that blocked the way. They soon competed in finding artifacts.

Finds—three tons in all—went into sacks keyed to square and depth. One thing the crew didn't uncover: train robber's gold of local legend.

One culture's skills may be lost to the next. Woodland peoples knew only the one-piece deer-bone fish-hook, shown above in two stages of carving. Earlier men hinged two pieces; this more efficient hook (right) resembles those of the Far North.

**bone fishhooks and needles, shell rings and necklaces, and the plugs that adorned pierced ears.**

keen edge. With such a valuable ax, a primitive man might buy a wife, as the artist depicts on page 456. We also discovered two hairpins of polished bone.

Four feet down, in the early Woodland period, we found the grave of a newborn baby. Twenty-five feet away, at the same level, Ruth came across the remains of an adult male. Very carefully we brushed the earth away.

"Carl," Ruth said suddenly, "this man was killed!"

Close beside the backbone lay a large quartz projectile point. The spear had been driven in from behind, probably in the way described. It had struck a major nerve, and must have left his legs paralyzed. Neither in these graves nor in a third at the nine-foot level was anything buried with the dead—no ornaments, weapons, or provisions for the journey to the hereafter. Perhaps possessions were too few, or were owned in common.

At the five-foot level we had entered the time of Archaic man, who knew neither pottery nor the bow and arrow. His chief weapon was a spear and throwing stick or atlatl. We found two atlatl parts of notched deer antler.

At six feet the soil changed to sticky clay, and we had to knead each handful, like dough, to find hidden objects. Here we began finding artifacts of a type never before discovered in the southeastern United States: hinged fishhooks, unlike the single-piece hook of the Woodland peoples; and polished foreleg bones of large bears, cut cleanly and scraped out so that bear fat and a wick could be stuffed into the cavity. Cave man could carry this torch like a candle.  How did such artifacts, heretofore found only much closer to the Arctic, come to be used so far south? During the last Ice Age, 10,000 years ago and more, there was apparently a slow movement eastward across the continent. Later, peoples of Archaic culture moved north and south along the Appalachians. Those coming south, perhaps bringing tools of the Far North, met people from the West and

464

**Alabamians of 8,000 years ago** work by firelight. Artist Peter V. Bianchi reconstructed this scene from such clues as bear-bone lamp above and fishhook (page 463) found on the spot.

Archaic hunter skinning bear with stone knife downed it with a spear thrower, the atlatl, which preceded bow and arrow of Woodland times (page 456). These people are probably "overdressed." Author found no sign they wore even these scanty garments.

South at the southern end of the mountains—the region around Russell Cave.

Then, at 23 feet, we found a pocket of charcoal by the north wall. I sent a sample to the University of Michigan's radiocarbon laboratory. There Professor H. R. Crane determined that the fire had burned some 9,000 years ago—well within the era of Early man. No other site in the Southeast has yielded a layer-by-layer cross section of continuous human life over so long a period.

465

**Painted braves** chipped stone for ceremonial pipe bowls from the ledge at ranger's back.

# PIPESTONE

IMAGINE you are in another century, visiting a Sioux chief in his great tepee. Plains Indians sit in solemn council, perhaps negotiating a tribal treaty or an agreement with white men. Whatever the occasion, etiquette decrees its climax. A coal from the fire kindles tobacco in a richly ornamented pipe. The pipe passes slowly around the circle. With each puff, smoke spirals from its carved stone bowl. This aromatic "handshake" binds the parties.

To Indians, the peace-pipe ceremony was sacred, a ritual with beginnings deep in tribal lore. Also sacred were the sources of soft red stone from which pipe bowls were shaped. Quarries were common ground, where hostile tribes met in peace. Pipestone National Monument in southwestern Minnesota preserves the most famous of these ancient sites—first described by artist George Catlin in 1836. You can see the vein of catlinite that Indians still work today; and in the museum, pipe bowls their ancestors laboriously carved and polished. Legend says the Great Spirit hovered over the quarry and set Indian maidens to guard it. Three huge boulders—the Three Maidens—stand vigil there today.

# EFFIGY MOUNDS

A HAWK'S SPREADING WINGS, a bear's burly outline—these effigies, fashioned in dirt, covered the graves of Midwestern Indians a millennium ago. Thousands of these burial mounds, large and small, simple and elaborate, were scattered through the upper Mississippi Valley. Many have been leveled by the march of civilization. Others survive, notably at Effigy Mounds National Monument on the river bluffs near McGregor, Iowa. Beads, earthenware pots, copper ornaments, and other artifacts buried in the mounds help tell the story of their builders, who, never seen by white man, were ancestors of the Indians we know.

# OCMULGEE NATIONAL MONUMENT

IN A COUNCIL CHAMBER domed with logs and covered with Georgia's red clay, 50 warriors sit in a circle planning an ambush. Before each seat a receptacle holds pipe, tobacco, magical charms. A raised platform represents a sacred eagle. Beside the central fire pit a squatting figure chants. The powwow follows strict ceremonial procedure, for rite makes might.

Here at Ocmulgee Monument, near Macon, visitors can see the 900-year-old earth lodge and flat-topped temple mounds where priest-chiefs worshiped the sun. Museum exhibits trace Indian cultures of the Southeast: first the primitive hunters, then the Shellfish Eaters of 5,000 years ago, the Early Farmers, the Master Farmers who raised the earthen mounds—finally the historic Creeks, who built a village here and ushered in their New Year with midsummer corn rituals.

# MOUND CITY GROUP

**American artists** fashioned the copper headdress (above) and effigy pipe in stone (right) when Rome was in its glory. Dug from man-made hillocks at this national monument near Chillicothe, Ohio, they show the skill of the Hopewell people, whose Burial Mound culture reached its zenith 300 B.C.–A.D. 200.

Mound City, like other monuments on these pages, is open all year, has no camping or picnicking facilities, but is near towns with accommodations.

# ISLE ROYALE NATIONAL PARK

THIS WILDERNESS PARK lies in the western half of Lake Superior, a score of miles from the mainland shore where Canada meets Minnesota. True devotees spend chilly nights in sleeping bags beside wooded lakes teeming with pike, perch, and walleyes, or they putter among the archipelago's 200 rocky islets in outboard cruisers. The more faint at heart stay in the comfortable lodges at Windigo or Rock Harbor.

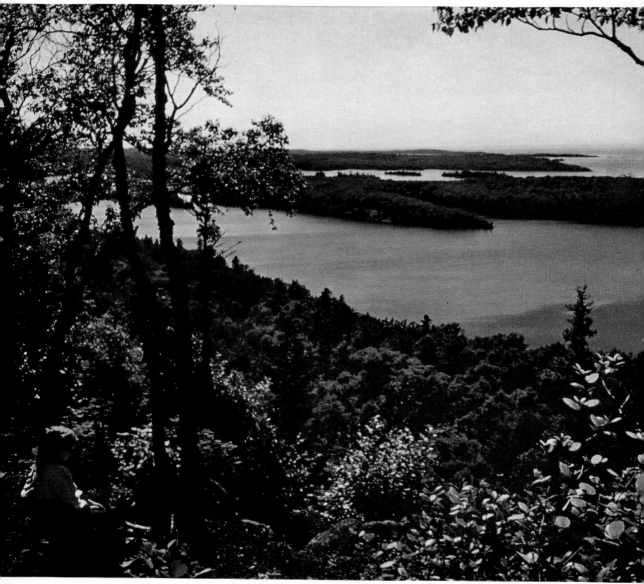

468   **Dense forests blanket** the 210-square-mile island, masking the scars of Ice Age glaciers. Moose, wolves, minks, muskrats, coyotes, and foxes have migrated from the mainland across Superior's ice, but bears, deer, porcupines, and skunks have not. One of isolation's boons: no snakes, ragweed, or poison ivy. Visitors embark at Houghton or Copper Harbor, Mich.,

Everybody hikes; they must, for there are no cars or horses. But hiking is a joy. Trails springy with pine needles and damp moss lead past flashing beaver ponds and glades purpled with wild iris. Pits deep in blueberry thickets mark where Isle Royale's Indians long ago mined native copper with fire and hammerstone—copper that found its way to Florida along the amazing trade trails of the red men. Orchids peep from the underbrush, and Indian pipes gleam by rotted logs. Here, as nowhere else, one can envision the Great Lakes region as it was when Champlain struggled up its rivers, or when Nicolet stepped ashore at Green Bay in clothes he donned to meet the Emperor of China.

NATHANIEL T. KENNEY, NATIONAL GEOGRAPHIC STAFF

or Grand Portage, Minn. Deck-load your boat, or rent one on Isle Royale. For lodgings (June 25–Labor Day) and information, write park supt. at Houghton.

**Colored pebbles,** even semiprecious greenstones adorn the island's shores. Indians mined pure copper here nearly 4,000 years ago. In 1669 French trappers took possession of the Michigan island and named it in honor of Louis XIV.

DUFF JOHNSTON

Mt. McKinley
NATIONAL PARK

Katmai
NATIONAL MONUMENT

Fairbanks○

A L A S K A

C A N A D A

○ Anchorage

Glacier Bay
NATIONAL MONUMENT

○ Juneau

1440 MILES

○ Vancouver

○ Seattle

C A N A D A
U S A

Chicago ○

Honolulu

Denver ○

St. Louis ○

○ San Francisco

Maui

Hawaii

Hawaii
NATIONAL PARK

2570 MILES

○ Los Angeles

U.S.A.
MEXICO

New Orleans ○

© N. G. S.
Irvin E. Alleman

## PART SEVEN

# ALASKA, HAWAII, AND THE VIRGIN ISLANDS

AMERICA'S CROWN JEWELS are her national parklands. On her perimeter gleam three alluring gems.

Rough-cut Alaska weighs out big. It dazzles with Mc-Kinley's blue-white spire, the glistening ice of Glacier Bay, and Katmai's sparkling lakes. Here the sun shines at midnight; the aurora borealis explodes into a thousand rainbows. "If you are old, go by all means," counseled Dr. Henry Gannett, a founder of the National Geographic Society. "But if you are young, wait. The scenery of Alaska is much grander than anything else of the kind in the world, and it is not well to dull one's capacity for enjoyment by seeing the finest first."

A gentle climate enhances Hawaii and the Virgin Islands, lustrous pearls of the tropical seas.

Mauna Loa, its heart aglow, crowns the 50th of the United States. "When will it erupt again?" asks the Honolulu visitor on his way to see Pele's Pit, the black sand beach, and the rare silversword that blooms but once.

Six thousand miles to the east, in the Caribbean where pirates roistered and islanders still hint of buried treasure, vacationists find tiny St. John, unflawed gem of the Virgin Islands, our newest national park.

471

**Inching up West Buttress** on slopes "slippery as greased glass," weary climbers hack a new trail to the continent's roof. Indians call 20,320-foot McKinley "Denali," the Great One; few other peaks in the world tower so far above the surrounding terrain. "Denali's Wife" (beyond) is 17,395-foot Mount Foraker, second highest in Mount McKinley National Park.

*Landing by light plane on one of Alaska's biggest
and roughest glaciers, climbers pioneer a new route
to conquer the white-crowned monarch of North America*

# MOUNT McKINLEY

By *BRADFORD WASHBURN*

*Photographs by the author*

**B**ELT FASTENED TIGHT?" shouted Terry Moore above the idling engine. I nodded, my heart pounding, and our little plane bumped down the runway at Chelatna Lake. Ahead towered mighty Mount McKinley, loftiest peak in North America. We were going to try the "impossible": climb McKinley's rugged West Buttress—a third of the way by airplane.

Beneath stretched unexplored Kahiltna Glacier, snout buried under boulders, ice so broken nothing could land on it. Rock walls towered on both sides; above was a solid ceiling of fog. It was like flying through a gigantic tunnel.

At last a rift split the clouds. Far up the valley, where snow covered the glacial ice, we made a perfect landing. Supplies unloaded, Terry sang out, "So long, partner!" and roared away in a swirl of snow. I was alone, 7,700 feet up, close under McKinley's flanks. Lightly it began to snow.

When the weather cleared, Terry flew in my three companions. We then broke trail up to Kahiltna Pass at 10,300 feet—first to set foot on this lofty saddle. It took us till midnight; the sky was deep red as twilight merged into dawn.

Another day we scaled "Peak Z" and built an igloo. When a storm struck that afternoon, we retreated inside and at the height of the tempest enjoyed a cup of tea. For several days we surveyed for the first complete large-scale map of the region. Finally, joined by four other team members who had circled the mountain by pack train, we launched our assault on McKinley's western barriers.

Skirting crevasses, we made our way up snow-and-ice slopes that ended abruptly in a massive granite shoulder. Above towered the 16,000-foot crest of the West Buttress. Right under it, at "Windy Corner," we set up our first advanced camp. After a cozy night in our igloo, we dug out into a howling storm, gusts hitting 80 miles an hour. It was 14° above zero. For two days we carried supplies up; then Jim Gale and I started for the next camp site. Our snowshoes slid back at each step. Shedding them, I broke through crust up to my waist. So with shovels we carved flat steps. After an hour's work I looked back at where I had left my pack; it was only 100 feet behind us.

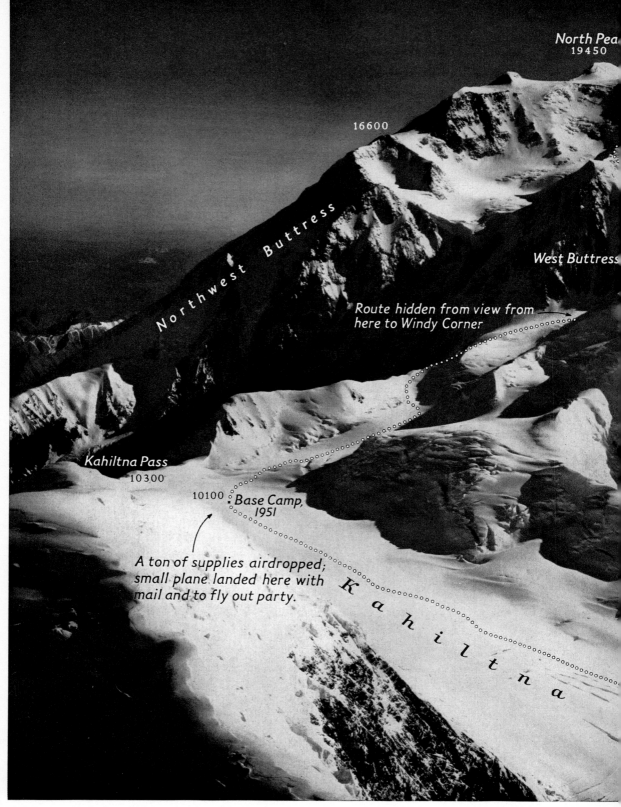

North Peak
19450

16600

Northwest Buttress

West Buttress

*Route hidden from view from here to Windy Corner*

Kahiltna Pass
10300

10100 *Base Camp, 1951*

*A ton of supplies airdropped; small plane landed here with mail and to fly out party.*

Kahiltna

474    **Regal McKinley's "impregnable" western face succumbed to a fly-and-hike assault**

The author's 1951 expedition made climbing history: the Great One had been conquered only six times before—never from this side. In a plane equipped with both wheels and skis, the explorers landed far up Kahiltna Glacier. Later

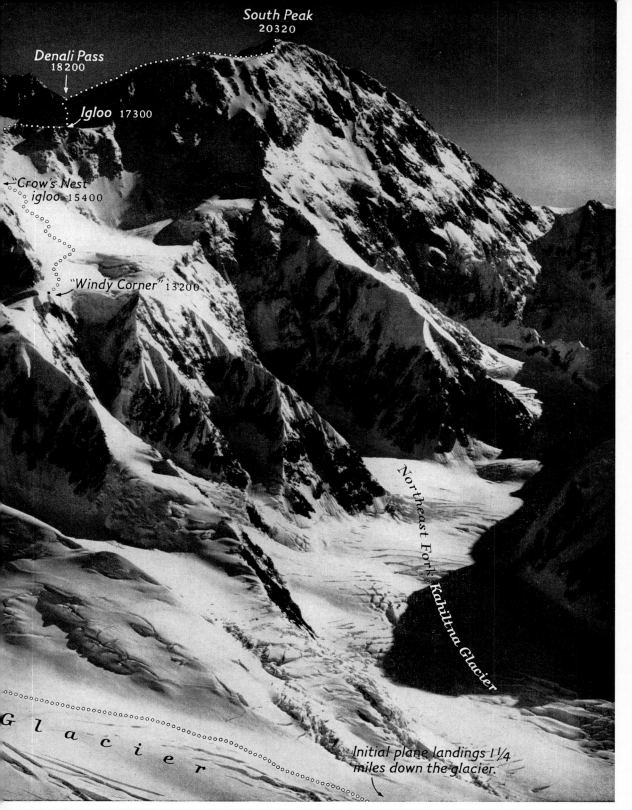

**South Peak** 20320

**Denali Pass** 18200

**Igloo** 17300

"Crow's Nest" igloo 15400

"Windy Corner" 13200

Northeast Fork Kahiltna Glacier

Glacier

Initial plane landings 1¼ miles down the glacier.

landings at 10,100 feet were the highest in Alaska to that time. One object of the expedition, sponsored by Boston's Museum of Science, the University of Denver, and the University of Alaska, was to make the peak more accessible for weather, cosmic ray, radio, and other research. In July's 18-hour days the team also mapped and studied the granite mass, its upper reaches blackened by slate, once the bottom of a prehistoric sea. All eight men made it to the top.

**McKinley's front porch offers a spectacular view—but watch that first step. It's a lulu!**

"Like looking out the very windows of Heaven," said Archdeacon Hudson Stuck, first to scale the true summit, South Peak, in 1913. Standing 3,000 feet from the top, near the author's highest camp site, a climber here looks over the ridgepoled West Buttress. Kahiltna Glacier flows like a sluggish river toward the lowlands where haze hides Anchorage, Alaska's largest city. Mount Spurr, 130 miles away, shows plainly through the cold, dry air.

All is not ice and snow in McKinley National Park. Beginning in early June, arctic plants, including Alaska's state flower, the forget-me-not, chase retreating snows off meadows and ridges.

Winding within sight of glaciers, a park road slips through spruce forests that cloak valleys and lower slopes, leading motorists to Eielson Visitor Center and on to Wonder Lake. Linked to the famed Alaska Highway, the park road makes North America's highest peak (page 42) accessible to any traveler. Climbers must get the superintendent's permission.

Wildlife thrives in the park— as the following pages show.

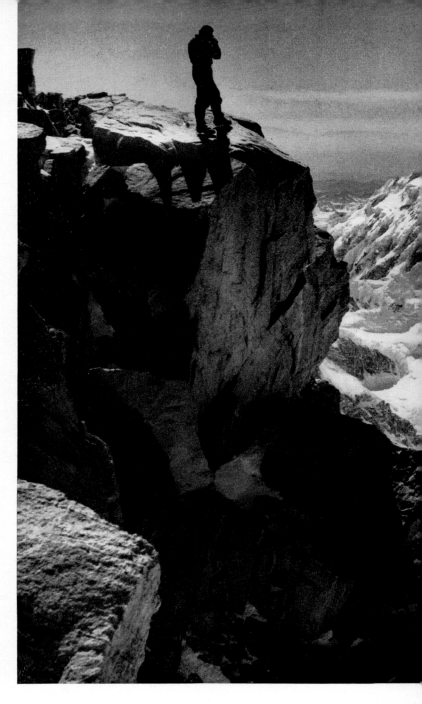

We reached our "Crow's Nest" camp site on a 15,400-foot shelf utterly exhausted and suffering from anoxia—lack of oxygen—which saps will power and impairs judgment. The last slope to the crest of West Buttress rose sharply 600 feet above our shelf. Jim and I took turns chopping steps in the most wretched snow imaginable. Roped together, we just chopped and chopped; neither of us spoke. Still a stone's throw from the ridge, rising wind drove us down, and roared over camp all night. Next day, fresh and rested, we made it.

In gale winds that day and dense fog the next, Jim, Bill Hackett, and I packed our loads over a granite knife edge studded with boulders and across a snow field to the foot of Denali Pass. At 17,300 feet we built an igloo.

July 10 dawned clear, and we started toward the pass. As the grade finally lessened I saw a shapeless bundle—a cache left by our 1947 expedition which had climbed the other side. I gave a shout of joy! We had conquered McKinley's western face. Four hours later we topped the summit and the panorama to the east burst upon us—100,000 square miles of Alaska in a single sweeping glance! Our new route had proved an ideal approach to the roof of North America.

477

*Golden Eagle*  Sharp talons clutch a hoary marmot; powerful wings spanning more than seven feet will carry it to the eagle's cliffside nest. Predators and prey live unmolested by man in this spectacular arctic refuge.

# Wildlife of Mount McKinley National Park

*By ADOLPH MURIE, Biologist, National Park Service*
*Paintings by WALTER A. WEBER, National Geographic Staff Artist*

I N THE CREEK AHEAD we saw a dark object that reached almost from shore to shore. We stopped for a better look. A grizzly bear was lying in the water enjoying the cool play of the current; a cub frolicked at her side. "It's probably Nokomis," I said as we scrambled from the rattletrap truck. "She's the only grizzly in the area with one cub."

Suddenly the old bear, 80 yards away, stood up and eyed us. I thought she was standing up to stretch, but my confidence vanished when she nervously chomped her jaws together. We could see her yellow teeth.

Squalls and barks erupted behind us! Another grizzly cub was pacing back and forth on the hillside directly above. This was not Nokomis at all. Our bathing bear must be Old Rosy, mother of *two* cubs. Now we found ourselves between an irate grizzly and her frightened cub—a classic example of the wrong place to be. We grabbed our cameras, sprinted down the road, jumped into the truck, and drove away. Seconds later the grizzly broke out onto the road. Stopping at a safe distance, we watched the family's reunion.

Walter Weber said that he wanted to see grizzlies (page 9). Here, on our second day in the field, we had found them. The National Geographic artist-naturalist (page 403) had come to Mount McKinley National Park to study and paint Alaskan wildlife. It was my pleasant duty to act as his guide.

In a few days we drove to Wonder Lake, near the base of Mount McKinley, and set up headquarters. It was late August, and hill and tundra blazed with brilliant crimson, yellow, and gold. Forests of white spruce and cottonwood clung to semi-frozen soil; fireweed, aster, and larkspur huddled in bright patches. Against this vivid backdrop we set out afoot to stalk that handsome relative of the domesticated reindeer, the caribou.

I have counted as many as 4,500 in a single band when these restless migrants cross the park in spring and early July. Now we found scattered groups. We circled downwind on two fine bulls with sweeping antlers and slowly set up our cameras. The caribou's eyesight is poor; only sudden movement would betray us. The bulls looked our way as if suspicious, but finally lay down contentedly. Suddenly both jumped to their feet and dashed off. Our comments were sulphurous. Probably the animals had been set upon by nose botflies or warble flies.

Caribou are the chief source of food for the timber wolf. I told Walter how I had discovered a wolves' hideaway one May morning, and, crawling inside, found six dumpy, blunt-nosed puppies, eyes still closed. I wrapped one in my parka and carried it home. The little female grew rapidly on canned milk. She became a pet and my 5-year-old daughter Gail named her Wags.

For three years I watched Wags's family and made notes on their habits. Surprisingly, besides Wags's mother and father, two adult males and a female lived at the den, all friendly with one another and the pups. Before a night hunt they often ceremoniously wagged tails and rubbed shoulders, and sometimes romped. Several times the unattached female baby-sat with the puppies while their mother hunted!

Once I watched the five adults stage a memorable battle royal with a big grizzly. The bear was heading straight for some meat, cached by the wolves near their den, when the pack attacked. The grizzly ran, but was soon overtaken and encircled. The wolves nipped at him, easily avoiding his

### Dall Sheep

Handsome targets for camera-toting climbers, these white-robed lords of Alaska's high country display slender, wrinkled horns. Rams' keen eyes watch for wolves.

### Stone's Caribou

Majestic nomads of the North scent the wind for danger as they cross a ridge near Mount McKinley. Caribou's antlered kin, the moose (page 45), is park's biggest animal.

### Timber Wolf

Wary of man, who has exterminated wolves in most other parts of the United States, these nimble, powerful-jawed night prowlers stalk caribou and other game.

481

lunges. The battle lasted 10 minutes, but its outcome was never in doubt. The bear retreated slowly, and eventually the wolves permitted him to lumber off.

McKINLEY PARK holds many a treat for ornithologists. They invariably inquire about two of its most elusive residents, the wandering tattler and the surfbird, whose nests were unknown to science until the 1920's. Raising its family above timberline in Alaska's interior, the surfbird winters along rocky Pacific coast beaches as far south as Chile. The wandering tattler winters as far away as New Zealand.

Not so mysterious is the powerful golden eagle, to me one of nature's most splendid creatures. Some years ago the park eagles were suspected of preying upon the lambs of mountain sheep, so I turned detective. Visiting many cliffside nests, I gathered pellets of undigested bones, feathers, and fur which the eagle regurgitates after a meal. More than 90 percent of the bird's diet proved to consist of ground squirrels and hoary marmots (page 43).

482    The bird that perhaps best typifies the North is the willow ptarmigan. We met

*Alaska Red Fox*  Foxes become fairly tame in the park. Some will even take food from visitors' hands. Lean winters, with rabbits and ptarmigan hard to catch, follow summer's feast of rodents, fledgling birds, and berries.

many of them prospecting for gravel along the road. Also present in the park are two other ptarmigan species: the rock and the white-tailed. All three change dress with the seasons, matching winter's snow with white outfits, donning brown-and-gray plumage in the spring, and displaying snowy underparts and brownish feathering in late summer and fall.

While camping in a spruce woods we studied the activities of a winsome little field mouse, the Toklat vole, named for Alaska's Toklat River. Each summer it harvests hay to feed on in winter. Near our cabin we found many miniature haystacks piled between branches of dwarf trees.

Too soon mid-September was upon us, and there was only time for one more camera hunt. We set out for the high, craggy ridges in search of Dall sheep. For 60 miles the park road passes through sheep range. Rattling along in our truck, we sighted 20 rams in the cliffs high above us. A dry river bed promised an approach. Afoot, we began a slow, laborious climb.

The park sheep, though they possess keen eyesight, can often be stalked in the open. They seem to feel at ease so long as they keep you in view. As we neared our ridgetop goal, the sunlight, which had been brilliant, began to grow dim. Soon the entire ridge was bathed in a curious half-glow. To add to our woes, a stray ram jumped from behind a rock and stampeded the band.

*Willow Ptarmigan*  Fly south for the winter? Not this tundra dweller with the feathered snowshoes. Like the magpie, Canada jay, and chickadee, he's set for the cold. Soon he'll doff late summer plumage for wintry white.

## MOUNT McKINLEY NATIONAL PARK

You can now drive here on new Denali Highway via Alaska Highway, or come by rail or air via Fairbanks, Anchorage, Seward. Hotel at park entrance is open June to Labor Day. Bus service in park. Camp and trailer grounds, foot trails, pack horses, good fishing await the vacationist. For further information write to Superintendent, McKinley Park, Alaska.

### Goshawk

"Nevermore," quoth the goshawk, "will I attack ravens when a pigeon hawk is on my tail!" The words are fancied but not the scene. From a hilltop the author saw a scrappy pigeon hawk break up the aerial dogfight and chase his larger rival all over the sky.

### Lynx

Snowshoe hares are this big cat's main food, though supply doesn't always meet demand. The hare is a cyclic animal, alternately plentiful and scarce; consequently, so is the lynx. Other rabbit fanciers: coyotes, foxes, owls. McKinley's chill climate excludes snakes and turtles, and all but one species of frogs.

"Four hours reaching these sheep," Walter grumbled. "Finally we get here, then no luck and no light. The sun is out, but what happened to the light?"

Returning to camp, we learned the answer: an 82-percent eclipse of the sun! But luck, and the sun, favored us a few days later. We maneuvered to within 40 yards of another band of rams and photographed them for several hours.

It was Walter's last day in the park. For a month we had roamed an unspoiled wilderness, enjoying the same majestic scenery that trail-blazing Charles Sheldon, the hunter-naturalist, had explored in the early 1900's. Largely because of Sheldon's accounts, part of the Alaska Range was set aside in 1917 as a national park. McKinley covers 3,030 square miles, and 130 species of birds and 36 species of mammals have been identified within its boundaries. A 100-mile road through the refuge provides ready access to wildlife areas. Sheep and caribou can often be seen from the road.

As we clambered down the mountainside, I noticed that Walter's gaze lingered on the magnificent sweep of horizon, the dark, tumbled ridges, the jagged crags, and the aloof, snowy hood of distant Mount McKinley. He seemed to be etching the scene in his memory.

**The Valley of Ten Thousand Smokes** spreads before its discoverer's 1917 camp. Five years earlier

# KATMAI NATIONAL MONUMENT

EDITOR'S NOTE: *In June, 1912, cataclysmic volcanic explosions devastated the Mount Katmai region on the Alaska Peninsula. Ash blanketed Kodiak, 100 miles away, and darkened skies over half the world. After National Geographic expeditions revealed Katmai to be the world's most remarkable volcanic region, President Wilson proclaimed it a national monument. Following is an account of the discovery in 1916 of . . .*

## The Valley of Ten Thousand Smokes

*By ROBERT F. GRIGGS, leader of five National Geographic expeditions to Katmai*

JULY 31 DAWNED CLEAR, but small clouds were gathering so we knew it was the last of the good weather. Planning an easy day, we climbed toward Katmai Pass, eyes peeled for signs of rising steam. None were visible. Starting back, I reached a little eminence and turned to urge my companion on. Far down the valley, over some rising ground, I saw a puff of steam. Late as it was, I decided to have a look.

The sight that flashed into view as we topped the hill was one of the most amazing ever beheld by mortal eye. The whole valley was full of hundreds, no thousands—literally, tens of thousands—of smokes curling up from its fissured floor. Some columns of steam shot up a thousand feet. We had stumbled into this sand-blasted wasteland was a green and fertile valley. Today only a handful of jets remain.

another Yellowstone—unsuspected by man until this hour. It was as though all the steam engines in the world, assembled together, had popped their safety valves at once and were letting off surplus steam in concert!

Returning to the valley a year later, our party camped within it for the first time, wondering what dangers might lurk in its steaming vents. Mixed with sulphurous gases were other strangely organic smells recalling burning wool, the musky smell of fox den, and the odors of decay. Would carbon monoxide attack us? I must confess that I chose to sleep next to the tent window, to get the best air possible. How I was paid for that selfishness! I took the brunt of all storms. The tent always leaked first on my side. My bed was always the first wet, my position the coldest and most uncomfortable.

Our camp had "all the comforts of home." Fifty yards to the rear was our refrigerator—a snowdrift. Just in front was our cookstove—a mild-mannered fumarole—into which we hung pots. Since the pots were surrounded by live steam just at the point of condensing, nothing ever boiled away or burned, no matter how long neglected. One drawback: our "stove" would not fry bacon.

The ground under our tent was hot. A thermometer thrust six inches down promptly rose to the boiling point. We put most of our bedding under us to keep cool! Blankets became as hot as the ground, but the air was cold; so we steamed on one side, froze on the other. We soon found our beds were not only hot, but wet from seeping vapors. The sensations of awakening in warm, wet beds can be compared only with certain distressing memories of childhood.

As we explored we could hear the ground ring hollow beneath the "tunk" of

487

**Mount Griggs lifts its mantled head above the jade lake that laps Katmai Crater**

Mount Katmai once raised a cone-shaped peak among its sister volcanoes; the shattering explosions of 1912 sheared it down to its present stump.

Scientists see evidence that the biggest eruptions belched from Novarupta Volcano, six miles west of Katmai. As Novarupta "cleared its throat," seething lava deep inside Katmai burst into volcanic conduits leading to Novarupta's crater.

Two and a half cubic miles of white-hot ash, much of it from the interior of Katmai, blasted high into the sky and smothered the area. Then, with a roar that was lost in the thunder of eruption, Katmai's peak collapsed—a 20th century counterpart of ancient Mazama's fall that produced Crater Lake (page 389).

Katmai's caldera is 2.5 miles across. Its lake ebbs and flows mysteriously, a blue-green tide tinted by minerals.

Highest volcano in Katmai National Monument, 7,600-foot Mount Griggs (renamed from Knife Peak in honor of the National Geographic expedition leader) still rumbles and steams at times.

our staffs, and more than once we felt it shake under our blows. What if it should suddenly give way and plunge us into a steaming caldron? We knew that once a man fell into such a place he would be instantly parboiled. At first we roped up. Later we discarded the ropes. If a man broke through it would be more merciful to leave him than attempt to pull him out. Gradually we learned to pick our way safely. Most dangerous were fissures bridged by ash and mud. When we accidentally put a foot through a thin crust, steam would spout. But it was always one foot only, and the owner was quick to back out.

We approached the valley again in June, 1919, curious to see what changes time had wrought. Despite decreasing activity, the geophysicists found vents much hotter than any that had been measured before. The highest temperature, nearly 1200° F., came from a fumarole not more than two inches in diameter. We cut the end of a stick into a brush of shavings and thrust it in. Instantly it began to smoke and char, and when jerked quickly into the air burst into flame. Since the vapor was almost pure steam—that is to say, water—what we really did was to kindle a fire by plunging a stick into water!

**Floatplane lands the author** on the pebbly shore of 19-mile-long Lake Grosvenor.

# My Visit to Katmai

*By ELSIE MAY BELL GROSVENOR*

I HAVE JUST VISITED Lake Grosvenor in Alaska," a friend wrote my husband. "It is a very beautiful lake; the fishing is excellent, the accommodations are good, and it is easy to reach by air. You really should go and see the lake that was named after you in 1919."

The idea was intriguing. We knew a great deal about the area from the many expeditions that Dr. Grosvenor, as President and Director of the National Geographic Society, had sent to explore the Alaska Peninsula. It was here that one of the greatest volcanic explosions in history took place. Only the eruption of Krakatau in Indonesia (1883) is known to have surpassed it in violence.

In 1912 the area was practically unknown, inhabited only by a few Indians and Eskimos. Early in June of that year a series of earthquakes and deep rumblings frightened the natives, and they packed up their belongings and left. A little later a great stream of hot, glowing sand burst from the earth and covered 53 square miles of the valley floor. Beginning June 6, the top of Mount Katmai disappeared in a series of catastrophic explosions. A great cloud of ash and dust darkened the sky. So dense was the fallout on Kodiak Island, a hundred miles away, that the people had to shovel ashes off their roofs to prevent cave-ins. Ships in the harbor were loaded down with dust, and sailors shoveled continuously to keep them from sinking.

The whole atmosphere was filled with volcanic debris, and even in far-off Cape Breton Island, on the other side of North America, we did not see the sun for nearly 40 days. All around the world there were evidences of dust filling the air—gloomy days and beautiful sunsets.

Society-sponsored explorations of the Katmai area discovered the Valley of Ten Thousand Smokes and several beautiful lakes. One was named for my husband; another, Lake Coville, for the then-chairman of The Society's Research Committee, Frederick V. Coville.

Eventually the land around Mount Katmai was set aside as a national monument. It now covers 2,697,590 acres—more than twice the size of Delaware and larger than any other United States national monument or park. There, in a part of the monument roughly 20 by 80 miles, 15 volcanoes have erupted in recent years—more than in any other place in the world of comparable size. The volcanic belt that girdles the earth seems to concentrate here.

For years the only way to reach Lake Grosvenor was on foot, a long overland trek, and you had to carry your own equipment. Now, we learned, there are comfortable fishing camps on the lakes and frequent plane flights from King Salmon airport. In Anchorage we met Mr. Ray Petersen, a former bush pilot, now president of Northern Consolidated Airlines. This line, with headquarters in Anchorage, serves Katmai and operates its visitor accommodations: tent camps at Brooks River and Lake Grosvenor, where Mr. Petersen invited us to visit his family.

On the plane with us rode men going to work in the fisheries and salmon canneries near Bristol Bay. Our first stop was at King Salmon, near the western edge of Katmai Monument. Here we left our airliner to board a small twin-engine floatplane. From this we had a more intimate view of the scenery than from the big plane. We were watching it all through the windows when someone pointed to a sparkling lake ahead and said: "That's Lake Grosvenor."

A few minutes later our plane settled on the water. We were welcomed by Mrs. Petersen and a group of dancing, excited children. The camp, on a neck of land between Lake Grosvenor and

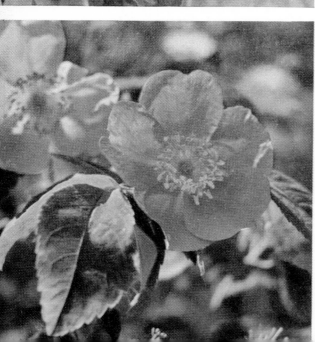

Lake Coville, has a gorgeous view of bright-blue water and lofty mountains, still snow-covered in late June. The guests wasted no time admiring the view, but started fishing immediately. In a short time Mr. Petersen pulled out a beautiful 16-inch rainbow trout, while his small son showed with pride a two-foot trout he caught.

The camp was simply furnished, but comfortable. Our rooms were canvas-covered; our beds were sleeping bags on cots. There was no electricity in the sleeping tents, but we had a lantern—and it stays fairly light all night in June this far north.

A short walk through the brush and a pause to watch the children playing badminton (without a net) on the gravel beach brought us to the communal dining tent. Delicious meals were spread on planks set on wooden horses, with the inevitable canned milk on the table. Every time I see a can of milk now I think of Alaska.

We were invited to tour Katmai by air; our guide was the chief ranger at Mount McKinley National Park who was making an inspection of the monument.

Our route took us down Lake Grosvenor, past Mount La Gorce, and com-

**Red salmon,** in silvery pre-spawning garb, hurdles Brooks Falls in Katmai National Monument.

**Summer comes fast to the 49th state,** and wild flowers burst into bloom across the land.

UPPER LEFT: Buttercups push a fragrant bouquet through an icy blanket. Hardy *Ranunculus* is one of the most primitive of flowering plants.

LEFT CENTER: To keep rain out of the nectar, *Geranium* wears an eyelash at each petal's base.

FAR LOWER LEFT: Fruit of the wild rose (*Rosa*) gives Alaskans a citrus substitute.

LOWER LEFT: Where the rice lily (*Fritillaria*) abounds, Indians grind the bulbs into flour for bread. Ricelike bulblets inspired the name.

ABOVE: Alaska's *Iris* floods fields with purple, may produce blossoms four inches in diameter.

LEFT: Dwarf fireweed, a member of *Epilobium*, gains its name by sprouting first on the scene of a fire. Also known as river beauty, it likes gravelly stream beds and lake beaches.

493

pletely around the 4,215-square-mile monument. As we approached Mount Katmai, we had a spectacular view of Mount Griggs, with its cone almost as perfect as Mount Fuji. We circled Mount Katmai several times, looking into its green crater lake, strikingly different in color from the blue one we had just seen. There is a glacier on the crater wall, creeping down to the water. Born after 1912, it is the only glacier in the world whose approximate age is known.

On our way back to camp we looked down on the Valley of Ten Thousand Smokes, now almost quiescent. Only seven large fumaroles remain of the original thousands. Down the whole long valley not a green thing was visible, and not a sign of life until we came to a small stream. Then the pilot excitedly pointed out a big brown bear making its way down the stream bank.

I asked Mr. Petersen, "Do bears ever bother you?"

"Not this year," he replied, "but last spring one broke into the Grosvenor Lake camp and tore the canvas walls to pieces, searching for something to eat. He found only soap flakes, which he mistook for food—with disastrous results. We spent days cleaning up after him. He never came back."

494

**Alaskan brown bears,** world's largest land-dwelling carnivores, drop their berry-and-marmot diet to feast on salmon. Prize fishing sites go to big, aggressive males who may weigh 1,500 pounds and stand nine feet on hind legs. Awkward cubs learn to fish from their mothers.

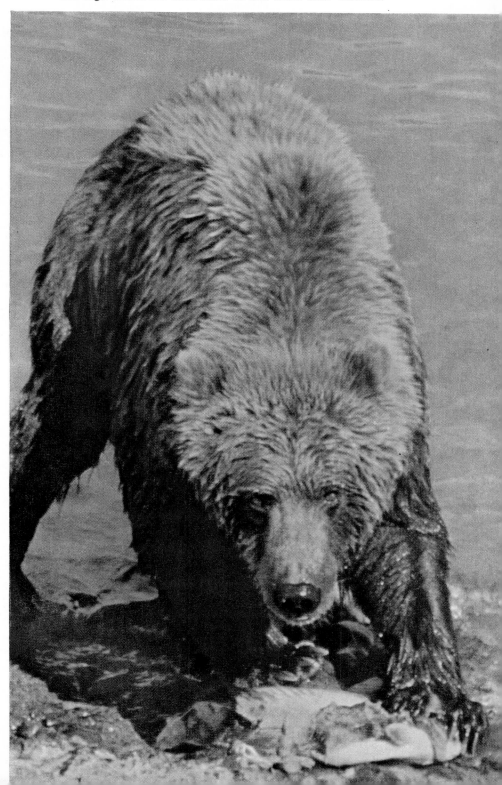

# GLACIER BAY

NATURALIST JOHN MUIR believed that the Creator taught His children with every sublime expression of nature. Glacier Bay was one of Scotsman John's greatest teachers; and, since his discovery of the 50-mile fiord in 1889, this scenic wilderness on Alaska's southeastern coast has taught the world much about glacier behavior.

Within the 3,554-square-mile national monument, created in 1925, visitors can see at work the same glacial forces that sculptured California's Yosemite (pages 322-25) and scoured Maine's Acadia and Michigan's Isle Royale. Alaska's frozen cataracts, some of them thousands of feet deep and several miles wide, grind irresistibly down the towering Fairweather and St. Elias Ranges like giant plowshares, carving their own valleys, wedging into, even splitting apart whole mountains, carrying within their icy bowels the composites of crushed landscapes. Many flow into the Pacific Ocean or into Glacier Bay, terminating in ice cliffs, such as Muir Glacier's 265-foot face.

Here in Muir Inlet, from a cautious half-mile out, the mariner might see the

**Stranded berg** awaits the tide; adrift, it can roll over and swamp a near boat.

shore line change before his eyes. Great chunks of ice crack off and crash into the water, sending out huge waves and crowding the inlet with bergs. Thus a glacier retreats, exposing new shore. John Muir built his cabin near the foot of the flow; today the receding snout is more than 13 miles away.

Not all glaciers in the monument reach the sea. Many melt in warm lowlands, depositing vast rock-strewn moraines as they recede. Mosses and lichens attack these barren ridges to help make soil for fireweed and alpine flowers. Dwarf willow thickets follow, and clumps of alders. Giant spruce and hemlock forests complete the camouflage. But tree stumps, standing like grotesque tombstones on the bay's western shore, bear witness that glaciers recede but to return, to crush relentlessly those bold growths again and again as the pendulum of climate swings in the ponderous rhythm of the ages.

From nearest tourist facilities at Juneau it's less than 100 miles by boat or plane to Point Gustavus, entrance to Glacier Bay. Ashore, the camper invades virgin forest, haven for bear, mink, and black-tailed deer. Afloat, he shares the bay with spouting whales, seals basking on ice cakes, waterfowl nesting by the thousands. He marvels at the glaciers, especially that named for Muir.

Here in its cavernous crevasses God-fearing John Muir became lost one day. Stumbling back to camp in the middle of the night, he exclaimed to his partner: "Such purity, such color, such delicate beauty! I was tempted to stay there and feast my soul, and softly freeze, until I would become part of the glacier."

**Reid Glacier's snout** gets a close look by seagoing rangers. In 1700 the entire bay was under 3,000 feet of ice. Today glaciers crawl to open water an inch or two a day—a foot is fast. Muir Glacier's speed: 20 to 30 feet!

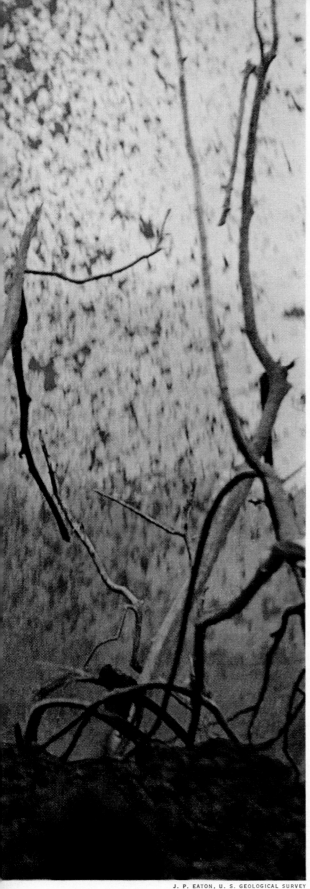

*Volcanic fires of the 50th state
draw 500,000 visitors a year to . . .*

# HAWAII
## NATIONAL PARK

*By PAUL A. ZAHL
National Geographic Staff
Photographs by the author*

LURCHING and bucking, our jeep climbed through a world of blue sky and black lava.

"When is Mauna Loa's next eruption due?" I asked geophysicist Jerry Eaton.

"It averages one every three years," said Jerry, "but it's already five years overdue. Let's hope she can hold off just a little longer."

We attacked the 13,680-foot volcano on foot, camping on the top, where July's night temperature drops below freezing. Next day we crossed the crater floor, past fantastic crevasses and red-lipped spatter cones glowing as if hot.

This scorched land is part of Hawaii National Park—362 square miles of unpredictable, lava-built scenery here on the large island of Hawaii and across 30 miles of Pacific on Maui. Mauna Loa's eruptions have made news since

**Roaring fountain** of rock blasts 400 feet into the air during 1955's eruption of Kilauea on the island of Hawaii. A shift in wind could fry the watching scientist—lava often reaches 2000° F. The park's volcanoes are the most accessible, best studied in the world.

**A fiery juggernaut, shod with clinkers, rolls down a green-banked roadway, turning it to black desolation**

From a vent on Kilauea's lower slope, this remorseless tide of molten rock oozed through a forest of 100-foot ohia trees, toppling them like matchsticks. Here it moved slowly—but Hawaiian lava can flow a frightening 35 miles an hour. Its fluidity explains the comparatively gentle nature of the island's eruptions. Sightseers flock to watch them.

Traditionally, Hawaiians attribute their volcanoes to the erratic goddess Pele. When Kilauea's long inactivity in 1934 slackened the tourist trade, the innkeeper of Volcano House on the crater rim implored Pele to manifest herself. He tossed a lei of ohelo berries into the lifeless fire pit, then added a bottle of gin, since the goddess is said to hanker for strong drink. That did the trick. Smoke mushroomed, lava flooded the crater, and visitors filled every room at the inn!

Pele's handiwork includes the 15-foot spatter cone clearing its throat at lower left and the black river of abrasive aa, below, surrounding islands of sugar cane. From such eruptions and deposits the Hawaiian Islands were formed.    501

**Haleakala, one of earth's largest craters,** could almost swallow Manhattan. Cinder cones pock the

Captain Cook's days. More sporadic is Kilauea, joined to Mauna Loa by a tract of park land. I looked down into its 2,600-acre caldera, wreathed in steam caused by water seeping onto hot rock hundreds of feet below the surface. Lava slopes changed from gray to blue to pink. Kilauea's awesome fire pit, Halemaumau, held a lava lake of cold stone. How different it must have looked on May 31, 1954, when a long fissure opened and lava spurted 500 feet high (page 47).

I was spellbound by the fern forest on Kilauea's eastern slopes. Hawaiians

502

half-mile-deep bowl on the island of Maui. Mauna Kea (left) and Mauna Loa jut 80 miles away.

say "little folk," menehunes, peek from behind each lacy frond. The flutters I saw came from birds, reminding me that Hawaii's official bird, the nene or Hawaiian goose, struggles to return from near extinction on these lava slopes.

Airhopping 30 miles of Pacific to Maui, my family and I plodded down Sliding Sands Trail on horseback into 19-square-mile Haleakala Crater and discovered another rarity—glittering spheres of slim, curved leaves. These were silverswords, found nowhere on earth except here on Maui and on Hawaii.

**Tree ferns** on Kilauea's windward slope are fed by up to 180 inches of rain a year; on leeward slope, in rain shadow, Kau Desert exposes naked lava. Snow at times whitens nearby Mauna Loa.

**Tropical incongruity:** waving palms, creamy surf —and a black beach! Lava from Kilauea met cool seas at Kaimu on Hawaii and exploded into obsidian fragments. Waves smoothed them to sand.

## HAWAII NATIONAL PARK

**Features:** Volcanic wonderland on islands of Hawaii and Maui. Craters, lava tubes, fern jungles, Kau Desert, rugged coast.

**Activities:** Visitor center at Kilauea (Hawaii); observatory at Haleakala (Maui). Scenic roads; rim and crater trails; horses at Haleakala. Talks, films, field trips.

**Weather:** Warm days, frequent showers, cool nights at lodges. Park open all year.

**What to bring:** Thick-soled hiking boots, rough-it clothing; woolens for high-altitude camping. Rain gear, hat, canteen.

**How to get there:** By air (several flights daily) or ship from Honolulu and mainland. Limousines to park; car rentals at Hilo (Hawaii), Wailuku (Maui). Write Hawaii Visitors Bureau at Honolulu, Hilo, Wailuku, or 323 Geary St., San Francisco.

**Accommodations:** Volcano House at Kilauea (write c/o park); Silversword Inn at Haleakala (Box 62, Kahului, Maui). Cabins and campgrounds at both sections.

*For further information write Superintendent, Hawaii National Park, Hawaii*

**Pasty red lava** belched from Mauna Loa's cone in 1949; then pahoehoe swirled down like blackstrap molasses. Actually it's as brittle as thin glass.

**Silverswords** rear golden candles; after flowering, they die. Found only on Maui and Hawaii, these bundles of saberlike leaves topped by ornate stalks here enliven cinder slopes within dormant Haleakala Crater.

507

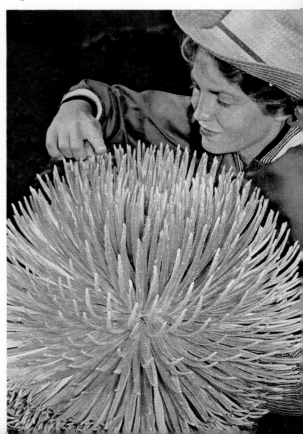

# VIRGIN ISLANDS NATIONAL PARK

PEARL-WHITE SANDS mark a jagged border round the island of St. John, Johnny-come-lately of U.S. national parks. In 1956 three-fourths of its 19 square miles was dedicated. Long before, in 1493, this little jewel of the Caribbean greeted its first tourist, Christopher Columbus. Struck by the myriad islands of its setting, he named the archipelago "Las Vírgenes," honoring Cologne's martyred St. Ursula and the 11,000 virgins.

Earlier, Carib and Arawak Indians inhabited St. John. Their stone picture writings can be seen today at Reef Bay, Congo Cay, and Carval Rock. Dutch, English, Spanish, and French adventurers followed; then in 1717 Danes moved in, bringing slaves to work the sugar plantations. In the mid-1800's, after slavery was abolished, planters abandoned their estates to the creeping for-

**Caribbean Shangri-La:** Caneel Bay Plantation, St. John's major guest facility, basks

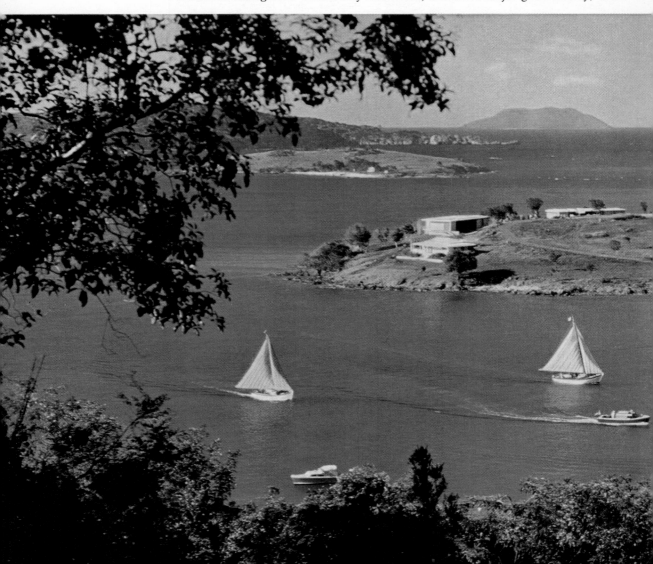

ests. In 1917 Denmark sold the islands to the United States for $25,000,000.

Not influenced by Miami's glitter 1,000 miles away, and unlike domesticated neighbors St. Thomas and St. Croix, St. John retains its primitive charm. Philanthropist Laurance S. Rockefeller, a National Geographic Trustee, worked to keep it that way. On behalf of Jackson Hole Preserve, of which he is president, he donated 5,000 acres to the Federal Government, and the park was assured. Here coconut-laden palms, breadfruit, guava, and wild orange trees grow eagerly in the mild tropical climate. Ferns, orchids, flamboyant and hibiscus shrubs, and cactus 20 feet tall flourish. Game fish thrive in the coastal waters. Bird life abounds. There are no snakes, few flies and mosquitoes.

For accommodations write Caneel Bay Plantation, 30 Rockefeller Plaza, N.Y.C., or Superintendent, Virgin Islands National Park, St. John, V.I. Awaiting you are crescent coves, and trails leading to bush-covered ruins. This is where civilization takes a year-round holiday. This is where the living is easy.     509

in a soft climate varying only six degrees winter to summer. St. Thomas is four miles by ferry.

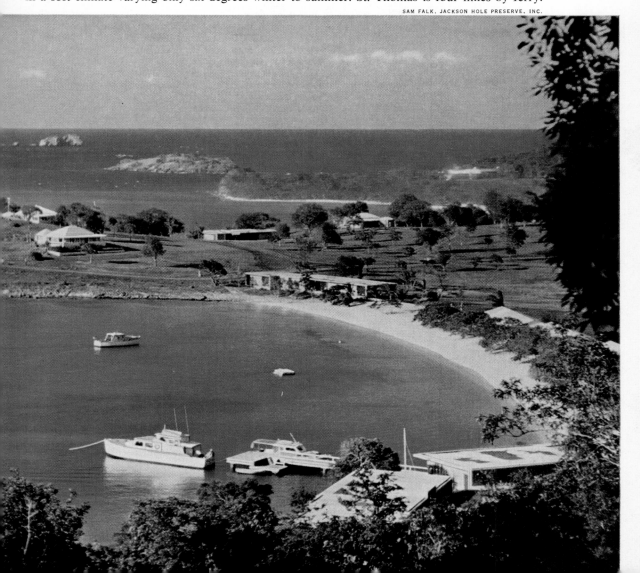

# HOW TO MAKE THE MOST OF YOUR NATIONAL PARKS VACATION

- Get oil-company credit cards (don't carry too much cash)?
- Make overnight reservations?
- Tell milkman, postman, paper boy, police (to spot prowlers)?
- Arrange to board pets?
- Leave extra key with neighbor?

PHILEAS FOGG, *the imperturbable hero of* Around the World in Eighty Days, *embarked on his journey with a valet and a valise full of money.*

*The average vacationing American, however, is not so nobly equipped. In place of Passepartout he has a wife and headstrong children. Instead of a bag bulging with money, he has a budget stretched thin, and his holiday is all too short.*

*In his shoes? You'll find tips here to enhance your trip.*

## PLANNING IS VITAL

First, decide what you want to see. Geysers? Caverns? Cliff dwellings? Wildlife? This book will help you make up your mind. Do you want to boat, fish, climb, camp in the wilderness, or just absorb the view from your car? The choice is yours.

**BUDGET YOUR TIME.** How many days in the park, how many to and from? Use maps in this book to rough out your itinerary. *Pick a theme* (Indian ruins) or concentrate on a region (the northern Rockies). Better still, plan an extended stay in one or two parks. You can spend all summer in Yosemite, Yellowstone, or Glacier and never run out of things to see and do. (Park Service has a pamphlet on each area; write Supt. of Documents, Wash. 25, D. C. for Price List 35.)

**BUDGET YOUR MONEY.** How much for transportation, how much for lodging, food, tours, horses, incidentals? Will it be a luxury hotel or lodge, a modest cabin, a free campground? (For listing, *Visitor Accommodations,* write National Park Service, Wash. 25, D. C. For out-of-park spots, write chambers of commerce.) *Make reservations early to avoid disappointment.* Remember, more than 70,000,000 others are planning park vacations too!

## HOW TO TRAVEL

Before loading the car, investigate other transportation. Fly-and-drive plans save travel time; trains, buses save driving; group tours (see travel agent) take planning details off your mind.

**AUTO TOURING.** Get road maps and travel data from your auto club or oil company touring service (get request card at gas station; allow two weeks' mailing time for marked route maps).

Have car checked thoroughly. Take jack, tool kit, flashlight, gasoline can, extra fan belt. Attach a bug screen to radiator grill.

Don't plan more than 400 miles a day on long trips (exhaustion invites accidents); snack rather than feast (big meals make drowsy drivers); don't dawdle along the way (save sightseeing time and energy for destination).

*About wee travelers:* For a long, taxing trip think twice about taking tiny tots (perhaps grandmother would be so kind . . . !) or pets (they grow restless in car, get lost, and in parks must be kept on leash, off trails, out of caverns and boats).

Coloring books, simple toys, car games (counting cows, identifying state auto tags), cookies hold children's interest, cut down rest stops and backseat brawls.

**DID YOU REMEMBER TO . . .**
- Buy traveler's checks (allow extra for emergencies)?

## WHAT TO TAKE

**CLOTHING.** Take comfortable, drip-dry apparel that looks neat without ironing. Don't overload. Include denims, khakis, if planning to rough it; long underwear to prevent chafing on horseback. Be sure to take sweater and warm jacket (park nights can be surprisingly cool), comfortable walking shoes, swim suit, raincoat. In most parks informal sportswear is all you'll need.

**OTHER ITEMS.** First-aid kit is a family must; include Red Cross text, motion-sickness pills, salt tablets, suntan lotion, insect repellent. Take laundry bag, litter bags, knife, bottle opener, stationery, tissues, extra flashlight batteries. Also thermos jug or water bag (porous, cools when hung on branch or outside car). For baby: a bottle warmer (plugs into dashboard lighter), disposable diapers.

Wear glasses? Play safe—take an extra pair, also prescription. And don't forget sunglasses, binoculars, camera, portable radio.

**TIPS ON PACKING.** Keep overnight essentials in separate, easy-to-reach bag (don't unpack car to find toothbrush or change of socks!). Put wet washcloths, swim suits in plastic bags. Carry hangers, clothesline. *Pack light,* especially if going by plane, train, or bus. *Don't be a slave to your luggage.*

## CANADA'S MAGNIFICENT NATIONAL PARKS DELIGHT U. S. VISITORS

For information on parks in this 29,000-square-mile system, write Canadian Government Travel Bureau, Ottawa. Here is a sampling:

**ROCKY MOUNTAINS.** *Mount Revelstoke,* B. C. Alpine plateau; skiing. *Glacier,* B. C. Climber's paradise. *Yoho,* B. C. Peaks, falls, lakes. *Kootenay,* B. C. Canyons, hot springs. *Jasper,* Alta. Ice fields; resort. *Banff,* Alta. Famed resorts Banff and Lake Louise. *Waterton Lakes,* Alta. (pages 122-28).

**PRAIRIES.** *Elk Island,* Alta. Buffaloes. *Prince Albert,* Sask. Lakes. *Riding Mountain,* Man. Wildlife.

**GREAT LAKES.** *Point Pelee,* Ont. Lake Erie beaches, bird refuge. *St. Lawrence Islands,* Ont. Among the Thousand Islands.

**ATLANTIC COAST.** *Fundy,* N. B. Rugged bay shore. *Prince Edward Island.* Coastal strip, beaches on Gulf of St. Lawrence. *Cape Breton Highlands,* N. S. Mountains meet wild Atlantic coast; golf, beaches.

Camping in the parks can be a most rewarding, inexpensive family vacation. For success take proper equipment (but not too much), get to your camp site by 5 p.m. ("full up" signs greet late arrivals), assign specific tasks to each member of family. Most park campgrounds are free, or nominal in fee, and provide tables, benches, rest rooms, water. Some even have showers and electrical outlets. Most parks offer trailer sites (check access road conditions in back areas).

**BASIC CAMP SUPPLIES.** Umbrella tent (or new 10½-lb. igloolike "pop-tent," erects in 90 seconds), sleeping bags, air mattresses (don't overinflate), wool blankets. Veteran campers also suggest:

| | |
|---|---|
| tarpaulin | plastic plates, |
| flashlight | cups, utensils |
| lantern | can opener |
| folding shovel | spatula |
| hatchet or saw | pot holder |
| sheath knife | dishpan |
| water bag | soap |
| insect bomb | scouring pads |
| camp stove | aluminum foil |
| aluminum nest- | paper towels |
| ing pots | toilet tissue |
| skillet | matches |
| coffee pot | whisk broom |

*Optional:* ice chest. (Canned, packaged, instant foods allow variety, need no refrigeration. Fresh foods, anchored in plastic bags, can be cooled in brooks.) Forget about bulky cots (chill air freezes you from below) and gadgets (keep things simple).

Some auto campers tow a rental utility trailer; most find everything (including packsacks, canteens) fits into car and waterproof case on roof rack. Collapsible boat, life preservers ride on top. You can rent camp and sports gear in some parks.

*Caution:* Bears will rip open tent to get food. Keep it covered so odors won't attract them; hang it from a line high between trees or put in closed car. Burn or bury scraps. *Don't feed wild animals.* Drinking water impure? Boil it.

**WHERE TO CAMP.** Most parks in this book have campgrounds. En route you can camp in hundreds of state-park and national-forest campgrounds. For listings:

*Camping Facilities,* National Park Service, Wash. 25, D. C.

*National Forest Vacations,* U. S. Forest Service, Wash. 25, D. C.

*Campground Guide* ($1), Campgrounds Unltd., Blue Rapids, Kans.

*Handbook of Auto Camping* ($3), Harper, 49 E. 33rd St., N.Y.C.

*Campground Directory,* American Automobile Assn. (members).

Director of State Parks at the various state capitals.

Nat'l Campers & Hikers Assn., Nat'l Newark Bldg., Newark, N. J.

Park scenery begs to be photographed. Heed the plea and you can relive summer's pleasures on many a winter evening. Follow these hints for better pictures:

*Include people* in the scene; have the camera look beyond them and record what they see. A picture of a giant tree alone is static—a child at its base feeding a chipmunk gives scale and interest. Hikers heading toward a mountain focus attention on it.

*Avoid self-conscious posing* and staring at lens. Have subjects walk, talk, examine something, do as they would if no camera were near. Close-ups are more dramatic than full-figure shots.

*Always frame your picture;* don't just point and shoot. Take a broad general view, an "establishing shot," then move in on details. Don't overlook signs; they can take place of copious notes.

Use telephoto lens for distant peaks, birds, animals; portrait lens for flower close-ups. *Obey your light meter,* but make different exposures to be sure: mountain, desert, seashore light is deceptive.

The more than 700 issues of the *National Geographic Magazine* contain a wealth of information on American travel, exploration, geology, plants, animals, Indian life. Check the Cumulative Index.

These stimulating National Geographic books will make your trip more meaningful:

*INDIANS OF THE AMERICAS.* 432 pages; 392 illustrations, 262 in full color. $7.50 postpaid.

*THE BOOK OF FISHES.* 340 pages; 377 illustrations, 207 in full color. $7.00 postpaid.

*THE WORLD IN YOUR GARDEN.* 248 pages; 148 illustrations, 102 in full color. $6.50 postpaid.

Order from National Geographic Society, Washington 6, D. C. Brochure on request.

# NATIONAL GEOGRAPHIC Society

16th & M Streets N.W.     Washington 6, D. C.

## National Geographic Magazine

ORGANIZED IN 1888 "FOR THE INCREASE AND DIFFUSION OF GEOGRAPHIC KNOWLEDGE"